GROWING UP
IN COLLEGE

GROWING UP

Liberal Education and Maturity

IN COLLEGE

Douglas H. Heath

Jossey-Bass Inc., Publishers
615 Montgomery Street • San Francisco • 1968

378.01
H35

GROWING UP IN COLLEGE
Liberal Education and Maturity
     by Douglas H. Heath

Copyright © 1968 by Jossey-Bass, Inc., Publishers

Jossey-Bass, Inc., Publishers
615 Montgomery Street
San Francisco, California 94111

Library of Congress Catalog Card Number: 68-54946

Printed in the United States of America
by York Composition Company, Inc.
York, Pennsylvania

FIRST EDITION

Code 681017

THE JOSSEY-BASS SERIES IN HIGHER EDUCATION

General Editors

JOSEPH AXELROD and MERVIN B. FREEDMAN
San Francisco State College

Preface

To become mature, or fulfilled, has long been a prized goal of individuals in most cultures. How a man grows healthily in response to different demands of the environment is the concern of parents, educators, therapists, and social workers—of anyone, for that matter, who cares about the growth of another person. Yet who can say of another person that he is "mature" or "mentally healthy" and then describe what he means—even to his own satisfaction? Many wise persons have long puzzled about the meaning of terms like *maturity, mental health,* or *self-fulfillment.* Despite the interest of professionals—psychologists, psychiatrists, teachers, and philosophers—in maturing and becoming more healthy, they have no acceptable theoretical model that is empirically verifiable by which to integrate their findings and insights.

Growing Up in College examines the adequacy of a theory of maturing. The book extends the work begun in *Explorations of Maturity* (Heath, 1965) by studying young adults who are growing in a powerfully maturing and liberally educating environment. Although the study analyzes only a small number of men in one college, it starts with the assumption that their maturing describes the potential developmental trajectory of any person regardless of where and when his maturing occurs. The book seeks to go behind the apparent differences that distinguish us from one another to discover that which is common to all of us as growing human beings.

The theory of maturing was initially induced from biological, psychoanalytic, and psychological theories and data. It has been validated on American college men and its generality is currently being tested in the principal religious-cultural areas of the world with gratifying results. Preliminary studies show it to be applicable to children. This book extends the test of the theory's adequacy by determining how well it orders and clarifies the developmental process and goals of which educators have spoken. If one of my more immodest hopes is fulfilled, *Growing Up in College* may suggest how a model of healthy development could assist educators to clarify the goals of a liberal education, which I attempt to do in Chapter Nine.

Another ambitious hope is that *Growing Up in College* may also illustrate how to determine—approximately, of course, for this work is only a beginning—what types of environmental determinants affect healthy development in young adults and, more specifically, what types of maturing effects different determinants may produce. Chapters Seven and Eight report the methods used to show how healthy development and its environmental determinants can be conceptually integrated and systematically studied.

Although not written expressly for students, the book has been useful to students who have read parts of it. Chapter Three could show contemporary students what many of them may be like and Chapters One, Five, and Six what they could become if they are fortunate enough to have powerfully maturing college experiences. Neither students nor teachers have many adequate models of the ways students can grow in these days. Some students may also discover the kinds of changes their colleges could make to help them become more liberally educated and mature persons.

The book is intended to be a scholarly study, disciplined by the guidance of objective methods, and interpreted, hopefully, dispassion-ately. But it was not until the work was completed and its implications were being examined in Chapter Nine that I sensed a less dispassion-ate hope emerging. Out of the work has come a deep conviction, shared also by Nevitt Sanford (1967), that the power of liberally edu-cating institutions to be maturing agencies in contemporary society may be declining. He suggests that the primary hope for strengthening the colleges lies in their students, who must be the ones to demand that their colleges and universities begin to educate them to be more full human beings—the historic goal of a liberal education. By de-scribing in detail how a person may become a more "full human being," the book perhaps will serve to further the efforts of every edu-cator who is true to that tradition.

The book's research strategy is akin to a disciplined case study. It examines a phenotypically unique institution and its students in order to identify a more genotypic order by which to understand any educational institution and the process of maturing. I identify and analyze a powerfully maturing college in some detail and study in-tensively the development of small groups of randomly selected fresh-men and seniors. Although the methods described in Chapter Four varied widely in their precision and reliability, I took the advice of Aristotle when I began the studies: I chose to use, in making observa-tions, only as much precision as was warranted by what was being observed. It seemed at the time that greater precision depended on the prior development of a more comprehensive map of the changes students might undergo in college. Otherwise, I might have measured insignificant changes precisely and ignored significant changes.

Few books so fully reveal the life and problems of one college and its students. To evaluate the studies and their conclusions properly, the reader should know about my relation to the college. Consonant with its Quaker tradition that emphasizes honesty and plain speaking, none of the administrators, faculty, and students who reviewed those chapters relevant to their interests sought to suppress any of the find-ings. I mention, in the book, when readers disagreed with the interpre-tations. It is I who have suppressed for ethical reasons some data, but my failure to report them affects neither the pattern of the results nor any suggested generalization.

Because of my involvement in the life of the college as an ob-serving participant, I have taken great care to check the findings, not to go far beyond the data, and to understate rather than overstate generalizations. Some may feel I have failed to be objective at times and too selective at others, particularly in the use of quotations from interviews. They may be right; but they would mistake the book's purpose if they discounted the book on such grounds alone. The purpose of *Growing Up in College* is to illustrate how a model can be used to order the developmental process, to illuminate potential types of maturing effects, to explore in detail the relation between an institution and the growth of its members, to suggest new hypotheses about healthy growth—in other words, to examine the adequacy of a theory of maturing in all of these ways. Its purpose is *not* to make some definitive test, to claim Haverford College had such an effect on 37 per cent of its students, or to prove some preconception about a college. In fact, it makes no difference to the purpose if some of the results and interpretations are incorrect—as some most certainly must be. It is the pattern of the findings and generalizations, not the validity of particular ones, that should be the focal issue.

Some readers may also argue that an observing participant is not able to separate his generalizations from his own particular biases and attitudes. Although my interpretations have been modified by the comments of many Haverfordian readers, I cannot claim that my analyses of the college's manifest peculiarities have thereby become freed of personal bias. But not to be able to make such a claim does not invalidate the book's generalizations. By inducing more general principles from the college's particular characteristics, one's personal values about particular manifest forms become irrelevant to the test of the validity of the hypothesized generalizations. Their validity can only be determined in other, different types of, settings or studies. For example, as may be sensed, I am deeply sympathetic—as a psychologist, as an educator, and then as a Quaker, in that order—to the college's religious tradition; and I believe, as do the alumni, that that tradition is the source of much of the college's power to have maturing effects. But the generalizations made in Chapter Eight about the *psychological* characteristics that define a powerfully maturing environment are basically irrelevant to Quakerism, Unitarianism, or half a dozen other -isms. It would be a mistake, to cite another example, to interpret comments about the immaturing effects of the college's dominant intellectualism to mean that I believe high academic expectations are not crucial for the development of students. They are. The purpose of such comments is to illustrate an induced principle of the theory of maturing: that the shortest path is not always the quickest. Helping a student to become more intellectually mature requires appreciating him as a person who must at times develop in other ways before his energies are freed to grow intellectually even more.

Colleges change. They may change very rapidly. Haverford College has changed in some very significant ways since the studies of the college were completed. The more detectable changes made since 1965 are indicated in parentheses in Chapter Two. Prospective students who discover Haverford through this book should examine the college themselves. Just because the conditions that made it a powerfully maturing environment for many years until 1965, when the studies were completed, since may have changed does not necessarily mean it has become a less powerful college—or a more powerful college.

Although *Growing Up in College* is based very closely on objective data from extensive empirical and statistical studies, to make the results communicable to those not trained in psychology, only the barest statistical and methodological considerations are described. I invite researchers who may feel that I have not adequately supported the findings to inquire about the procedures and data. Another limitation of the book is that its results have not been placed within the full context of other studies of college students. Newcomb and Feldman of the Institute for Social Research, University of Michigan, have recently summarized all such studies for the Carnegie Foundation. It seemed wiser not to do superficially what they have done exhaustively. The book should be read within the perspective of their monograph (Newcomb & Feldman, 1968).

This book is more than the result of the studies it reports. It is the outgrowth of the influence of many persons. For almost two decades I have waited for the most appropriate way to express appreciation to two educators who enduringly influenced my own development. This book tries to integrate the developments each furthered in me as a student at Amherst College: Theodore Koester introduced me to psychology and Gail Kennedy to educational philosophy. This book is a measure of their lasting influence. Robert White's *Lives in Progress* (1952) and observation that psychologists knew little about the maturing process sparked the interest that eventually led to this work.

Nevitt Sanford's pioneering studies (1956, 1962) and encouragement to apply my ideas to the development of college students inspired the more formal studies of the book.

The book is also the result of many warm and intimate experiences with very perceptive and delightful Haverford students. It could not have been written without their willing cooperation and unfailing honesty. The book does not adequately describe their liveliness, warmth, and humor. I am particularly indebted to the two students, who must remain anonymous, who permitted me to describe them in Chapter Four. I am also grateful to the faculty and deans who made judgments for the studies.

Of the many persons who have read parts of the book, the comments of Gail Kennedy, James Lyons, William Ambler, Sidney Perloe, Archibald MacIntosh, John Nicholson, and Elva Pepper deserve a special word of thanks. Although helping to correct my biases, they are certainly not responsible for those still remaining. Emily Kingham, Lester Alston, and Hazel Pugh have been most helpful with more technical aspects of the research. Mildred Hargreaves, Doris Houpt, and Elaine Doyle have patiently and expertly typed their way through many drafts of the manuscript.

The research was supported by grants from Haverford College and the National Institute of Mental Health, #10987 and 11227. Part of the book was written while I was on a Fulbright Traveling Fellowship in Italy and Turkey in 1966.

But my greatest debt is to the Haverford community. At no time did it close itself to my questions and procedures. It faithfully and generously helped in every way I requested. The college in its own quiet Friendly way worked its maturing effects on me as well. The book is dedicated with much affection and appreciation to those of the Haverford community between 1955 and 1965.

September 1968   DOUGLAS H. HEATH
Haverford, Pennsylvania

Contents

GROWING UP
IN COLLEGE

CHAPTER I

Becoming Mature

Man uses different phrases to express his insistent need to become whole: to grow healthily, to become more mature or mentally healthy, to fulfill or actualize himself. And just how does a man become more mature or whole? For answers man has always sought out gurus and therapists, read his bibles like *The Tibetan Book of the Dead* and *The Power of Positive Thinking,* and even listened to philosophers and, more rarely, his parents. As the mythology of his religion and the traditions of his family have become less compelling guides to wholeness for modern man, he has turned increasingly to others, like educators, for a vision of how to become a more mature person.

From the tradition of the Greek *paideia* to Dewey, educators

1

have shared the vision that education should promote the growth of the individual, his self-realization and maturity. "The valuable intellectual development is self-development" (Whitehead, 1916, p. 13). Man should seek to learn "the skills of being" (Van Doren, 1943, p. 67). "All education is the effort to make maturity the more it might become" (Raushenbush, 1965). Educators are agreed that a liberal education *is* a very potent and effective means to further the self-realization and maturing of a person. But it is not the only means; it may not even be a very powerful means for many persons, if we are to believe some of the studies that show liberally educating colleges do not have many enduring effects upon their students (Newcomb & Feldman, 1968). Responsibilities of a regular job and family have more potent maturing effects for many.

Yet education remains the principal institutional agent for promoting the growth of young people in contemporary society. Faith in the power of education to encourage maturing has led to the investment of enormous resources in the educational system. But what has been the consequence of such high expectation and affluence? Have our schools really become more powerful maturing influences in our society? By the standards some use the answer is yes, if we measure "powerful" by the size of the school, the diversity of its faculty, the adequacy of its course "coverage," the size of its computer, the number of honors its graduates receive.

By the standards implied in the vision of educational philosophers, however, it is not at all clear that today's schools produce as powerful maturing effects as they did even a decade ago. Certainly increasingly larger numbers of students don't think so. They speak of "irrelevance" and "empty academicism." They turn off and drop out. They demand power to organize and, ironically, "liberate" the university. They boycott classes and even imprison their administrators. Furthermore, if the vision implies that a school helps its students become more educable—that is, more open to further growth, rather than just educates them academically, which is only one way to further their educability—then schools are indeed failing. As later chapters will suggest, contemporary students may be better educated but they may well be less educable than earlier students—at least for the type of education colleges are increasingly providing.

Faculty also question the power of their colleges to educate liberally. Puzzled by the vague criticism, stubborn intransigence, and anarchistic temper of students more privileged than any in history, some educators claim that colleges face an identity crisis; some assert a deepening nihilistic malaise to be *the* threat to the existence of the university (Bell, 1966); some speak of the dying liberal arts tradition (Barzun, 1963).

Why is there this paradoxical gap between the munificence and unexcelled opportunities of our schools and colleges and the emerging student and faculty doubts about their power to educate? Could it not be due to a fundamental lack of clarity and consensus among both educators and students about the priority goals of a liberal education? Has not the humanistic goal of human excellence or maturity been supplanted by a much narrower goal of academic excellence in most colleges (N. Sanford, 1967)? Students sense that faculty view them as anonymous walking heads, not as growing individual persons. What college really does measure its effects by the maturing of its students?

The dilemma of the educator is that terms like *growth, maturity, the whole person,* and *human excellence* are insufferably vague. In recent years, there has been a renaissance of research and theoretical effort to identify and order the principal traits that define ideal or healthy growth of young adults (Brown, 1960; Erikson, 1959; N. Sanford, 1956; Warren & Heist, 1960; White, 1952, 1959, 1963), but no comprehensive model of maturing is yet available. The consequence is that the goal of human excellence remains embarrassingly barren and useless.

The purpose of this book is to give substance to the concept of maturity and to identify the determinants that promote such maturing. Although our basic aim is to test a theory of maturity in young adults and illustrate how the specific maturing effects of different social and institutional practices can be discovered, our findings may also enable us to suggest more specific types of goals that define becoming liberally educated.

How shall we proceed? Dewey suggested that "the only way which does not lead us into the clouds . . . is discovery of what actually takes place when education really occurs" (1934, p. 2). That is what I have done. I have identified a college that has been widely regarded to have had very powerful maturing effects, and I have intensively studied just how its students did mature and why.

If we are to discover how persons do mature, what do we look for? Certainly a principal reason why so many other studies of the development of young adults detect so few changes is that they did not investigate many of the types of maturing effects that educators describe. We use as the scaffold for our studies a psychological model of the growth process that, hopefully, comprehends most of the historic goals of educators. If so, it may help to order more systematically some of their very diffuse ideas and bring greater clarity to them and their students about how young persons can and should grow when becoming educated.

MODEL OF THE MATURING PERSON

To become a more mature person is to grow intellectually, to form guiding values, to become knowledgeable about oneself, and to develop social, interpersonal skills. Although these ways of defining a mature person may seem arbitrary, they are important to both the psychologist and educator.

Judgment, analytic and synthetic thinking, logical reasoning, and imaginativeness are man's more important intellective skills. They constitute the core of the ego for the psychoanalyst. With such skills, man transcends the limits of both time and space, reconstructs and thereby learns from the past, forms models and thereby anticipates the future. For many educators, *the* measure of becoming educated is the extent to which a person has developed and perfected such skills.

A person's needs, motives, interests, convictions, and values determine the choices he makes, steer his behavior, and give him a sense of purpose and direction. Psychologists do not have an adequate theory of how values develop to offer the educator who, whether he likes it or not, is intimately involved in teaching attitudes and values like intellectual honesty, integrity, tolerance, and objectivity.

It is also important to understand what a person knows of himself because his self-concept decisively regulates how he adapts. What a person believes to be his strengths and weaknesses determines what he will attempt or not attempt. As Socrates said, to "know thyself" leads to wisdom, the ability to use knowledge effectively for adaptive purposes.

Finally, skill in interpersonal relations interests psychologists, perhaps more than educators. Most of life's problems require interpersonal skills for their solution. Furthermore, the development of the different parts of a person is inextricably woven into one's maturing relationships with others, as we shall later demonstrate over and over again. Impairment in the capacity to respond to another results in a distorted self-concept, retarded intellectual skills, and impulse-ridden values. Educators tend to ignore the powerful maturing effects a young person's personal friendships may have, for example, on his intellectual skills.

What pattern, if any, marks the development of intellectual skills, the crystallization of one's values, the growth of self-knowledge, and the maturing of one's interpersonal skills? Certain recurring themes or underlying developmental dimensions, which help define the maturing person, emerge from biological, psychoanalytic, psychosocial, and mental health theories and research.[1]

To become a more *mature* person is to become more able to symbolize one's experience and to become more allocentric or other-centered, integrated, stable, and autonomous. If we now combine these five developmental trends that define maturing with the four structures that define the person, we arrive at twenty specific hypotheses about how a person grows: a *maturing person* develops more symbolized, allocentric, integrated, stable, and autonomous values, intellectual skills, social interpersonal skills, and ideas about himself.

A person is more than a collection of unrelated trends and structures. He has organization and unity. He grows and acts all in one piece. For this reason, the analysis of our mature person into different structures and dimensions will be preoccupied with their relationships. Growth is an organismic process. It assumes that the development of one structure is not independent of the development of others; dimensions like integration and stability are interrelated and merely represent different ways of analyzing the same growth process. The theory of maturing is holistic. The maturity of any particular behavior cannot be assessed apart from the maturity of the person. For example, a young man who had participated in the studies on which this book is based sneaked over to the neighboring woman's college one dark night, took off all his clothes, and danced an Indian war dance around a tree outside his girl's dorm. His joyful war whoops woke her

[1] The sources from which the model was induced, the methods developed to test it, and the empirical results that verified it are reported in *Explorations of Maturity* (Heath, 1965). This chapter draws on the evidence the book cites. Our statements, though made without qualification, should be read as tentative until replicated.

and, unfortunately, higher powers. From the Dean of Women's point of view, his behavior was not quite excusable or healthy. In the light of my analysis of this student as a total person, however, his behavior was a masterful act that burst the bonds of too stabilized or rigid inhibitions that had prevented the integration of some very deep needs into his personality. He had become, by this interpretation, more inwardly free to grow more wholly. My only regret was that he whooped so loudly.

What does it mean to become more mature in the ways predicted, and what is the evidence that supports our hypotheses about the growth process? Most of the evidence comes from the lives of college men—the critical age group that philosophers believe to be most receptive to a liberal education. One theoretical test of the model's adequacy is that it include the specific developmental changes educational philosophers have claimed a liberal education should produce. Appendix A summarizes their viewpoints and illustrates how the model of maturing does indeed organize the process of becoming liberally educated.

REPRESENTING EXPERIENCE SYMBOLICALLY

To become mature is to develop the power to represent one's experience as hunches, words, thoughts, or other symbols. A growing person becomes able to reflect on his past and current experience, to imagine, anticipate, plan, and hope. He develops an inner private world that gives him the resources for happiness and the potentialities for anxious torment. A rich inner life frees him of physical and temporal constraints. He can roam through the past and the future, the possible and the impossible, even heaven and hell, with abandon and delight, remedying the mistakes of his past, creating visions of his future. A mature person has a rich, differentiated awareness and an accurate internal representation both of his own needs and of reality. The power to symbolize experience vastly increases a human being's adaptive possibilities.

The maturing person develops more reflective intellective skills —an insight Timothy Leary and the hippies also share. Whether by LSD or starvation or retreats into the wilderness, man has always sought to sensitize and heighten his consciousness and his power to reflect, and to represent clearly ever elusive immanent and even transcendent experiences. With increasing maturity, a person not only can readily recall his past defeats and triumphs but also can accurately monitor his own ongoing thoughts for consistency and logicality. And when he solves a problem, he can, unlike a child, explain how he solved it. Thought turns back on itself, so that he can tell himself, almost simultaneously, if this thought is appropriate, that one groovy, this one logical, that one just plain crazy, this one brilliant. Hard data supporting the hypothesis that more mature persons have more developed reflective skills are scarce; but more mature people have been found to be more imaginally productive, capable of producing more images, thoughts, and combinations of ideas. They also use reflection more frequently to gain perspective about their lives.

Maturing is also associated with an increasing ability to bring into awareness what one believes and values. A mature person knows his motives. To bring a patient's motives and values to consciousness has long been a principal goal of therapists. Such awareness leads to and defines the patient's increasing maturity. In a questionnaire designed to measure maturity, it is the immature student who answers "True" this item: "Because I seldom reflect about why I believe and act as I do, I find these questions difficult to answer."

Similarly, maturing brings greater awareness of oneself. The Buddhists talk of man becoming more and more awake. Fromm says all education is but the attempt to wake man up more and more. But what the Buddhists and Fromm mean is that man develops a more accurate understanding of his own powers. That more mature persons do have more accurate insights about themselves is true. Those who do have more accurate self-images have also been found to be more interested in other persons and to have warmer and more enduring relationships. They describe themselves to be more adaptable, independent, self-driving, conscientious, enthusiastic, and purposeful persons. These self-evaluations are corroborated by independent judges. Also, as our theory predicts, they have more stable, integrated, and allocentric self-images as well.

Finally, a mature person can reflect about his personal relationships and their sources of strain and satisfaction. His past interpersonal experience is not shut off from his present awareness by repressions; nor is it cast into vague and elusive memories only fleetingly available when needed. Concomitantly, he is able to understand why other persons feel and act as they do. Therapists identify such skill to be central to healthy personal relationships. Much effort is expended to help persons who are blindly caught in repetitively unhappy personal crises to learn how to understand more clearly why they act as they do. However, there is still little firm experimental evidence, other than clinical observation, to support the hypothesis that more mature persons are more reflective and insightful about their relations with others.

As Appendix A suggests, most educators also agree that the expansion of the inner symbolic world of the individual is a principal goal as well as effect of a liberal education.

BECOMING ALLOCENTRIC

A mature person is not as egocentric as an immature person, nor is he as dominated by his own immediate needs. He is more socialized and "other-centered." The process of maturing is a pervasively social process. Parents, educators, clergy, and everybody else combine forces to suppress our childish autocentricism. To become more mature is gradually to incorporate into oneself the social world into which one is being pushed and pulled. Just what form does a maturing person's growing allocentricism take?

A mature person can communicate with other persons. He incorporates the grammatical and logical structures of his culture; his thought becomes more realistic and his concepts more precise and accurate. His private world is no longer "private"; it is a social world organized around memories, thoughts, and wishes that involve other persons. Inadequate social relationships may well impair the development of logical thinking (Piaget, 1928; Sullivan, 1953), for in social discussion and argument, a person learns how to take the viewpoint of other persons toward his own ideas and to check, through the eye of the other, the logical consistency of his own thought. That more mature persons have more allocentrically organized thought processes than immature persons may well be true. Immature persons have been found to have impaired and less socially organized intellectual skills; that is, their intellectual skills are fused by singularly personal emotions and coordinated in strange and unrealistic ways. Their thoughts belong more to the world of night and dreams, where no social reality against which to test their practicability or appropriateness can be seen.

Similarly, a maturing person's motives and values become less autocentric and more centered around other people. Today, he values only his own acre or city, but tomorrow, his nation or the world. He values being a citizen of the world for whom color and language and custom are not barriers but means to appreciate and respect diversity. With greater understanding of how different people live and believe may come greater sensitivity and sympathy for others. It is not only an American bias our data reflect when they confirm that mature persons value social, loving, altruistic relationships more than immature persons do. Mature Turks and Italians share these values, too. The mature person is tolerant; he is not authoritarian.

What of the values of the less mature young adult? Interestingly, he tends to value more highly aesthetic and creative activities; his values are congruent with his temperamental preferences, which are aesthetic as well as intellectualistic and impersonal. But his strong aesthetic orientation does not mean he is more creative; the relationship of maturity to creativity is something more complex. Instead, he is more deeply caught up in his own bodily impulses, not yet having found more adaptive means to communicate them creatively to others. His aesthetic values express his narcissism more than his identification with the discipline of a genuinely aesthetic way of life. More immature students seek out those academic courses where private self-absorption and vicarious immersion in the subjective problems of others are both possible and permitted.

The mature person's ideas about himself are also more allocentric. He begins to think of himself as a human being who also hates, lusts, envies, loves, fears, and enjoys like other human beings. A more mature person agrees with questionnaire statements like: "Fundamentally, I am like most other persons." It is the immature person who believes himself to be so unique, so alone, so isolated that he cannot possibly be understood. Some immature persons so value their own autocentric concepts of themselves as precious individualists that they are insulted if you tell them you "understand" them. Adolescents, not notoriously allocentric in their self-concepts, frequently become incredulous if you suggest that their parents—their *own* parents—once probably felt just like they did. To consider that one's own father or mother was once an adolescent who probably was like oneself is a distinctly uncomfortable experience to many youngsters. They find shockingly obscene the possibility that their own father, during his adolescence, probably also bolted himself in the bathroom when *his* parents were away and masturbated while reading a dirty book. A more mature person, with a more allocentric view of himself, knows that there is probably nothing he has ever felt, wished, or done that at least 85 per cent of the rest of his friends and even those over thirty have not also felt, wished, or done. It is our autocentric view of ourselves that creates the generation and communication gap. As a person learns to take the view of other persons, even toward himself, he also begins to understand more accurately what other persons think of him. In contrast to an immature person, for example, a more mature person replies "True" to the questionnaire statement: "I usually know what other people think of me."

Finally, a mature person cares for others. We expect his relationships with others to become more allocentric. The flowering of friendship, love, and devotion become more prominent. He can love, not just romantically—for much romantic love is only an autocentric fulfillment of compulsive sexual urges—but he can love in the sense of St. Paul, who wrote in his epistle to the Romans

> Owe no man anything, but to love one another; for he that loveth another hath fulfilled the law . . . Love worketh no ill to his neighbor. Therefore love *is* the fulfilling of the law (Ch. 13, verses 8, 10).

Scientific evidence about the characteristics of allocentric personal relationships is scanty. Informal observations reveal that more mature college students are more social—perhaps less lonely; they more frequently live with other people, retreat less frequently into single dormitory rooms; they have many more devoted close friendships that persist than do immature students. Mature persons will also agree with questionnaire statements like: "I have so liked a friend that I did things for him even at the expense of my own interests."

The basic developmental trend is toward increased allocentricism. We expect that the development of more allocentric personal relationships will be accompanied, for example, by more socialized intellectual skills. Some elusive hints in the available data suggest this may be the case. Our holistic stance also leads us to expect that development on one dimension will co-vary with development on the other dimensions that define the growth process. Freud (1900) thought development from dreamlike or illogical (autocentric) to socialized or logical (allocentric) thinking is paralleled by development from less conscious to more conscious concepts and ideas. We don't yet have the evidence to confirm these systemic assumptions.

Almost universally, educators agree that one function of a liberal education is to transform a youth, particularly his intellectual skills and values, into a more socially-centered adult (Appendix A).

BECOMING INTEGRATED

Life moves toward greater differentiation and complexity; we begin to die the moment that movement reverses itself. A person's internal environment changes as he ages; his external environment, particularly in contemporary times, changes ceaselessly. These challenges require new adaptations, inner modifications and syntheses. Some individuals, like the intellectually curious, have an incessant need to spin new syntheses and theories, to make meaningful what seems to be meaningless. Others seek environmental diversity and contrast by which to grow or develop their potentialities further. To speak of *progressive* integration is to emphasize that the maturing person is continually open, flexible, curious, and actively engaged.

A perceptive educator close to maturing students knows that their thought processes and interests do become more subtle, complex, and integrative. Frequently, he is witness—or midwife—to the blossoming of creative ideas and new syntheses that surprise both him and the student. He sees them slowly, sometimes miraculously, begin to organize their thoughts and become more coherent and consistent in their arguments. Reflection monitors the ongoing thought process as effortlessly as a gull scans the ocean for signs of herring. Hypothesis formation and testing become coordinated; problem solving becomes more systematic. Analytic and imaginative skills identify the possibilities from which judgment then selects. The maturing person develops the perfected intellect and the socialized intelligence of which educators like Cardinal Newman and John Dewey spoke. Persons whose thought processes are more integrative and organized, not infused by what the psychoanalysts call primary process or dreamlike images, are more mature. They have been found to possess more accurate and integrated self-images, to control their impulses more appropriately, to not be alienated from other persons, and to be more persistent, energetic, mentally quick, predictable, and realistic than those whose thought processes are disorganized. The person whose thought processes are chaotic and inconsistent is unimaginative, less concerned about people, and tends to devalue altruistic or loving relations with others.

The maturing person's values also become progressively integrated and more consistent. He slowly evolves a workable Weltanschauung, a way or philosophy of life that gives him both direction and consistent purpose. He moves out of those dark periods when he feels torn and divided, pulled between competing values or ways of life. He is no longer like one student who, experimenting with LSD, smashing furniture when drunk, defying authority by blatant sexual escapades, rejecting the affection of other students, in a private moment with his own less acceptable fantasies, composed this plot outline of a short story:

> A young boy, left outside in a bitter snow storm, watching a party of friends within a warm and inviting home, longing to enter into the warmth of the gaiety and fun, remains outside only to fall down into a snowbank to sleep—and to die.

A maturing person finds some greater synthesis that brings increased integrity but reduced defiance.

The movement toward progressive integration is reflected in the increasing congruence of the self-image. What a person thinks he is becomes more like what he wants to be; what a person thinks he is is what he believes other people think of him. A person who has a reasonably consistent view of himself does not need to "play a role," does not need to appear what he isn't since he has no contradictory images of himself. He can act out of wholeness and therefore spontaneously be himself. Mature persons have been found to have more congruent self-images. Persons who have more integrated self-images are more realistic, adventurous, purposeful, and energetic. Those whose ideas about themselves are divided have been found to be alienated from others as well; they suffer an internal world that is composed of primitive and bizarre fantasies over which they have little control. Such divided persons are illogical, unconventional, and frequently impulsive. Although the causes of every suicide are complex, the tragic suicide of Norma Jean Baker was undoubtedly caused, in part, by her inability to reconcile her image of herself as Norma Jean and her image as Marilyn Monroe.

Finally, with increasing maturity comes more integrated personal relationships with men and women. Freud postulated a universal Eros impulse which drove man to seek integration—popularly misconceived to mean only sexual—with other persons. Others, like Angyal (1941), speak of man's need to belong to some larger collective group or community. A maturing person who knows and accepts what he is can open himself to his friends, not holding back, hiding, or defending himself in his intimate relationships. A mature male would not say, "I rarely feel I can just be myself with a close girl friend; there are parts of me she doesn't know." With growing intimacy and openness to the other person also comes the development of new interests, an increasing sensitivity to the thoughts and feelings of others, and an expanding inner world as new information, transported by affection and love, is assimilated into the self and integrated with old values and other feelings.

The progressive integration of the person occurs in all sectors of his life. As the research evidence cited indicates, increasing integration of the self-image is accompanied by increasing organization of one's intellectual skills. Furthermore, the growing integration of the self is accompanied by increasing stability, just as any hierarchically organized system tends toward increasing stability. A young child reacts to pain with a massive temper outburst, pervasive physiological reactions, and possible loss of consciousness. A more mature youth responds selectively. He marshals his energy to find ways to avoid or eliminate the pain. He is not drawn into a catastrophic reaction, because with his more differentiated adaptive means he preserves his stability as he searches for ways to alleviate the pain.

That a maturing person becomes more integrated is strongly seconded by educators, particularly when they discuss the development of relational, coordinating, and synthesizing intellective skills. As Appendix A illustrates, educators, in different words and from different points of view, consistently agree that a liberal education should stimulate man to quest after new connections and organizations of experience.

BECOMING MORE STABLE

To say that a person becomes more stable is to say that his intellectual skills, values, image of himself, and interpersonal relations become more resistant to disruption by threat. As educators know, it is the more immature student whose thought becomes disorganized and illogical when blocked by a temporary frustration. If his cognitive efficiency has become disrupted, a mature person is able to recover from such disorganization more quickly than an immature person, even though the two do not differ in intelligence. Those whose intellective skills are not yet stabilized tend to be anxious, unconfident, moody persons with poor control of their impulses.

Most meaningful adaptations require persistent directed activity and commitment over long periods of time. Not to be certain about what one believes—to be a militarist today and a pacifist tomorrow, to waiver in one's allegiances—paralyzes effective adaptation. Reasonably stable value systems result in consistent and predictable choices. To know what one values is to make adaptation immeasurably easier, for then many of the decisions that must inevitably be made are made without struggle and conflict. One knows what is right. The hardest decisions become the easiest ones.

Erikson (1959) has identified the young adult's central developmental problem to be the achievement of an identity, a synthesis of his leading potentialities that stabilizes his concept of himself. He comes to know who he is and what he wants. His concept of himself is similar to what it was yesterday and what it will be tomorrow. He has a growing certainty about his future, an understanding of his past —he knows, in part, his destiny. And when one compares persons whom others judge to be mature with persons judged to be immature, the more mature person does have a more stable self-image. Furthermore, the person with a more stable self-image has available energy for a wider range of adaptive problems as well as for more spontaneous involvements in the lives of other people. Persons who have made a meaningful identity are not as disturbed by challenging and threatening information. Their self-knowledge gives them a resilience to absorb contradictions and threats without losing their self-control or self-esteem.

Similarly, a maturing person grows out of fleeting adolescent crushes, impetuous attractions, and quasi-hysterical identifications into more enduring and stable friendships. In early adulthood, male and female atttachments and unions are made that persist for a lifetime. Relations may be more quiet than they were in adolescence, but they are usually more steadfast. The relationship between such growing interpersonal stability and other self-structures is unknown.

However, the person grows and matures as a totality. His values do not stabilize independently of the crystallization of his self-image, for example. Or, settling down to a more enduring relation with another, as with a roommate or one's beloved, may affect one's developing intellectual skills. As a person matures, the characteristics associated with his increasingly stable self-image are probably also mirrored in his developing values and interpersonal relationships.

BECOMING MORE AUTONOMOUS

A maturing person becomes less manipulable by his environment and less driven by infantile wishes and conflicts. He develops an internal buffer zone between the immediate demands of his external and internal environment. He becomes discriminating in his decisions; he can postpone and delay, suppress or ignore. A mature person is free to make decisions that are appropriate to the evident facts at hand; he is less imprisoned by prejudices and less fettered by the smiles of environmental seducers, like TV commercials. Without involving ourselves in the "free will" controversy, we can say that maturing is directly correlated with an expanding area of "freed" decisions. This is not to imply that there are no identifiable determinants of a mature person's decisions; rather, the locus of the decisions has been moved from both the environment and his past history into his own contemporary self-structure.

To speak of autonomous intellectual skills is to speak of thought no longer tangled by personal fears and impulses, as one sees in animistic, anthropomorphic, superstitious, and magical thought, or tied to the appearance, the illusion of sensory reality, as one sees in the thought of children. A mature person is able to analyze and judge information, even that most personally relevant to him, in terms of the demands of the information itself, without being influenced by either his own personal desires or by the persuasive opinions of others. Thought becomes objective; judgment, independent. The mature person, confronted with powerful public opinions that contradict his experience, retains autonomy in his judgment, selecting the relevant, discarding the irrelevant. The evidence is scanty and indirect, but it suggests that the thought processes of the mature person are less intruded on by primitive and childish images and content than those of the immature person. Presumably, mature persons are thereby "freer" to reason objectively, even with disturbing information, without allowing their thought to be absorbed into the networks of irrational ideas that surround every conflict.

Many psychologists and educators identify maturing with the

increasing capacity to stick by one's values and convictions, even in the face of severe opposition or pressure. The search for one's identity is frequently fought over emerging values that differ from those imposed earlier by parents or the community. Much adolescent conflict and defiance find their source in this growth trend toward greater autonomy. Ideals and conscience become contemporary, that is, autonomous of many of the early formative and irrational pressures by which one was conformed to parental, school, or society's expectations. Interestingly, mature persons often report themselves to be in less conflict with their parents and other authorities than immature persons. Noted in college for their personal strength and independence of mind and character, such mature persons frequently come from families whose values are resonant with their own identity. Defiance of parental standards may not be a necessary stage in the development of autonomous values.

To speak of an autonomous self-image is to speak of a set of ideas about oneself that cannot be sold to a high bidder, ideas that are not shadowed by residual conflicts and anxieties or earlier childhood experiences. That is, with increasing maturity and greater certainty about what one is like, one can discriminate more effectively between the opinions that others have of him and what of the past is worthy of influencing him. He no longer defines himself in terms of either the world's or his parents' evaluations—unless, of course, they be appropriate evaluations. The available evidence confirms that the more mature person is more *selectively* open to "believable" information about himself. It is the immature person of inadequate self-esteem that indiscriminately resists information that contradicts his image of himself (Tippett & Silber, 1966).

A maturing person also does not sacrifice his own integrity or independence in his relations with men and women to secure some evanescent pleasure or token of respect and love. An immature female, not certain about her own identity, would agree with this statement: "A man I love could persuade me to do something I might otherwise consider to be wrong." A mature man will not barter his soul for a Helen. The view is widely held that the style of a person's adult relationships only repeats that of his earlier relations with his parents, but it is characteristic of the maturing person to outgrow such persisting emotional ties. His responses to others are not compulsive repetitions and intricate manifestations of lingering infantile patterns. They are based solidly within the reality of the present relationship. Persons who are more autonomous of their parents—that is, are less compliant or oppositional—have been found to be more discriminating in their acceptance of information about themselves (Tippett & Silber, 1966).

Although the two dimensions, allocentricism and autonomy, appear to contradict each other, in reality they are compatible. A mature person resolves the apparent contradiction this way: his increased allocentricism makes him aware of others' views and motives, including those views about him; he is able to understand and converse with others, tentatively taking the position of the other. But his autonomy permits him to retain command of his own decisions, to accept selectively what the other person may say. Much youthful defiance is an exaggerated form of autonomy *not* leavened by a comparable appreciation of the point of view or feelings of the person toward whom his rebellion is directed—a proposition to which centuries of suffering parents surely would agree. A more mature person asserting his intellectual or emotional autonomy still is aware of the ins and outs of an opposing view, can still project himself through empathy and intuition to understand and sympathize with the views of the other.

The implied assumption, fundamental to understanding the systemic nature of the maturing process, is that too extended development of one of the dimensions or self-structures eventually inhibits its own future development. Too extended allocentric development not approximated by a comparable development in autonomy produces a rigid conformism, which may in turn stifle allocentricism; too great autonomy not balanced by a comparable allocentricism produces an insufferable aloofness or unreasonable rebelliousness. This central assumption remains unverified, but it will affect many of our subsequent analyses of the psychological effects of a liberal arts college on its students.

Finally, educators also talk about a liberally educated person as an independent person, freed to use his intellect, himself, and his values as means for more creative adaptations (Appendix A).

Of the several problems that must be troubling the reflective reader by now, we examine three. We must distinguish between the characteristics we have been describing and what they become in excess. Thus, symbolization does not mean an obsessive introspection; allocentricism is not conformity; an integrated individual is not the same as the inhuman organization man; stability is not rigidity; and autonomy is neither a hermetic existence nor an inhibited coldness. Too rigid a self-structure prevents the assimilation of new information and the creation of new adaptations. Obsessive introspection limits the formation of stabilized integrations and their implementation in decisive action. Excessive allocentricism prevents the development of a meaningful identity. While development on the five dimensions may not be equal at various points in the maturing process, too great an advance or a lag in development on one dimension may limit development on the other dimensions. Maturing depends upon the reciprocal development of all dimensions, with development of some dimensions perhaps leading at one time, other dimensions at another time.

Second, a mature person, by virtue of his maturity, can permit himself to become disorganized when adaptation or his need to play requires such disorganization. A more stably organized person, centered in his own identity, aware of reality, trusting in his control, and conscious of the forces that can affect his behavior, can allow himself to regress selectively with an inner certainty that he can recover his former self-structure at his decision. He can allow himself to get potted, with or without liquor or LSD. The available evidence suggests that more mature persons can control their regressive thoughts and images and can recover their former level of thought organization more readily than immature persons.

To be educable means to be in a potential state of disorganization, to allow oneself to plunge into contradictory theories and points of view sharply contrasting with one's own, to entertain the prejudices and biases of others. To be educable even means to permit oneself, in the search for new ideas, to slip into the dream world of hunch, reverie, and narrowed awareness where the form of life's images is blurred, where strange and frightening and monstrous combinations of the familiar and unfamiliar romp and play, and where no words are either powerful or subtle enough to capture emerging feelings, intuitions, and vivid sensory impressions. While maturity is no guarantee against some disorganization, it is a guarantee that disorganization can be used for adaptive and playful purposes when such disorganization is felt to be necessary or desirable.

It follows, therefore, that an educator should be more leery of the student who sails through college with complete equanimity and poise, brilliantly accommodating himself to professorial demands, than he should be about some of those students whose disorganized floundering is preliminary to a new creative personal synthesis. The trouble is that it takes rare perceptiveness to distinguish, at times, between a maturely and an immaturely disorganized student.

The third problem is related to the second: What is the relation of maturity to creativity? And here answers are unknown. Much work proceeds about the nature of creativity, very little about maturity, and less, if any, about their relationship. Surely, creative persons are not sealed off from those ideas that emerge during periods of controlled disorganization, sleep, mystical experiences or other irrational states. To be creative also requires special talents and skills that are probably closely tied to hereditary or constitutional factors. To be creative probably also depends to some limited extent on being reasonably mature, particularly in the more intellectual fields, but to be mature does not depend on being very creative in any narrow technical sense. True, a more mature person should be able to create more adaptive possibilities by which to solve a wider range of problems, but to define creativity without reference to the type of medium with which the creative person works is to rob the term of any legitimate meaning. Our insubstantial research evidence does not suggest mature persons are any more intellectually creative than immature persons. We have no evidence to determine if more creative persons are more mature than less creative ones. The issue remains open, awaiting more knowledge about both creative and mature persons. A recent collection of essays (Heist, 1968) presents some evidence on this matter.

While some evidence supports the theory of maturing described in this chapter, future research will undoubtedly sharpen and alter the model, perhaps suggest a more comprehensive set of defining dimensions, and surely produce evidence that challenges many of the empirical relationships already found. But the worth of a model lies not so much in its eternal truth as in the help it offers to order and organize thought and in its power to suggest new ideas and relationships. Of even greater importance is its ability to predict how actual students in a powerfully liberally educating institution do mature. This is its most rigorous test. To that test we now turn.

CHAPTER II

A Liberally Educating College

To test the theory of maturing and identify those conditions that promote maturing we must study persons in a situation that has the power to mature them. If to become liberally educated is to become more mature, then we want to study the students of a powerfully liberally educating institution, that is, one that produces a wide range of maturing effects that endure in a large number of its students. But not every institution that claims it liberally educates does. Its range of maturing effects may be so limited and ephemeral, and the number of students who mature so small, that there is no test of the comprehensive adequacy of the theory of maturing. Independent educators and conventional criteria of the power of a college to educate suggest Haverford College to be one of the country's best examples of a liberally educating institution that historically has had a wide range of maturing effects upon its students.

To mature is to increase one's potentials for adaptation. To adapt is to find an optimal relation between adjusting to the demands of the environment and fulfilling one's own demands. To understand the maturing process we must describe the types of demands that Haverford College makes to which the students must adapt. This chapter analyzes the college, not by merely describing it, but by trying to capture the spirit of the demands and their effects that characterizes the invisible college.[1]

HAVERFORD COLLEGE, 1955–1965

For the many who have never heard of Haverford College, it is *not* Harvard University, a confusion some Haverfordians like to perpetuate by saying "Harvard is the Haverford of the East"; it is *not* a coed college located at nearby Swarthmore; it is *not* what *Life* magazine quixotically said, "Haverford: grind school—a place only for brainy students with exceptionally strong academic interests—sound preparation for the business world—an abundance of spit and polish —an introvert would probably not be happy here—;" and finally, it may or may not be what the *Chicago Tribune* called it, after an intensive survey of educators and institutions of higher education, "the best men's college in the country." To support its view, the *Tribune* said, in part,

[1] The analysis relies heavily on many different sources, including student papers written about the college, student publications and reports, published commentaries, extensive psychological test material, and student-faculty criticisms of the analysis itself. We describe the college as it was during the decade 1955–65, during which the principal studies of the book were conducted. The analysis was written prior to and independently of the results of the actual studies. The findings reported in Chapters Seven and Eight have not been influenced by either this chapter or the theory of maturing, for no student participant was aware of either. The chapter has been briefly abstracted in *Explorations of Maturity* (Heath, 1965).

The eminence of Haverford College for undergraduate education . . . in the liberal arts is comparable to that of Harvard among American universities . . . [it] was rated first among men's colleges by an overwhelming majority of scholars and scientists . . . some rate it above all other educational institutions in the country (April 21, 1957).

More objective criteria of the liberally educating power of the college that others might cite are these indices: the percentage of its graduates who have received Woodrow Wilson, Danforth, and all other types of major graduate fellowships is either the highest in the country or one of the highest, depending upon what year one selects to study. Again, in proportion to its size, the college has ranked either first or is one of the five highest ranking colleges or universities in the country in the number of its alumni who have completed their doctorates in the humanities, sciences, and social sciences, who have received Public Health research grants, or who have been cited in *Who's Who in America*. By these criteria, there would be little doubt we study a powerfully liberally educating college.

But just how effective is the college in *really* liberally educating its students? No firm objective evidence exists. Insofar as the Wilson and the Danforth fellowships are awarded partially on the basis of personal qualities and maturity, the college may indeed have powerful maturing effects. Observers who know the college and others well claim it does liberally educate. Jacob, for example, although not citing the evidence in his famous report (1957), singled Haverford College out to be one of those few that had potent effects on changing the values of its students. More critically, the students themselves, the final experts, do claim the college changes them. These judgments and indices are subject to qualification, of course, but they suggest we fairly test the hypotheses of Chapter One about maturing when we study the liberally educating effects of such a college.

What kind of college was Haverford during the decade between 1955 and 1965? It was a small residential, intellectually demanding, and Quaker college.

A SMALL RESIDENTIAL COLLEGE

The college is located along Philadelphia's Main Line on two hundred odd acres of fields, woods, and landscaped lawns of flowering dogwood, apple and cherry trees and towering elms, poplars, and beeches. Almost all of the students and many of the faculty live on the campus. Until recently, every major building on the campus could be seen from one spot. Except for some grand and stately Tudor homes converted into apartments for faculty, the buildings are plain and gracious but unostentatious, in conformity with Quaker views about simplicity. The most conflictual building is Barclay, the freshman dormitory, scarred by many years of exuberances encouraged by its long open corridors ideal for midnight bowling, soap slides, water fights, and riots. Since its appearance in 1877, it has been the "storm center of . . . discipline" problems. Prudently, almost all subsequent dormitories have been divided into small groups of rooms collected around individual entryways.

The number of students is small, and according to 61 per cent of one entering class, the principal reason for selecting the college. Entering classes averaged about 125 during the 1955–65 decade. To those surrounded by tens of thousands of students, a world of 450 to 500 (555 in 1966) students and 60 (65 in 1966) faculty members may seem unreal. Few courses contain more than thirty students and even then many are divided into sections. Faculty are adamant about increasing the size of courses and much departmental jockeying has ensued about whether fifteen or twenty or twenty-two students is an ideal seminar size. Almost all freshmen participate in a weekly English tutorial with one faculty member and three or four other freshmen. No student is taught by graduate students for the faculty has resisted this seductive lure of a graduate program. Advanced seminars average ten students, a few of which meet regularly in faculty homes. The number of majors per department is small and much faculty time is spent with those concentrating in the department or conducting independent but faculty supervised research. Any student has the opportunity to visit with and seek the advice of the incessant stream of distinguished departmental and college visitors. Faculty-student relations are informal; some of the younger faculty are called by their first names. Students frequent some faculty homes for meals, desserts, and as baby sitters. During the decade of the study, the former dean of the faculty and his wife entertained more than a thousand students in small groups with home-cooked roast beef dinners. While most students are known to the deans and most students know something about most faculty, few faculty know at least casually more than about 15 per cent of the student body, if that many.

The small size of the college also makes it easier for students to recognize almost everyone on the campus, though it is the rare student who knows everyone by name. It is easier to become known than it is to remain unknown. In contrast to students at larger colleges, where a student may never meet any other member of one of his courses outside of class, Haverford students live and eat, study and play, worship and date always in the presence of the same students. One can become too intimately known in such a situation, for there is little opportunity to flee into anonymity or escape the gaze of others. The small community both facilitates and limits the formation of friendships. It is easier to know more about a larger number of students, for neither class nor academic major bars friendships with others. Because of his close proximity to the same persons for four years, his social community stabilizes itself earlier, thus preparing the ground for maximizing the influence of one's friends as well as for developing enduring friendships. On the other hand, a small college finds it difficult to provide the diversity in social class background, ethnic origin, and temperament that the cosmopolitan university does, so that some students feel acutely lonely in such a homogeneous community. Although a student may know more about his environment and come under social pressure more readily at Haverford, the psychological effect of smallness, somewhat paradoxically, is not conformism but a heightened individualism, a subject to which we will return later.

In a small college where the person with whom one disagrees cannot be avoided and where personal disputes and sharp intellectual disagreements disrupt the social fabric of the community, certain informal means of preserving the texture of social relations into which all are woven have evolved as the Haverford way. It is difficult to live too closely to stimulating if not irascible geniuses. The college does not suffer—or profit—from the famous feuds that so often mark larger institutions. At Haverford, people disagree by a heavy silence, humorous sarcasm, or gentle chiding. For example, in writing about colorful and disruptive editors of the college newspaper, *The Haverford News,* yearbook editors have written, "Using a minimum of truths, he stands somewhat off from the throng and quickly fashions a sheaf of paper"; "The *News* had at the time of this encounter the vocal and vigorous support of perhaps as much as 3 per cent of the student body"—the 3 per cent represented the staff of the *News.* Or another instance of how disagreements are resolved occurred when a freshman, complaining in a letter to the *News* that other students had suggested he was too unkempt and unwashed even for Haverford, which is almost inconceivable, said these students violated what should be a "free individual's responsibility to himself." The next issue was a lively one. Letters from other students argued quite abstractly the meaning of "responsibility to self." They suggested (1) "There is a difference between struggling to comprehend and answer one's inner call, and compensating for failure to do so through offensive external mannerisms," and recommended that (2) "Mr. [A] start to channel his treasured individualism into some constructive areas and help his witness to his principles by patching the hole in the seat of his pants." Mr. A remained an accepted member of the community. He also got another pair of pants. More recently, as divisive issues, like the Vietnam war, have deeply troubled the community, disagreement has had a sharper edge, frequently personal, with both students and faculty criticizing each other more directly and personally.

AN INTELLECTUALLY DEMANDING COLLEGE

The college, since its founding in 1833 and chartering in 1856 to grant the bachelor of arts degree, has been claimed by its historians to have maintained high intellectual standards, to have consistently demanded much of its students, and to have had a Board of Managers that has sympathetically sought to implement such standards by seeking highly competent and scholarly faculty. In the 1880's the college emerged as a strong liberal arts institution and the intellectual tradition of the college became fixed. In 1918, one of its most influential presidents wrote, "If [Haverford] was to be a small college, with limited resources, it must strive for excellence in the one field, *i.e.*, liberal arts, toward which its past history has been driving it" (Sharpless, 1918, pp. 103–104).

The college has historically maintained such an intellectual tradition by keeping its classes small, maintaining a large faculty relative to the number of its students, paying its scholarly faculty well, and emphasizing informal faculty-student relationships that helped to maximize the faculty's influence on students.

That the intellectual ethos of the college is perceived by the students to be so dominating is revealed by studies of the college using objective measures for which comparative data about other colleges are available. For example, several randomly selected samples of Haverford students described the college to be more "eggheadish," "bookwormish," scholarly, theoretical, and philosophical than 95 per cent of the students of nineteen other liberal arts colleges and universities (including Antioch, Dartmouth, Middlebury, and Princeton) described their own institutions (Pervin, 1966). Other randomly drawn samples from the freshman and senior classes described the college similarly on the College Characteristics Index (CCI), that is, more theoretical and intellectual than 95 per cent of the colleges for which normative data were available (Stern, 1963). Furthermore, the Pervin study suggested the students' perceptions of the college were very similar to their perception of the faculty, which is the college's principal interpreter of its intellectual tradition.

So let us now turn to the faculty. During the decade of the studies, the college, like many others, has been subject to considerable faculty and administrative instability, due to retirements, resignations, and increases in the size of the faculty. The average age of the faculty is forty; only about one-fifth of the faculty has been at the college more than a dozen years. There has been a 100 per cent turnover in faculty in 60 per cent of the twenty-one academic departments within the past twelve to thirteen years and, as of 1967, a 100 per cent change in the administrative posts within ten years. The increased faculty mobility, combined with the increasing gravitational effects that positions of greater responsibility and associations with graduate universities have for professional scholars, may be symptomatic of that observed national trend away from deep faculty attachments to their colleges to a more embracing attachment to their own professions and personal advancement (Caplow & McGee, 1958). The tempo of the faculty procession through the college has been spirited. Such a trend poses a serious threat to colleges like Haverford, as the *News* has been quick to editorialize, where its "atmosphere" and values, two of its more precious assets, depend upon a continuing stable core of respected faculty and administration temperamentally understanding of and sympathetic to its traditions.

Just what kind of faculty does the college have? It has sought not just scholars but those scholars who are also excellent teachers, temperamentally congruent with the values of the college community, and sympathetically interested in students. The scholarly tradition has historically been dominated by the Ivy League. As of 1965, almost 50 per cent of the faculty came from Harvard, Yale, and Princeton. The

Harvard crimson was worn by one-fourth of the faculty at commencement. How do the students describe the faculty? Of twenty colleges and university faculties rated by their students (Pervin, 1966), the Haverford faculty was judged to be the most (or at least in the top 5 per cent of the faculties studied) "eggheadish" and "bookwormish," theoretical, philosophical, research-oriented, sophisticated, and avocational. The faculty was also perceived to be the most motivated, aspiring, challenging, skeptical, examining, and uncertain of the other faculty groups. More than the faculties of most of the other reporting colleges, it was perceived by the students to be very warm, permissive, guiding, personal, democratic, tolerant, and moral, though not prudish. Whether the faculty is in fact so "eggheadish" or aspiring or personal we do not know.

When the students' image of the typical Haverford student is compared with their image of the typical faculty member, we find the faculty is believed to differ from the students on a variety of intellectual traits. In decreasing order of difference, the faculty was judged to be more "grinding," scholarly, research-oriented, intellectual, ritualistic, philosophical, "eggheadish," erudite, aspiring, and nonathletic.

The hardworking and demanding faculty clearly sets the intellectual pace of the college. Young teachers just out of graduate school bring expectations and standards unconsciously molded by their recent graduate work and associates. Since many of them have been the outstanding but unmellowed graduate students of their day, they expect of their students the same intellectual perseverance, motivation, and dedication that undoubtedly contributed to their own recent successful performance. With the strengthening of most departments by the infusion of vigorous young men and a few women, in their late twenties and early thirties, underclassmen find few "gut" courses left by which to lighten their demanding five-course programs. Alumni express persistent concern about the faculty pressure on the students. The high expectations of the faculty can be illustrated by the awards it gives. Despite the exceptionally high aptitudes of a conscientious student body and the recognition of their achievement by other educators, not more than two or three students in a class achieve even a low *A* average at the college. The faculty has a policy of awarding only one or two *summa* and three or four *magna cum laudes* to a graduating class. Students feel these high expectations; many accept them and try to respond but often at the expense of their personal maturing in nonintellectual areas. While students are aware a solid *C* or a low *B* grade average may get them into graduate or professional schools, the college definitely is not a "gentleman *C*" school. Such a tradition violates almost everybody's expectation of what a Haverford education should be. Students respect those teachers who demand much from them and may complain if new faculty do not teach courses of substance. It is not unusual to hear students with solid *C* averages deprecate their ability and achievement (even though they may score on the ninetieth percentile of the Graduate Record examinations) and feel unworthy of the college. Students do not rebel against the intellectual demands of the faculty. They introject them, identify with the faculty, and guiltily blame themselves for failing to reach their expectations.

A young faculty has other subtle effects. There is not as wide a psychological or communication gulf between young men in their late teens and faculty in their thirties as there so often is between young adults and venerable faculty of fifty. Students expect more equalitarian and democratic relations with younger faculty; they expect to compete more successfully with an inexperienced than an experienced intellectual; they may find it easier to find themselves, their identities, mirrored in someone close to their own age and contemporary cultural experiences. Many younger faculty themselves are also strangers to the recent events of history—the depression, Korean War, or Joseph McCarthy's attacks on academic freedom.

The curriculum, which expresses the faculty's conception of a liberal education, is conventionally organized by departments ranging from astronomy to Spanish. The faculty has resisted including applied courses, like computer programming or the creative arts, which are provided in various ways outside of the formal curriculum. The first two years of courses are intended to broaden a young man by introducing him to the liberal arts spectrum; the last two years deepen his control of a more limited academic discipline. All students are required in their first two years to complete four semester courses in the humanities, in the social sciences, and in the natural sciences (Requirements reduced in 1967) and the equivalent of two college years of a foreign language. The principal distinctive characteristic of the faculty's curricular expectations is that a student's liberal education not be bereft of systematic work with issues that deal with values. Two of his four humanities courses must deal with religious or ethical values (This requirement was abandoned in 1967). In addition, the freshman had to complete a one-year tutorial English course whose content also dealt with values and ethical problems (Requirement modified in 1967). The faculty resists defining more precisely than this what knowledge it considers central to a liberal education.

The college's intellectual tradition is so valued that competing traditions offering alternative foci around which to organize one's life or by which to rebel against the dominant value system either don't exist or play only a secondary role. Students stumbling along with grade averages of sixty and seventy find few nonacademic traditions with which to identify and secure some measure of self- and peer-group respect. Unlike many other colleges, Haverford does not "institutionalize" social partying, heavy dating, drinking, and other ways of fulfilling youthful needs as group values, although they are, of course, frequently expressed. The college has no fraternities to which students alienated from the principal values of the campus can flee. Also, athletics and its associated flamboyance have seldom been a competing focal point for status on the campus. In 1918, President Sharpless wrote, "The athlete, if fair in his methods, was something of a leader but not the great hero, unless he were also a scholar" (1918). In 1960, the sports editor of the *News* wrote, "The good ball player who is also a good student is not uncommon on our campus; moreover, many of our most accomplished athletes, originally unmotivated academically, have become scholastically concerned and have developed tremendously in capacity for academic achievement" (June 3, 1960, p. 5). The students are not anti-athletic aesthetes. They participate extensively and well in thirteen varsity sports, particularly in soccer, basketball, and cricket. Each year, about 50 per cent of the students engage in a varsity or junior varsity sport, and most of the rest in many intramural activities. But a person who centers his life around athletics becomes a "jock," and "jocks" have little status as jocks at the college. Alumni, as they have for years, lament the absence of pep rallies and the sparse attendance at athletic contests.

The one major viable competitor to the intellectual life is extra-curricular activity. Both the number of (fifteen to twenty campus organizations and innumerable Student Council committees) and heavy participation in such groups attest to a strong need not only to achieve outside the circle of faculty influence but also to balance an ever-present abstract intellectual way of life by activity that has immediate consequences.

What are some other reactions to the incessant intellectual demands of the college? Most students, aware of the expectations of the college, enter as freshmen open to the faculty's intellectual standards. They accept many faculty as intellectual models, but find they too seldom develop the level of competence both they and the faculty hold them to. Some students, in order to achieve, turn their ambition and great capacity for action and resourcefulness to extracurricular activities, civil rights, or political activity—without ever abandoning their basic value of the importance of academic achievement. Others remain deeply ambivalent in their loyalty to the college, sharply critical of it when at college, insufferably proud of its intellectual tradition when at home with former friends, perhaps because they do not have successful football seasons or orgiastic fraternity parties about which to boast. Other students carry away from the college a deep abiding sense of guilt for having failed, so they feel, to realize what they expected of themselves—even if they graduated near the top of their class.

Most students would have the college no other way. They entered expecting to be stretched intellectually. Most leave stretched, some out of shape. Of any graduating class, about 80 per cent go immediately on to graduate and professional schools where many distinguish themselves. Of the 25 per cent that fail to graduate with their class, 5 to 10 per cent return to complete their academic work. Compared to the attrition rates of other colleges, the college permanently loses few of its students, perhaps due to its liberal policies about leaves of absence and its sympathetic forbearance and patience with students in academic or personal difficulties.

A QUAKER COLLEGE

What gives the college the ineffable but recognizable uniqueness that was sensed by a visiting evaluative committee and claimed by the students and alumni? It is not its size, nor its faculty and intellectual tradition, nor its students, but some combination of all of these factors within a spirit, an atmosphere of value and belief that, perhaps, stems from or is at least associated with the Quaker (Friends) philosophy of man and his communal relationships. The Friends value independent thought, continuous confrontation of oneself and one's relationships, respect for others and their way of life, man's inherent corporateness, and consistently democratic and liberal social concerns. These values permeate the invisible college we now discuss.

Haverford was during the decade a Quaker college more in tone and temper than in numbers. Twenty-nine per cent of one entering class said a reason for selecting the college was its religious tradition that valued the worth of each individual. But not every suitor speaks directly out of his heart; some whisper what they know the coy maiden wants to hear. No matter. What are the facts? About 10 per cent of the student body (7 per cent in 1966), about 15 per cent of the faculty, few of the administration, and most of the Board of Managers are Friends. No Quaker has been appointed to the faculty since 1960. These numbers are too few and the spirit of the Friends is not one to make the college a parochial or provincial one—which it certainly isn't.

How do the students feel about the invisible atmosphere of the college? Comparing Haverford to other similar colleges, Pervin found that it ranked within the top 5 per cent in its liberal concerns for social welfare, pacifism, acceptance of integration and intermarriage. It was also more idealistic, concerned, humane, sympathetic, as well as nonconformist and rebellious than most of the other nineteen colleges in the study (Pervin, 1966). This picture is supplemented by studies with the CCI (Stern, 1963) that showed the college to be more sharply defined than 95 per cent of its normative colleges in the following ways: the college places little value on social appearance and grooming (personal narcissism) or on submissive and deferent behavior to authority. The college is a protesting, rebellious, restive place. It is judged to be highly self-depreciatory and critical, open to constant self-evaluation and valuing a nondefensive adaptability. What keeps the college from becoming anarchic and diffuse? The CCI suggests that the college, whether in physical plant, in academic regulations, or in faculty expectations is very ordered and structured. The college is certainly not perceived to be chaotic or disorganized. But more important, perhaps, is the college's strong value of commitment and involvement, whether in personal, social, political, international, or other outwardly directed activities. These more objectively measured characteristics reflect much of the college's historic religious values and traditions that have shaped its distinctive "atmosphere" and given it an organizing center of purpose.

Students and faculty do not agree about the value or the effects of its religious tradition. Many of the alumni, older faculty, and some students believe the Quaker tradition and its emphasis on religious and social values made the college unique. From this viewpoint, the Quaker heritage not only impressed its spirit on the college but also silently guaranteed to both the faculty and students many freedoms and opportunities each might eventually lose if the college lost its mooring lines to its Quaker traditions. In times of crisis, for example, the Quaker way of life and values have given direction to college policy. They served as the unconscious apperceptive moral framework within which specific ethical judgments and values were consciously formed. The Quaker ideals have frequently been used by the *News* as a measuring rod by which to criticize the administration. For example, the use of a large tent in which to feed over 1700 guests at one president's inauguration elicited strong words about the violation of the Friends' value of simplicity; permission for the armed services to put up posters and to recruit on the campus and hesitation in rejecting the use of Defense Department funds for faculty research projects were cited as a betrayal and erosion of the Friends' peace testimony. Postponing the abolition of two alumni semi-secret social fraternities involving selected upperclassmen excited prolonged agitation and recriminations that the Friends were not consistent in their beliefs about non-discrimination and equality. A non-Quaker European alumnus expressed his feelings this way:

> This spirit made Haverford a community—for all . . . and at no other school, be it in the United States or Europe, have I ever found a student and teacher community tied better together, spiritually, as well as socially. There was an atmosphere of intellectuals, of liberals, of young people who kept their eyes and ears—and their hearts—open to everything going on around them, on campus and in the world. These people would never think a moment of segregation, secrecy, social discrimination (*The Haverford News,* February 10, 1958, p. 10).

Other faculty and students, probably a considerable majority in recent years, believe the college has outgrown its Quaker tradition, which now is and should belong more properly to its history. Many wish to preserve the college's historic value on the right of individual self-determination and its democratic and social concerns, values that resonate with the cast of mind of many academic intellectuals, but not its associated "religious" roots, connections, or forms, with which the more secular faculty are unsympathetic. Many would deny that the Quaker philosophy or its more distinctive institutions, like its Meeting for worship, had any liberally educating or maturing effects on its students. Much of what the following section describes, from this viewpoint, would exist even if the college had not been Quaker. They would sharply disagree with the hypothesis that it was the constellation of the college's small size, intellectual tradition, *and* Quaker philosophy that made the college peculiarly potent in liberally educating its students in the past.

FAITH AND TESTIMONIES OF QUAKERS

What are the values and attitudes that defined the invisible college during the period of the studies? How were they expressed in the college's educational policies, and what were their effects on the maturing of the students?

The Friends' central religious belief is that there is a part of God in every man, referred to as the "Inner Light," and that the responsibility of each man is to look inwardly and follow the guidance of that inner spirit. From this simple point of faith, for no other doctrine defines all Quakers, follow the well-known Quaker values and testimonies.

Since each man shares a part of God, each man, regardless of his status, wealth, color, or creed, is of equal value and worth. A Quaker believes in equality, individuality, and individual freedom; he rejects status symbols, self-aggrandizement, display, and luxuriant living that imply one man is worth more than any other. Quakers address each other by their full names or first names, avoiding such status marks as "Doctor" or "President." To display a Phi Beta Kappa key is ostentatious; some students have refused such awards. Within the student body, there is little social class consciousness. Friendships cut across academic class and other artificial lines. Although the college has some very wealthy students, status is not achieved by expensive cars or social entertainment. Family background or income is not a prerequisite for acceptance and respect. The students prize the lack of social snobbery and status competitiveness and make deprecatory comments about "the Princeton man," their biased image of social snobbishness. All but two of one group of academic honors candidates refused to stand for oral examinations, one alleged reason being that such honors created unjustifiable distinctions among students. They value personal integrity and individuality, the expression of what a person is, although they recognize many do not know what they are. The students know they do not have to appear what they aren't—except to appear, if they can't be, individualists who seem to know what they are. The farewell words of one departing senior about his classmates expressed the college's strongest value this way: "And then one dare not forget those individuals who have spent their four years trying to transform the Haverford legend of intellectual integrity into a reality" (*The Haverford News,* June 9, 1961, p. 3).

Students value not only the pursuit after what one "truly is" but also respect for others and their opinions. They do not value intolerance or authoritarian curbs on the freedom of others—or their own. Until 1965, any student or alumnus could command the attention of the entire community by writing to the *News* or by speaking in Quaker Meeting. He would be read or listened to, and responded to—usually with respectful and carefully worded pithy comments. This respect for any dissenting voice is revealed in the Quaker business meeting, which eschews the pitting of majority against minority as is done in voting procedures. The faculty, for example, does not act unless there is basic unanimity on an issue. It reaches decisions most slowly. The philosophy of the college values such respect and the small size of the community almost requires it.

I have quoted the students liberally. It is time to give the faculty its voice. To illustrate the spirit of honest and frank criticism that is valued, we cite one exasperated faculty member whose letter to the *News* said:

> *The Haverford News* is a monument of inexact and ungrammatical writing. Its pages demonstrate week after week that Haverford students not only do not know enough to say clearly what they mean, but that they know so little as to say at times what even those who teach them cannot believe they can possibly mean. Lately, the *News* has been concerned with the image of the Haverford man. It is not flattering. It reveals, to a larger audience than a long-suffering faculty, that in part the Haverford man is a pretentious illiterate (May 12, 1958, p. 2).

Participation in the current life of the community is not restricted to the student or faculty member. Alumni also participate actively in controversy at the college. In response to a faculty position about accepting defense grants, one alumnus wrote:

> To banish our moral confusion
> Six professors, in solemn collusion,
> Have pledged hospitality
> To debate on morality
> Provided it yields no conclusion!
> (*The Haverford News,* March 11, 1957).

STUDENT RESPONSIBILITY

From the belief that each man must bear his own responsibility for listening to the "inward word," the basis for the Friends' rejection of a professional ministry to mediate between the individual and his God, comes the Friends' strong emphasis on individual responsibility. The college has not always so interpreted the Friends' faith. From its founding, the Board of Managers struggled with student anarchy and discipline until it finally wearied of what were called "Cromwellian attempt[s] to enforce habits and conduct by authority." In 1871, the Board transferred disciplinary power to the college officials, who also struggled similarly for another thirty years with rebellious and ungovernable students. In 1900, self-governing responsibility was gradually extended to the students. Contemporary students have very wide responsibilities and powers. The Students' Association, to which all students belong, and its executive agency, the Students' Council, is one of the most powerful and independent self-governing groups in any American college.

The Council supports financially some fifteen to twenty student organizations, appoints its own numerous standing committees (as well as two student members to each of the faculty standing committees as of 1966). Like the administration, it exercises no policy or censoring control over *The Haverford News* and the college literary magazine. The *News* remains the Council's and administration's most vociferous critic.

The Council's most important psychological function is to maintain the ethical standards and sense of responsibility of the student body. For example, it shares with the administration responsibility for disciplining students who destroy property. It assesses the costs of property damage on individual students, the entire student body, or pays for damages out of its own treasury. One year the Council received 130 bills for damage, most of it nonmalicious. Pent-up tensions are released through massive water fights, randomly directed snowballs, the painting of the spherical concrete balls that line the campus roads Easter egg colors, and occasional more serious expressions. According to the Columbia Bureau of Applied Social Research questionnaire results, sent to some eighty-five colleges in the country, more Haverford students (28 per cent of the respondents) admitted having destroyed college property than students from the other comparable male colleges queried (*The Haverford News,* October 4, 1963, p. 8).

Excessive drinking does not play the role in student social life that it does in many other colleges. Earlier, the *News* chided the administration for hypocrisy "between the lip-service paid to Friends' teaching [that one should not drink] and the College practice" about drinking, which was to ignore all but the most flagrant violations. A jointly sponsored faculty-student policy on drinking was:

> Student drinking of alcoholic beverages is not consistent with the history of the College, with the tenets of the Friends' belief, with excellence in scholarship under the prevalent conditions of academic pressure, or with the maintenance of a healthy community. Prohibition is inconsistent with the freedom of individual development which is the proudest part of the life of the college. But liberty does not mean license. Drinking to excess in any form; drinking in public places on the campus; furnishing alcoholic beverages to minors; and any breach of taste induced or encouraged by drinking will not be tolerated (*The Haverford News,* March 17, 1958, p. 2).

Although the frequency of drinking may be increasing on the campus, students seem to have reasonable control over this behavior. Some confirmation of this assessment comes again from the Columbia questionnaire that reported that 51 per cent of Haverford men, the next to the lowest percentage for other similar male colleges, have "ever gotten drunk." The *News* commented, "The survey questions asked not whether Haverfordians habitually get drunk, but whether they have EVER gotten drunk," perhaps revealing skepticism that drunken behavior was extensive on the campus. (Since 1965, student use of drugs like marijuana has replaced concern about drinking.)

The Student Council has sole responsibility for implementing the honor system, which all entering freshmen pledge on their honor to obey as long as they are at college. The honor code is a viable and central moral influence with sanctions enforced by the Council, which may publicly and severely reprimand a student, recommend to the administration (which has never vetoed a recommendation) that he be placed on probation, suspended, or permanently expelled from college. The Council has not shied from recommending the more drastic measures.

The Haverford honor system is somewhat unique among honor systems, for it applies not only to academic honesty but also to social (sexual) relationships. Yearly, the students re-examine and redefine the code themselves, though within the context of preparatory discussions with the administration. The code is then presented to the student body every year for discussion and approval, thus insuring the contemporary students' agreement about its acceptance.

The academic honor system, first initiated in 1896, identifies the behavior considered to be intellectually dishonorable, for example, cheating on examinations, copying other person's papers, talking about an examination that other students have not yet taken. All examinations are unproctored and take-home examinations are frequent. Students initiated with faculty approval a highly successful self-scheduled and student-conducted system of final examinations. The students agree about what defines academic honor.

The students do not agree about the social code, the specific wording of which is a cause of often legalistic and fuming arguments by some who want the protection of an exact definition about the extent to which sexual relations violate the code. The code, revised in 1961–62, somewhat euphemistically said:

> Any act which, if it became public, would damage the reputation of the College, the student and/or the woman guest involved, shall be considered a violation of the Honor System (Handbook Student Association, 1961–62).

The "any act" phrase was subsequently elaborated by the Council to include sexual relations on the campus. This revision came under immediate attack and the strident arguments culminated in the elimination of the specific interpretation of the "any act" clause in 1965 to emphasize that a student is honor bound to show respect to a woman and regard for the community. The vagueness is just short of monumental and will probably be the cause for more arguments by a different Council. With the consent of their roommates, students may entertain women in their rooms any time except between 2:00 (3:30 weekends) and 9:00 A.M. (In 1966, the hour restrictions were removed.) Students must report any honor system violation about which they have knowledge. A student who fails to report a violation committed by another student is also held responsible for violating the code.

The honor system is a potentially powerful psychological determinant and regulator of behavior. How strongly is the system supported by the students? There is no doubt that the system is enforced when violations are brought to the Council. There is little doubt that most students strongly support the academic code and perceive any willful concerted attempt to subvert its spirit to be a threat to their own freedom and moral integrity. The reaction of the *News* to the violation of the code by ten sophomores, who collectively cheated academically one year, well expressed the prevailing sentiment of the shocked student body, a sentiment that was expressed in many forms throughout the rest of the year in a deep and troubled reflective concern about the honor system and the college:

> For the results of the hearings show that the student body harbored within its midst a sizable group of students determined to ride roughshod over the common moral standards which had been agreed upon as the basis for the Honor System. . . . For the previous superiority of the . . . Honor System resided not only in the extreme liberality of its provisions but also in the supposed collective moral conscience which bound one student with another, reinforcing the fragile camaraderie of our interpersonal relations. If this collective moral conscience . . . has become so diffused, scattered and ignored, no sound basis for an Honor System exists . . . (*The Haverford News,* October 7, 1957, p. 2).

The Columbia study revealed that Haverford not only reported the lowest rate of academic dishonesty, but that the amount of dishonesty was so infinitesimal to be practically nonexistent. The students assessed the poll results to be quite accurate; the percentage of reported students cheating was similar to the number of students reported to the Council.

Item	*Haverford Response*
"Have you ever copied from another student during an exam?"	3%
"Have you ever plagiarized from published material on papers?"	7%
"Have you ever turned in a paper done entirely or in part by another student?"	0%
"Have you ever used crib notes during an exam?"	1%

Student attitudes about the social codes are more ambivalent and ambiguous. There is neither consensus by the students nor information about how frequently the social code is violated, though most would agree it is violated more often than the academic code. The code is generally supported if only because it does not trespass too far upon the temperament of the average student. Upperclassmen, engaged to be married, tend to take the social code less seriously.

What are the effects of the honor system on the maturing of the students? Chapters Seven and Eight discuss more systematically some personal effects cited by the students. Our analysis differs somewhat from that of the students. Since the students are responsible for its interpretation and enforcement, the faculty and administration are not forced into the role of moral arbiters. Rebellion against and resistance to parental surrogates or other imposed authoritarian sources of ethics, if expressed against the honor system, destroy, instead, the trust among peers rather than the pattern of relations with a faculty member. Most students accept and internalize the ethical attitudes that undergird the honor system, particularly its academic code, and for this reason they react to deliberate violations of the communal trust in an often poignantly personal way. The students believe the college imposes few rules upon their behavior because the most important rules are those they themselves have helped to shape and which they have sole power to enforce. The sense of freedom to control one's actions is genuinely felt by the students.

A second effect of the honor system is that, through its gradual internalization and shared communal acceptance, the students are bound together, unified, by a meaningful common ethical concern. A community emphasizing individuality and freedom runs the risk of centrifugal fragmentation. Students perceive the honor system and one

or two other institutions to be the major positive counterforces that
blend a sense of community with a genuinely felt personal freedom.
The yearbook of one class reflectively mentioned:

> . . . [T]he most influential element which contributes to a
> community feeling at Haverford is the Honor System . . .
> for the majority of the students it provides a normal and
> healthy social atmosphere and . . . eliminates the need for
> less efficient means of regulating student conduct imposed
> by the administration. . . . The Honor System contributes
> in some part to the integrity and mutual confidence in aca-
> demic work which prevails at Haverford (*Record*, 1957,
> p. 69).

A third consequence of the honor system is that, to some degree, it frees many students from the sharply troublesome decisions
young men are sometimes forced to make when their own values conflict with those of a stereotyped masculine group. In such groups, to
retain one's honor and image of oneself as a male one must cheat academically as well as have—and brag about—many sexual exploits.
The men are not pushed to demonstrate their defiance nor their potency or to appear as if they are highly aggressive males constantly on
the make. At Haverford, a male can maintain his honor by *not* boast-
ing about the number of Bryn Mawr girls he has seduced. If one does
have sexual relationships, one broadcasts it very discreetly.

The absence, however, of a group-enforced myth that a man
is not a man until he has demonstrated his potency may not help some
students to mature. Socially immature members occasionally need the
pressure of a peer group to date, to date frequently and to experiment
with more mature or adult forms of behavior. There is remarkably
little social pressure at the college to date at all. The more shy and
passively dependent men, particularly, seldom date and thereby fail
to experience the maturing influences that may call out of them both
love and devotion to a woman. If peer-group expectations are important psychological spurs to social and heterosexual development, the
absence of such expectations tends to retard the allocentric maturing
of some students.

A fourth consequence of the system is that it accentuates the
awareness, if not the actual intensity, of the students' sexual needs
while it limits the one form of expression most highly valued by them.

Sex and the pressing personal problems it induces are brought frankly and honestly into the collective awareness of the entire student body. Open discussion and release from community and parental suppression, certainly less strong than formerly, may also free from inhibition sexual desires only dimly felt earlier by some.

What does happen to the men's sexual energies? They seem to be expressed in much that same way as they were before coming to college—fantasy, masturbation, and petting—except that their growing intensity may also be converted into more aggressive behavior. Some of the excessive property destruction that occurs during mid-fall and early spring may be outlets for unrelieved sexual tension, enhanced in part by prolonged inhibition and suppression. The constant but heavy intellectual demands obscure the intensity of some students' sexual desires, the suppression of which produces lethargy, apathy, impairment in concentration, and erratic motivation.

Although deviant behavior, like homosexuality, is not valued and occurs very infrequently, students, stimulated by American cultural obsessions in this area as well as by the intensity of monastery-type living are in conflict about the relation of affection, intimacy, and homosexuality. In contrast to the separation made by Europeans between demonstrative affectionate and homosexual behavior, American men generally confuse the two and shy away from and vigorously suppress affectionate tender feelings toward the same sex. Many intensely lonely young men fear too intimate an involvement with other males because of this confusion, and so suppress all expression of affection. Marriage during their college years satisfies such loneliness for some.

A fifth possible effect of the honor system is to induce considerable guilt and, for some, regression. Students are only too human and when prized goals are in jeopardy and urgent needs are aroused, saintliness and moral values sometimes are compromised—only to be followed by ever remindful signs inducing guilt. Guilt and regressive behavior may also be accentuated by the form of social life at the college. Social activities are not organized around fraternities, clubs or groups but around a student's room. The isolation of a couple from other activities that could absorb it in non-self-oriented activities is only reinforced. The centering of social relations within the students' rooms encourages intimacies and heavy physical involvement, the building up of tensions, and possible aggravated potential conflict with the social code. Some find the process too painful and after initial failures with a series of "blind dates" and rationalized by heavy academic pressures reduce their dating or eliminate it entirely. Often the accumulated internal tension, contributed to by unfulfilled sexual needs, is projected onto the academic work load which is then in turn blamed for causing the internal tension!

Another central attitude of the Friends is that they prize having values and concerns and doing something about them. This attitude was implemented in required courses like freshman English, which forced the students to examine their own value positions (The course no longer has this focus, 1966) and in the faculty's requirement all students take some courses in religion and philosophy that had central valuative concerns (Requirement abandoned, 1967). The principal noncurricular and most controversial means the college used to implement its concern for values was compulsory Fifth Day Quaker Meeting[2] that symbolized the context of values that made the college community more than just an intellectual one. One *News* editor said the "two fundamentally moral features of the Haverford education scene . . . [are the] teacher-scholar and the much-argued-about Haverford Meeting" (*The Haverford News,* February 17, 1958, p. 2). What is a Quaker Meeting and the tradition it symbolized?

Friends believe each person has the responsibility to open himself actively to the leadings of the Inner Light. Waiting in silence while actively meditating is the best way to receive its guidance. A minister, ritualistic prayers, music, cross and ornamentation only distract this inward search. A Meeting House has only benches on which to sit in expectant silence. Like the Meeting House, the worship service is plain —very plain. A student's reaction to a Friends Meeting was

> Then we enter, find an empty square foot of horsehair cushion, and settle down to receive an impression of simplicity, integrity, sincerity and profundity. With our new attitude,

[2] Fifth Day Meeting was effectively abolished in 1966 as a communal religious activity by making attendance voluntary. Because Meeting was a distinctive activity for over 100 years, embodied most clearly the spirit of the invisible college, and was alleged to have had maturing effects upon many alumni and members of the classes studied in this book, the analysis of its effects has been retained, but abbreviated, to illustrate the spirit of the college during the studies.

we find the stares facing us not altogether vacant; and the interior of the old building seems pleasingly simple (*Record*, 1959).

The Friends also believe that corporate or group worship adds another dimension to worship not found in solitary meditation. If Friends are indeed open to the inward spirit, they may be moved to speak of their inner perceptions which will help to formulate similar but unexpressed leadings in other waiting Friends. If the first speaker, when spontaneously moved to speak, catches the spirit of the Meeting, the others will center down on this topic. A deep quiet and yet emotional quickening may pervade the Meeting House. Meeting is not an intellectual experience. It is a corporate attempt to have a mystical experiential relation believed to be possible because each man shares part of that same Inner Light. The college's Meeting seldom achieved this ideal.

What happened in Fifth Day Meeting when it was a communal activity? (Following abolition of compulsory attendance in 1966, about twenty students attended each week.) The religious life of the Meeting directly mirrored the quality of the larger life of the college and so varied dramatically from month to month, year to year. Alumni reported unrelieved years of spiritual decay and student rebellion against Meeting. Students slept, read *Time*, or did their homework. Within the period of the research, Meeting reflected much of the turmoil and dissensions of the world outside of the college. Critics of American involvement in Vietnam, to convert one Meeting into a political forum, physically usurped the facing benches where the President of the college sat. Others used Meeting to work out a means to force the local barbers to desegregate. Meeting itself became an issue as student concern about compulsion and interference with their own private lives became prominent. Some students held a silent Meeting to protest both compulsion and irreverence on the front steps of the Meeting House; others rose to criticize Meeting, its purpose and spirit. On other Thursdays, in other months and years, the life of the Meeting deepened, became a more personally existential experience, as students and faculty reflectively raised moral issues relevant to the entire community, frequently eclipsed by the strains of everyday living, and then reworked and reinterpreted them. Meeting was always unpredictable and could be quite lively—even in its prolonged silences. The spirits of Haverfordians did not always move in the channels provided for them.

It is difficult to describe the faculty, student, and alumni response to Meeting. Faculty attendance steadily declined during the decade until only about 15 per cent regularly attended. The rapidly changing faculty, the increasingly agnostic and atheistic temper of young intellectual professionals (As of 1966, over 40 per cent of the faculty would not express a religious preference; 13 per cent and 8 per cent identified themselves as Jewish and Catholic respectively), the decline in the number of Quaker faculty, the increased subtle and overt pressures on the faculty to do research and to involve themselves in noncollegiate affairs, as described by Bell (1966), lessened the bonds the faculty traditionally felt to communal activities not directly related to their immediate lives or professional interests.

The student response to Meeting was also not unaffected by the changing character of the entering Haverford student. As of 1964, the only objective evidence about student reaction to Meeting came from a poll conducted by the *News,* which revealed that about one-third of the students favored the abolition of compulsory attendance and that over half of the students reported that Meeting had benefited them. A better index of the psychological value of Meeting was the extent and quality of student participation, which in its last decade was extensive and, while frequently contentious and bordering on the irreverent, was always perceptive. The student contribution consistently revealed a disconcerting and penetrating maturity. Wisdom was not always the province only of the older and—to use Quaker language— more weighty participants.

The alumni response was perceived by the students to be strongly supportive of Meeting. Alumni in retrospect claimed the corporate experience of Meeting was one of the most valued treasures of their college days. One alumnus wrote:

> In spite of all those portents of spiritual decay, the institution of Meeting survived and I found it a remarkable thing that so many of my class—during our 25th reunion last June—observed that of all values they took from college, remembrance of Quaker Meeting was the most enduring. Yet, I can assure you, we had our moments of irreverence and apathy as students . . . but I suspect that the deeper values will always remain elusive until one has reached an

age when he can discover them in retrospect (*The Haver-ford News,* March 17, 1958, p. 2).

What effects did or could Meeting have on its often rebellious members that made it so linger in the memories of alumni?

To attend Meeting for four years was to experience immediately and personally most of the basic Quaker values: simplicity, respect, responsibility, loving acceptance, equality of individual worth, corporateness. Meeting was the college's only communal means for kindling its students' sensitivity to moral and spiritual concerns. Each member was responsible for his own spiritual experience and the spirit of the Meeting. Anyone, regardless of his age or wisdom, had the responsibility and right to speak if so moved, though he was expected to exercise self-discipline and respect for others. Ideally, one sought to strip away the immediately personal to reveal the universal. Ideally, one spoke in a tone of reverent concern. When students were satirical or critical, they were not disciplined by the administration—though, more likely, some other student would rise to modulate rancor if its presence was sensed. A student visibly and concretely learned through the sufferance of the Meeting, and at times the Meeting did suffer, what it meant to listen with tolerance to the thought of another. In Meeting all were equal; a faculty member's witness was neither more nor less valid than a student's. This could be a meaningful lesson in democratic values to a student whose own intellectual worth had been diminished in his academic relations with the faculty.

The particular form of Meeting encouraged the community to reinterpret regularly its larger problems at a different level of experience and meaning than was usually possible in most other colleges. The significance of an issue was frequently explored from many points of view but usually within a fundamentally religious or ethical context. The result could be an expansion of awareness that transcended a shallow or only intellectual assimilation of a problem or issue. Meeting, by deepening and sensitizing reflection, could expand the boundaries of self. It provided the opportunity for students and faculty to participate in the lives of the other on a radically different basis than is the case for either in other colleges.

One might speculate about another very subjective effect of Meeting. It was the one common experience of the entire intellectual community in which the *irrational* was accepted and valued. The ceaseless demands of academic work for logical, rational, and ordered thought tend to overdevelop only one side of the student. Perhaps the real reason a college fails to affect its students profoundly is that it too frequently fails to find constructive ways by which to accept and then integrate into the intellectual lives of the students their deep needs to abandon their rationality, control, and order.

What, then, gave such a unifying effect to Meeting, an effect deeply cherished by some alumni long after graduation? Could it have been a young man learned how to be silent with himself among a group of silent others? In such a corporate silence, he may even have experienced a glimmer that his own identity included more than just a self-consciously exaggerated individuality.

THE CHANGING COLLEGE

In identifying that unique blend of characteristics that made Haverford a liberally educating college, President White in his last report advised the Board of Managers to "keep [the college] small, keep it Quaker, cultivate the inquiring mind, find good men with courage and integrity and then back them" (Haverford College Bulletin, 1954–55). A college, as he said, is a continuously changing procession of people. Reflecting the temper of the decade since 1955, the procession's tempo shifted from *adagio* to *allegro*. Its direction changed and became more focused.

What has been the measure of this change since 1955? The college began to expand its size by 60 per cent to a projected 700 students, still far short of the 4,000 students to which Bell claimed Columbia could expand "without losing its intimacy" (1966). Certainly, compared to the universities of America, the college remains infinitesimal. But no one seems to be clear what the liberally educating or maturing advantages of "smallness" are. Is a college still "small" when it can no longer be "seen" in its entirety from any one spot, like the President's window, when no one can know everyone in the community, when the members of the college can no longer meet meaningfully together as a democratic community to discuss its problems? By these criteria of smallness, then the college no longer seems to be small. But "smallness" may imply other conditions more central to the maturing process, perhaps not identifiable except by examining the actual empirical effects of smallness on student development. Chapter

Eight presents our own inductions about the criteria that define "smallness."

Since 1955, the intellectual tradition of the college has been so strengthened that it dominated an even larger area of the life of the community. The academic physical resources of the college have been increased impressively; the faculty has expanded to include many highly competent young scholars as well as postdoctoral research fellows; the autonomy of the academic departments has become possessively strong; the curriculum has undergone ceaseless change and is thoroughly contemporary. The students continue to be superbly prepared for graduate work.

These changes belong to the more visible and measurable college. How has the more invisible college changed since 1955? This is a troublesomely subjective question to which there is no one answer. The students and faculty, supported by the Board of Managers, have been spirited in dissenting to public policies, in participating in the movements of the day, in assuming wider social responsibilities and leadership, in taking nationally publicized stands on moral issues, in opening the cloistered college to the winds and storms of the outside world. Many of the Friends' historic principles and testimonies are those of contemporary liberals and have therefore persisted and been witnessed to even more vigorously. But within the college, the motivations for such activity have changed from religious or spiritual to social-political or more secular ones. Some say the foundations on which the college was built and liberally educated its students in the past have been narrowed. The Quaker community was too small to provide enough competent students, faculty and administrators for the expanding college. The demise of Meeting symbolically reflected the changing character of the college's community and the fracturing of the faculty's and students' identification with the historic religious tradition of the college, increasingly perceived to be external, to the basic identity of most members of the college. The basis for communal membership shifted even more to intellectual excellence. The most recent statement of qualifications for a faculty candidate emphasized his "enthusiasm . . . excitement . . . commitment . . . love . . . for his chosen field" but said little about a similar enthusiasm for educating students and nothing about supporting the college's corporate traditions and values.

Some faculty have spoken of the "new college." What was this "new college" taking root? Its past decade of change suggests it had become an ahistorical college no longer tied to a religious tradition. It progressively valued and channeled its restless energy and great vitality into an intellectual perfectionism, modified for a minority by a serious and responsible social activism. It became less small, less Quaker, more intellectually demanding.

But as a continually changing procession of people, a college consists of students whose character also shapes its direction. The next chapter describes how the entering freshmen changed during the decade.

CHAPTER **III**

The Changing Generation

ʕ\\ʕ\\ʕ\\ʕ\\ʕ\\ʕ\\ʕ\\ʕ\\ʕ\\ʕ\\ʕ\\ʕ\\ʕ\\ʕ\\ʕ\\ʕ\\

Part of the college environment is its interpersonal environment. The personalities of one's peers have both indirect and direct effects upon one's maturing. In contrast to more encrusted autocratic and larger educational institutions, smaller colleges of the temper of Haverford are more readily and immediately shaped by the character and values of their students. As a college's atmosphere and expectations change, so do their effects upon the students. Furthermore, as the students themselves say (Chapter Seven),

the type of person with whom they interact is one of the more important determinants of their development.

But to mature is to learn to adapt to more than just the demands of one's environment. To mature is to shape an optimal adaptation to the demands of both the environment and one's own structure and needs. It has been hypothesized that the changes a college
seemingly works in its students are due more to the potentials of its
entering students than to the demands of the college (Newcomb,
1962). A purpose of this chapter, then, is to assess informally the developmental status of the entering freshman's intellectual skills, values,
self-concept, and interpersonal relationships. How maturely developed
each self-structure is affects the kinds of maturing effects a college
educes. But to describe the entering Haverford freshman in depth is
to risk obscuring more general and important purposes. Our purpose
is *not* to analyze the particularistic effects of the practice of one college's admission department, but to discuss such effects as they affect
our test of the theory of maturing.[1]

The maturing process described in Chapter One we assume to
be perfectly general. As any person matures, he becomes, for example,
more stable and allocentric in his values and self-concept. For this
reason, whether the college's student body is sociologically representative of all American young adults, or even of a larger population than
a middle- and upper-class white suburban one, is irrelevant to the test
of the theory. What is crucially relevant to the test of the theory is
that we study persons who are educable or "maturable." The ideal
test of the theory would be to examine optimally educable young adults
who are inwardly ready and free to mature in an educative setting
that had the power to educe such development. By describing the
modal student as we did the college environment, we can perhaps
anticipate in what ways the theory of maturing may be tested fairly.
As we shall see later, Haverford College and its students only approximate but do not match these ideal conditions.

Another general purpose of the chapter is to present the only

---

[1] The chapter condenses a detailed analysis of extensive statistical
studies of entering Haverford freshmen since World War II and of the
relation between admission practices and changes in the personality
structure of freshmen. To have reported such detail and the supporting
data would have obscured the relevance of the chapter to the larger
purposes of the book.

known available data about characterological changes in student generations since World War II. Since most of the personality changes cannot be clearly associated with the college's admission practices, since other educators have informally noted similar changes (Keniston, 1965), and since guidance personnel, psychiatrists, and even students from many parts of the country have strongly agreed with published reports of the trends (Heath, 1968a, b), we hypothesize that they may describe beginning personality changes in white middle- and upper-class students from our more affluent suburban and metropolitan areas. If so, the personality changes this chapter later describes have important implications for educators whose goal is the maturing of young persons. Chapter Nine will explore some of these implications.

To identify the central organizing strands that depict a "type," a modal person, is to risk stumbling on the same stony path the researchers of "national character" have tripped upon: modal types do not exist and are statistical fictions; intracollege variability in personality traits may be greater than intercollege variability, small samples may limit the reliability of the trends we report, and the paucity of comparable normative data about students of other similar colleges clouds our understanding of just how different the Haverford freshman is from the students of other colleges.

Our study does have some unique strengths. The same psychological test data are available for all entering freshmen since World War II. It is possible, therefore, to determine if the character of the students has changed in the past decades and if the changes parallel those described about the college. To establish and check the consistency of the trends occurring in the decade 1955-65, students entering prior to and after the decade were also studied. Other strengths are that the men were selected by the same person using the same methods; the relative homogeneity of small classes makes them easier to comprehend; and the analysis did not violate the intuitive judgments of the person who admitted the men to the college.

The procession of students entering college since World War II was stopped every fourth year, at which point a 35 per cent sample of each entering class was randomly selected for the study. To check the reliability of the trends noted in the contemporary students, samples from two intermediate classes of the sixties were also studied.

Since the analysis includes only those data most relevant to our purposes, we summarize only briefly the social and other background data of a class. Sixty to seventy per cent of the entering classes came from the mid-Atlantic region. Since 1947, an increasing proportion (65 per cent in the sixties) came from public schools. The religious composition of the classes also changed. Since the late forties, the percentage of entering Quakers steadily declined from 15 to 7 per cent; that of Jews increased from 5 to 16 per cent; that of Catholics remained about 6 per cent over the decades. There was little change in the men's parents' occupations: doctors, ministers, managers of business firms, bankers, engineers and research scientists, lawyers, editors, and educators. The college does not attract students whose parents are in the arts, entertainment, outdoor, or technical and applied fields. Nor does it attract students from the very wealthy or politically powerful families. The median parental income of one contemporary class was about $18,000 a year (Astin, 1966). The men's parents are highly educated; 70 per cent of the fathers of one class were college graduates and 54 per cent had graduate degrees.

COGNITIVE-INTELLECTIVE SKILLS

It is not surprising that the men should be highly developed in their intellectual skills.[2] A stable high level of academic achievement and high scholastic aptitude have been primary criteria for admission to the college for years. Most entering freshmen have been in the top fifth of their secondary classes; over 50 per cent had maintained *A* averages. Since the twenties, when the college kept some records, the median quantitative and verbal aptitudes of the students have been higher than those of students of most other colleges in the country. Since the forties, the aptitudes of the entering freshmen have become not only significantly higher[3] but also consistently more homogeneous, that is, the classes of the sixties are 40 per cent less variable intellectually than those of the late forties and fifties. There has been a consistently progressive decline from 18 to 0 per cent in the number of fresh-

---

[2] Test data about the dimensional maturity of each self-structure were obviously not available for the samples studied. Whereas subsequent chapters are organized about the dimensional hypotheses of the theory of maturing, this chapter had to be organized about the different self-structures.

[3] All designated statistically "significant" results in this chapter meet a two-tailed .05 *p* criterion.

men who said they had been slow learners in school. These trends mirror the growing intellectual focus of the college described earlier.

Despite the freshman's impressive ability to think integratively and relationally, he is not as developed similarly in other educational skills. Any entering class will have a number of students who cannot read difficult prose passages with ready comprehension or who read three to four times slower than other students. The consistent increase in scholastic aptitude (SAT) in almost every successive entering class since the early sixties[4] has *not* been matched by any change whatsoever in tested rates of reading and comprehension. The disturbing consequence of such progressive discrepancies among different cognitive skills is that the freshmen actually are *not* as equipped as their allegedly higher aptitudes imply for the increased academic assignments of the sixties. Informal observation of their other educational skills, like outlining, selecting and organizing information, and writing analytic interpretative reports, suggests other discrepancies exist as well among their cognitive capabilities. Such developmental discrepancies produce severe strain and much frustration. In recent years, about 80 per cent of the freshmen sought counseling, primarily for inadequate reading habits, inefficiencies in learning, and reduced academic motivation.

How maturely developed, then, are the intellective-cognitive skills of the entering freshman? Our hunch is that his skills are much more maturely developed than those of most other students his age. His high aptitudes mean that he will adapt very quickly to the intellectual demands of the college, although his inadequately developed reading and organizational skills suggest that he will not stabilize his achievement until much later. Much time and effort will be drawn from other types of development before he will intellectually function with efficiency. His past academic achievement suggests he has already learned to think allocentrically and to use the logic and grammar of

---

[4] That the SAT increases have *not* been matched by any change in the median freshman ability to reason abstractly with verbal concepts (Terman Concept Mastery Test) raises provocative questions about what the verbal and quantitative SAT scores are measuring. We do not know if the national validity correlates of the SAT scores have changed in the past decade as a result of the major curricular changes at the secondary level. SAT scores account for only 10 to 20 per cent of the variance of any particular class's subsequent academic performance.

the academic world appropriately. The development of more reflective ways of thinking, of symbolizing his experiences, may be enhanced by his high verbal aptitude. The discrepancies between his scholastic talents and educational skills mean he will be susceptible to considerable discouragement. Loss of self-confidence may in turn affect the intellectual development of those who cannot function autonomously of personal frustrations and external distractions.

VALUES AND MOTIVATIONAL INTERESTS

For over two decades, the typical entering freshman has valued most highly the path of the intellectual who is interested in theory, abstract ideas, and general principles, and who pursues his understanding of truth into philosophy and science (Allport, Vernon, & Lindzey [AVL], 1960). Successive classes have valued the intellectual life progressively more highly. Reflecting the high value placed on intellectual activity are the interests of the freshmen: 80 per cent[5] report enjoying school and liking science; 75 per cent consistently enjoy reading history; eight out of every ten students enjoy reading editorials and attending lectures on serious subjects; two to three times more Haverford freshmen than men entering other colleges hope to contribute to scientific theory or write original works (Astin, 1966).

What other characteristics describe persons who value the use of their intellect so highly? Studies of six other samples of Haverford freshmen selected from classes in the late fifties and early sixties suggest that persons who value the theoretical way of life are temperamentally similar to men successful in the professions and sciences, both theoretical and applied, but that they are quite dissimilar to men successful in more applied social service and business activities in which the quality of one's interpersonal relationships is an important determinant of success.

More specifically, the modal freshman for two decades felt most comfortable with highly verbal people who had considerable independence and responsibility (Strong Vocational Interest Blank— SVIB). Successive classes of freshmen have become significantly more

[5] The reported percentages come from the Minnesota Multiphasic Personality Inventory administered to all students since World War II. Percentages are usually reported as multiples of five, approximating the average of the classes mentioned.

similar temperamentally to successful independent professional men who have had extensive specialized postgraduate education, particularly in scientific fields like medicine, chemistry, psychology, and architecture. Interestingly, although increasingly more freshmen claimed they intended to major in the sciences (from 34 per cent in the early fifties to 41 per cent in the mid-sixties), progressively fewer actually did (from 32 to 23 per cent). The difference between the 41 per cent who planned to major and the subsequent 23 per cent that actually did suggests that the plans of a considerable number of students were not completely integrative with their talents and personalities.

Consistently since the forties, the least valued way of life has been that of the businessman, the pragmatist preoccupied by practical affairs, the implementation of decisions in action, concerns for money, finance, the world of commerce and the marketplace. In fact, not one of the selected classes for the past twenty years ever valued "economic man" as highly as have the men of other American colleges for whom data are available (Allport *et al.,* 1960; Huntley, 1967). Successive classes have increasingly devalued the economic way of life. In contrast to 56 per cent of a national sample of entering college freshmen, only 39 per cent of Haverford freshmen claimed being very well off financially was an important goal. Sixty-three per cent of the same national sample but only 36 per cent of one Haverford entering class claimed success in its own business was a very important goal. Eighty-eight per cent of the national sample but only 62 per cent of the Haverford freshmen had discussed how to make money sometime during the preceding year (Astin, 1966).

The devaluation of the economic way of life has been reflected in the motivational interests of the freshmen. The entering freshmen of the twenty years since World War II would find little to discuss with bankers, purchasing agents, or accountants. Within the recent decade, the noneconomic orientation of the students has become even sharper, so that contemporary students are significantly less similar than the men of the forties and fifties in their preferences for activities that are more routinely impersonal, practical, and nonimaginative. Only 7 per cent of one entering class of the sixties intended to enter business. The Haverford student has not been an organization man anxious to wear a grey flannel suit.

Philip Jacob, whose controversial book on the values of students initiated much of the contemporary research on the effects of college on personality development (1957), said the Haverford freshman of the mid-fifties was, in comparison to some other men,

> obsessed with a success mania. . . . Well over half the students crave to be "leaders," "important," "successful," "outstanding," "renowned," "famous" in their careers. They even specify that they would like to make a contribution to society which "would be remembered." . . . Part of this drive for leadership spills over into social and civic concerns, so that the student body as a whole is markedly less "privatistic" and more interested in social problems than its Harvard or Miami counterparts. . . . (1957, pp. 106–110).

The need for achievement and leadership Jacob attributed to the entering freshmen has not been expressed in a high value on political activity or the use of power, which consistently ranks third or fourth as an attractive way of life for two decades of freshmen. Jacob also refers to the less privatistic orientation of the freshman, implying he is more interested in others and their problems than are other college men. But when compared to other college men as described by available normative data, the entering freshman does not stand out as valuing "social man" or a philanthropic and altruistic way of life any more highly than other college men (Allport *et al.*, 1960). A high social value finds its temperamental counterpart in those social service occupations that depend on their effectiveness in direct personal relationships with others. Although the freshmen have become since the early fifties significantly more similar to men in those professions concerned with other people and their welfare—physicians, psychologists, ministers, educators, and city school superintendents—this other-centeredness seems to be subsidiary to the primacy of the professional role. The students have not become more similar to men in applied socially-oriented occupations, suggesting that they find direct individual, group, or social participation to be less congenial. They prefer to maintain their distance by means of a professional intellectualism as is demanded, for example, by college teaching rather than by secondary school teaching, which were the intended vocations of 19 per cent and 2 per cent of one entering class respectively.

Although the modal student does not singularly value a socially altruistic way of life, one-third of an entering freshman group, in contrast to only one-sixth of a national sample (Astin, 1966), considered work with the Peace Corps or Vista to be an important goal. Persons who value the social and altruistic way of life have been found in our studies to be more tolerant, willing to accept social responsibility, and more actively energetic in their social relationships. They have more stable, integrated, allocentric, and mature images of themselves. They also believe others think of them as more mature and are, in fact, so judged by others. Such persons also think of themselves as being more intellectually, motivationally, and interpersonally mature, particularly in their male relationships, than do men who don't value the social altruistic way of life as highly.

The entering freshmen have changed most in their religious and aesthetic values. Within the past ten years, the students have declined very consistently in their interest in and appreciation of religious values and just as consistently increased in their appreciation of aesthetic activities. These trends have also been reported in freshmen of other colleges (Huntley, 1967).

Since the college experience is frequently alleged to make a student less religious and more aesthetically inclined (Newcomb & Feldman, 1968), we examine the psychological meaning of the contrasting trends in the entering freshmen in detail. In terms of religious beliefs and practices, the entering freshman has either been indifferent or quite liberal. For all classes sampled since World War II, about 20 per cent reported that they were more religious than other men their own age. In the late forties, slightly more than a third of the entering freshmen had attended church regularly. Then followed a decade during which about 50 per cent and by the mid-sixties about 30 per cent of the recent classes in contrast to 62 per cent of a national male sample attended church (Astin, 1966). About a third, in contrast to 40 per cent of other college males, reported praying; less than 10 per cent read the Bible during the week. Twenty per cent of the Haverford freshmen but 36 per cent of other college males said grace before meals. With respect to their beliefs, about 80 per cent of the freshmen of the immediate post-World War II classes believed in God but in the sixties only 65 per cent held such a belief. About 15 to 20 per cent of the classes believed there was a Devil or Hell, and about 45 an afterlife. About 20 per cent of the students throughout the two decades believed in the second coming of Christ. There has been a fairly consistent decline in the number of students who believed miracles were tricks (from 30 per cent to about 10 per cent). About a third of the entering freshmen believed Christ performed miracles. In recent years, a decreasing number of students (now about 10 per cent) believed there was only one true religion. A quarter of the entering classes had little patience with those who believed there was only one true religion.

The freshman of the sixties increasingly values the aesthetic way of life; this value is manifested in his significantly increased similarity to men successful in aesthetic occupations like art and architecture. Twice as many freshmen at Haverford than at other colleges had attended a ballet performance or listened to folk music before their matriculation (Astin, 1966). What is the psychological meaning of this aesthetic interest that emerges as the second most important value for the classes of the sixties? Allport defines the person who values an aesthetic way of life this way:

> Each single experience is judged from the standpoint of grace, symmetry, or fitness. He regards life as a procession of events; each single impression is enjoyed for its own sake. He need not be a creative artist nor need he be effete. . . . In social affairs he may be said to be interested in persons but not in the welfare of persons; he tends toward individualism and self-sufficiency. Aesthetic people . . . oppose political activity when it makes for the repression of individuality (Allport et al., 1960, p. 4).

Our own studies suggest that a person who highly values the aesthetic way of life has considerable mastery of his cultural tradition and language. He is consistently and strongly femininely oriented, both in his personality and in his strong temperamental congruence to men successful in the world of the arts and letters. He, as one might expect, feels out of place with men in the physically productive or applied economic areas. High valuation of the aesthetic in the freshman year is associated with immaturity as judged by others and seems to be directly related to an increasing readiness to be more socially irresponsible, with self-reported failure to mature in one's intellectual skills or values, and with limited allocentric and reflective development in college.

Allport's comment that a high aesthetic value suggests individualism and self-sufficiency, our data, and considerable experience with the Study of Values test, lead to this hypothesis. The combination of high aesthetic *and* theoretical values in a young male, not leavened by high social values and a willingness to value and express appreciation, sympathy, love, and consideration for others, is a sign of a strongly egocentric or narcissistic person. Energy is inwardly directed. One's body, as the experiential and subjective source for the appreciation of form and harmony, becomes the primary focus of gratification.

The shift within the past decade from valuing a religious to an aesthetic way of life suggests that the need to yield to or feel part of some larger external power, cosmic or human, has been replaced by a need to yield to bodily or self experiences—at least in wish and value. The national pastime of seeking ever new thrills and excitements, particularly sensual, whether sexually or drug-induced, may reflect this change. The increased aesthetic trend is healthy when it is channeled into active communication through artistic media, brings sensitivity and tact to social relations, or finds its way into economic or political activities. It may be unhealthy if it stays caught within the privatistic world of thought, of the theoretical value, expressed primarily through self-centered interests. These interpretations must remain hypotheses until we can return to them later, with more information.

To make an interpretative summary, those who entered the Haverford procession during the past twenty years have been remarkably similar in their distinctively high value of the theoretical or intellectual way of life and in their consistent devaluation of a life centered in the market place. In fact, the interests of the classes of the sixties are much more homogeneous than those of the forties and fifties; 60 per cent of the lowest standard deviations for the two decades of scores were found in the two most contemporary classes. Over the years, the entering freshman has valued even more highly the intellectual man and his ideas and even less the practical "man of the world" and his affairs. He also values less emotional or mystical religious experiences, finding the satisfaction of his needs for synthesis, union, or passive yielding of his self-control in his body and self. It is not yet clear how his social and political values modulate this increased narcissistic potential. He is perhaps more sensitive, more preoccupied by the use of feelings in forming judgments, perhaps not as ruggedly masculine, preferring words and ideas to physically manipulable objects. Rather than make wood cabinets, an activity once engaged in by students on the campus, he now makes collages or he sculps and pots. He is fiercely individualistic, and will be most at home in those professions where he can retain his autonomy and freedom but where, at the same time, he can relate to other people, protected by his knowledge and intellectualism from too intense emotional involvement in their lives. To return to Jacob's analysis, it might be inferred the freshman does have a strong drive to achieve intellectually, to be a leader in his profession, but there now is some doubt about what will capture his devotion: some external vision, ideal, or mission—or some part of himself, like his intellect?

How maturely developed are the men's values? The Study of Values (AVL) measures a person's more conscious image of himself and his goals; the Strong Vocational Interest Blank (SVIB) measures a person's less conscious temperament and motives. Inconsistent or discrepant patterns between the two tests indicate a failure in integration. By this criterion, the men's values are maturely integrated; the changes in their values have also paralleled the changes in their motivational interests. Another index of the developmental maturity of the men's values is their differentiatedness. Increasingly over the decades, not only the men's more consciously held values but also their motivational interests have become more crystallized and differentiated. Beginning with the students admitted in the late forties, the range between the highest and lowest SVIB scores has gradually and very consistently grown larger—15.8, 17.4, 21.5, 23.9, and 29.1—indicating that the student of the sixties is temperamentally more ready to accept and reject, to make choices, and to follow whatever of his inclinations are the most salient. Increasing numbers of contemporary freshmen have made their vocational choices before matriculation; they enter college determined to specialize as early as possible. Although the students' values are more definite and formed and may be more, in a limited sense, integrated, we do not know whether such early crystallization reflects forced "maturing" in a culture that now rewards and encourages more focused interests at younger ages by means of national contests and advanced placement courses. Whether such early solidification makes a young man more open to the development of new interests is not known.

The very consistent integration of the men's values and preferences suggests that they have accurately symbolized their values. Such integration also suggests that their pattern of values is probably quite stable and autonomous. The college will probably not effect too radical a shift in the occupational orientation of the modal student, just because its ethos matches the intellectualistic and professional character of the students. Finally, the men have developed allocentric, although intellectualized, interests and a significant minority are interested in serving others. The men are not authoritarian (Calif. F) and are tolerant of others (MMPI: To).

SELF-IMAGE AND INTERPERSONAL RELATIONSHIPS

The entering freshmen have been remarkably similar in their talents, values, and interests for many years. They have even become increasingly more homogeneous in the sixties. Have the men varied more in their personalities? Given that a college can more readily select for objectively measured talent or expressed academic interests than it can for more elusive personality traits, the answer is, surprisingly, no. For two decades, the entering freshmen have had singularly similar personalities and, as occurred for their aptitudes and interests, the freshmen of the sixties have become increasingly more homogeneous in their personal traits, that is, the classes of the mid-sixties were more homogeneous on 80 per cent of the tabulated twenty-five personality scores than the classes of the fifties.

Another index of the relative homogeneity of the student body is that the men agree very consistently in describing other students. Their peers are rated higher on 30 per cent of the 104 traits sampled in Pervin's study (1966) than are the students of other colleges when rated by their fellow students. The "typical" student was judged to be much more intellectual, "eggheadish," "bookwormish," scholarly, thinking, research-oriented, philosophical, brilliant (but not wise), and professional. He was judged to be an aspiring, challenging, but grinding, academically achieving person of excellence. More than most other students, he was considered to be inhibited, sober, not lustful or irrepressible, tense, introverted, sensitive, complex, sincere, idealistic, and restlessly nonconforming.

Although the admissions office has made laborious efforts to increase the variety of students by extending the geographical and school representation within the student body, its efforts seem to have been to no avail psychologically. The crystallization of a more defined value and temperamental pattern combined with increased intellectual, motivational, and personality homogeneity suggests that if a Haverford type did not come clearly into focus several decades ago, it almost does so now. The increasing psychological sameness of the students may be due to several interacting factors: personality homogeneity may be an inevitable accompaniment of increased intellectual homogeneity; students may be increasingly selected to fit a preconception of who can survive the intellectual rigors of the college; the homogenization of American youth, by means of the mass communication media and other cultural forces, may be reducing the variability of the population from which the college draws its students.

The greater homogeneity of the freshmen gives us more assurance in describing their self-image and personal relationships.[6] The typical freshman has consistently thought himself to be an effective person. Ninety per cent of every class studied said it was as capable as other persons, expected to succeed in whatever it did, was actively interested in its daily activities, and was happy most of the time. A small but steadily increasing number of young men said they never felt better in their lives (from 50 per cent in the late forties to 60 per cent in the sixties) and didn't tire quickly (from 70 to 80 per cent). But it is surprising to note that about 25 per cent of every class lacked self-confidence. From one-fifth to one-third of every class reported it was too high-strung, tense, restless, couldn't sit quietly or concentrate for extended periods of time. It took life too hard and constantly felt tired. Four out of ten freshmen said they were always worrying. One out of five reported he had dreams it was wiser not to reveal and that he felt unable to tell another person everything about himself.

Although these feelings of tension are not unusual in young men reaching adulthood, their extent, given that the admissions department selects for maturity, raises the question, "Is the entering student more unstable than other college students?" From the limited

[6] The analysis relies on a variety of test materials, including the MMPI, Bernreuter, adjective checklists, Stern's Activities Index, and Rorschach. Only MMPI scores were available for all sampled classes. Trends in responses to individual MMPI items were independently identified by at least two of three judges. A trend was defined by the consistency in the progressive change in the number of students agreeing with the question and the magnitude of the overall percentage change. Only thirty of the forty-two more reliably identified trends are reported; most of the remaining trends duplicated or only confirmed the reported trends. Table 3.1 illustrates the typical changes identified as a trend.

comparative data available[7] and the very small and contradictory differences found, we doubt that he is.

It has been frequently asserted that contemporary students are more maladjusted and neurotic than those of earlier generations. The data from two decades of entering students do not support such a claim, but they do suggest that more men increasingly feel themselves to be under much greater strain and pressure. For example, 40 per cent of the students of the sixties report working under a great deal of tension, in contrast to 25 per cent of the earlier classes; 75 per cent say their hardest battles are with themselves, in contrast to 60 per cent earlier; 40 per cent say they wake up fresh and rested in the morning, in contrast to some 60 per cent earlier; 60 per cent report they've worn themselves out by undertaking too much, in contrast to 45 per cent in the fifties. The percentage differences between the earlier and later classes are certainly not large in and of themselves. Yet, the consistency of the trends and the overall pattern of such items and numerous others suggest more contemporary students feel harried and under greater pressure than students of the forties and fifties.

Three salient personality changes best organize the mass of personality data of the entering freshmen. Compared to the students of even just a decade ago, the contemporary student has become an increasingly intellectualized and inhibited person whose energies are directed more toward himself and his own interests than toward others with whom he has become progressively less emotionally involved.

In comparison to the students of the forties and fifties, the students of the sixties have become significantly more over-controlled, inhibited, and tend to be more defensive and intellectually efficient. The students value playing life's game "coolly," denying and suppressing feelings and moods that, if expressed, would suggest they were not in command of themselves. For example, progressively more young men throughout the decades report that they seldom blush and are not easily embarrassed. Twenty per cent fewer freshmen now admit that they sweat when embarrassed. The young men intellectualize away, with the assistance of Freudian or hip and beat language, any feelings that smack of squareness, sentimentality, dependency, or weakness.

[7] Comparisons were made to the Manifest Anxiety Scale (Taylor, 1953), Bernreuter, and MMPI (Goodstein, 1954) scores. We are grateful to Dr. Loper for making available MMPI scores for selected classes of entering freshmen at the University of Minnesota.

The men are more tightly constricted, serious, and responsible. There has been a 20 per cent decline in the number of entering freshmen who said they had sometimes been sent to the principal for "cutting up."

It is not that many freshmen don't have strong feelings; some 45 per cent of every class believed it felt more intensely than other men. It is just that they do not want to be caught in situations in which they may betray their loss of control. Increasing numbers over the years dislike exciting crowds, lively parties, engaging in stunts at parties even when others are, singing and dramatics—all situations in which they risk the spontaneous expression of emotion.

But at a less manifest level, the over-control of the men is not fully integrative; this hypothesis suggests that their aesthetic intellectualism—the mode by which such control is expressed—is partly defensive, perhaps screening from the men other feelings and wishes. Suppression of emotions, particularly when they interfere with intellectual work, is highly adjustive to the nonemotional demands of the college. But such suppression is not adaptive or healthy to the young men, and if it persists through the college years, it could limit their maturing.[8]

What is the evidence that the constriction of spontaneity and emotionality, their premature seriousness and focused professional motivation may be robbing the freshmen of their humanness? Most symptomatic of the progressive constriction of the men in the sixties are covert indices of strain and repressed wishes. A small but consistently increasing proportion of freshmen report dreaming (from 60 per cent in the forties to 75 per cent in the sixties), dreaming frequently (30 to 60 per cent) and repetitively (15 to 30 per cent). More dream about sex (25 to 45 per cent), about which more are now worried (5 to 20 per cent). There has been a 15 per cent increase to about 40 per cent of the entering freshmen who have the urge to do something shocking or harmful; 55 per cent of a contemporary class said it felt like smashing things. Also symptomatic, but not as covert, is the slowly progressive rise from 8 to 16 per cent of the entering freshmen who

[8] It is provocative to note that the departmental chairmen rated their seniors graduating in the fifties, the less cool generation, to be not only significantly more emotionally stable but also more original and (though not significantly) consistently more personable than the seniors of the sixties.

report drinking excessively, the 10 per cent increase in more recent years of those who take drugs not upon doctor's orders. Other small signs that are part of a pattern of increased constriction that forces impulse and wish to be expressed in more covert ways are the larger proportion of contemporary students who are apprehensive about certain animals, more forgetful about where they put things, dislike the excitement of crowds, and have compulsive habits like counting inconsequential objects.

More and more entering students report that they fight themselves, feel tense, and don't feel rested upon waking. The consistent increase in the dream life of these freshmen, where it is safer to live one's suppressed desires with perfect anonymity, even to oneself, suggests they have much to learn and to accept of themselves, perhaps even more than their predecessors—ironically, in this age of Freud and the denuded wasteland of the unconscious. The cool kid in his intellectualized pursuit of knowledge, even self-knowledge, has isolated himself from much of what is warm and tender about himself. A further irony is that many of these same young men *know* very well what they can't yet allow themselves to experience, but have found no way to experience it. Does not the decline in religious values, the one value area most dependent on the abandonment of self and self-control to some greater ideal or value, and the increase in the aesthetic, the one value area that emphasizes disciplined form, manifest this shift to an intellectual controlled coolness? Could such a personality change in the student body have contributed to the demise of the college's Fifth Day Meeting, which relied heavily on spontaneity and a willingness to abandon self-control for a common religious mystical experience?

A second strand that ties the data together is that as a person becomes increasingly identified with his intellect and its products, with his ability coolly to endure excitement and all types of what used to be warm and hot thrills, he begins to magnify the importance of his head and his intellectual control. We hypothesize that too salient a valuation of the intellectual and aesthetic, when not externalized in some outreach, indicates a heightened narcissistic potential. Overvaluation of self-control and intellectualism in less mature persons eventually leads to an exaggerated evaluation of the possessor of that control and intellect—namely, oneself. There has been an increasing trend toward such overevaluation, stimulated by the societal adulation of youth and its intellectual gifts. Twenty-five per cent of the men of the forties thought they were important persons; 45 per cent of the freshmen of the sixties think so. Forty-five per cent thought if given a chance they could work great benefit to the world; over 60 per cent of contemporary students believe so. An average of 20 per cent of the early classes thought they knew more than many experts; now 40 per cent think so. On adjective checklists, the students themselves called other students self-centered, self-conscious, individualistic, not easily impressed, and hard to convince—traits that describe a fairly high impermeable barrier around a person's receptivity to others.

How is the exaggerated sense of self-importance expressed? Certainly, the freshmen value and defend the college that reinforces their individualism and self-sufficiency. They value themselves as individualists on a campus of individualists. The Friends' religious faith that insists each person be responsible for his own behavior is used by some to rationalize their own egocentricism. Unfortunately, such an overvaluation betrays, perhaps not quite unconsciously, a profound misunderstanding of the Friends' assumption about man's communal and social nature, which leavens the excesses inherent in individualism.

The meaning of self-sufficiency or even narcissism cannot be understood in isolation from the quality of a person's interpersonal relationships. The third inextricable strand of the emerging pattern is a trend toward increased interpersonal autocentricism, or, more precisely, decreased intensity of social feeling. Because this trend has been developing so consistently for two decades, some detailed findings are reported in Table 3.1 to illustrate how successively small percentage differences defined a trend.

The strength of the human and social ties that bind one person to the next seems to have declined consistently for two decades. Contrary to Jacob's assessment just a decade previously, the entering freshman has become increasingly privatistic in his personal relationships; he is more willing to accept an isolated, lonely life than to participate in a gregarious group or other-centered life. Such a tendency is certainly compatible with a growing preoccupation with intellectual matters, in which one works essentially alone and for oneself. Increasingly more students have spent much of their time either by themselves or with only a few friends. And when such freshmen (not yet a majority of the class) do emerge out of themselves into the lives of others, their relationships do not seem to be as compellingly based on affection, devotion, or loyalty to another as formerly. For example, relations with

TABLE 3.1

Sample MMPI Items for the Classes 1948–49 to 1968

Item	Per Cent True							
	48–49	52	56	60	64	65	67	68
When I was a child I didn't care to be a member of a crowd or gang.	33	35	35	38	49	58	49	47
I could be happy living all alone in a cabin in the woods or mountains.	23	28	31	38	33	35	42	45
I am a good mixer.	77	49	48	63	60	58	38	43
I like to go to parties and other affairs where there is lots of loud fun.	65	56	55	53	44	40	38	40
At parties I am more likely to sit by myself or with just one other person than to join in with the crowd.	23	35	40	27	44	38	47	50
My worries seem to disappear when I get into a crowd of lively friends.	71	69	73	68	58	65	56	55
If I were in trouble with several friends who were equally to blame, I would rather take the whole blame than to give them away.	63	56	50	57	47	43	33	45
When a man is with a woman he is usually thinking about things related to her sex.	29	37	15	27	35	28	36	43
I enjoy reading love stories.	55	49	35	25	44	30	18	25
I like dramatics.	80	74	73	75	60	73	67	66
I would like to be a singer.	51	47	37	36	33	38	31	23

women for the entering freshmen appear to be increasingly restricted to or defined in terms of sex, even more than for the older and more experienced veterans of World War II, who made up the classes of the forties. The exaggerated awareness of sex in American adolescent culture may accentuate the sexual character of transitory adolescent relationships. The concurrent decrease of interest in love stories, probably too sentimental for today's young persons, indirectly suggests that what is love to an older generation either may not be comprehended by many contemporary students or may now be primarily sex for a younger generation living in a culture that confuses the two. Recall that the recent classes expressed more concern about sexual problems and dreamt more about sex as well. Or perhaps the students of the sixties are just more frank, preferring not to use the euphemisms of earlier "unliberated" generations.

Finally, Table 3.1 suggests that the progressive decline in social feeling manifests itself in other ways as well. Although interest in dramatics and singing has several psychological meanings, certainly one intent of an actor or singer is to express something of himself, to communicate, even to move another emotionally. Does the cool generation, living more for itself than for others, not care to reach out to others?

What do these dramatic and troubling trends mean? Is the cool kid only protecting a stereotyped image of what he thinks he should be like? The weakness of all questionnaires is that they reveal what the person wants to reveal—and a little more—whether what is revealed is true or not. Or if a person believes what he reveals, what he reveals may still not be true. How can we check what he says? We must go back to the freshman's life his first few months at the college to see just how his autocentricism is expressed before the college begins to work its effects, if it works any, on its students' relationships. Extensive observation, research and counseling interviews suggest the entering freshmen are *not* becoming more withdrawn or schizoid (an observation confirmed by the formal MMPI scores, the consistently stable value on social altruism, and the increasing preference for more professional occupations that involve service to others). The analysis has relied too heavily on tests designed to elicit weaknesses, not strengths. When the students later speak for themselves, their hidden delightful warmth and liveliness, sensitivity and perceptiveness, and humor and wisdom will become more prominent. These traits are not measured by tests. If anything, many of the young men are much more emotional, sensitive, preoccupied by other people, and psychologically sophisticated than many preceding students *when* they feel secure enough to let you know them. In such a relation, more freshmen speak of loneliness, of a need for friends—even just one—to whom they can "open themselves up," whom they can trust, and with whom they can be just themselves. They don't trust others who give freely of themselves because they don't trust their own needs to give. One very lonely but sceptical freshman asked, "Why does a busy professor keep his door open to talk with any student who wants to bother him? What does he want?" He could not emotionally accept that another human being could genuinely want to listen to him. It is not that the students do not desire companionship; it is that many share a pervading fear that to initiate such friendships is to risk being misunderstood, "shot down," rejected, even thought "queer." To break the barrier surrounding an iconoclastic individualist is a formidable and risky adventure to the more inhibited freshmen, who are inexperienced in reaching out and initiating emotional contacts with others. Interestingly, many of these young men had held prestigious and responsible extracurricular positions, were leaders of their secondary schools, and had maintained superb academic records. And yet, apparently, they never had been drawn into the adolescent pal or gang stage to experience and trust their emerging affectionate feelings toward another. Rorschach data and observation merge at this point to suggest that the following developmental sequence might have occurred. By not experiencing the intimacy of the early adolescent years, when it is safer because sexual impulses don't complicate friendships so intensely, a person grows into young adulthood without either the self-trust or the social skills to initiate similar intimacy relations with young men and women. Instead, when sexual impulses later do become so imperious and insistent, relations with girls are focused on just the immediate impulsive goal. They shy away from too close relations with other young men because they fear that any feelings of affection, let alone their casual demonstration, may mean a homosexual involvement, which is, of all types of relationships, the most anxiety-arousing and conflictual for males (Heath, 1965). Overt homosexual behavior on the campus is rare; it is more a means to quell loneliness than to secure sexual gratification in the late teens. By confusing affection, loyalty, consideration, and friendship with sexuality and sensuality, some students inhibit all tenderness, thus robbing themselves of the opportunity to experience the difference. That the loneliness of so many contemporary students is so poignant and sharp suggests that much of the vaunted individualism, even apparent narcissism, intellectual inhibition and control, and perhaps the drive for achievement, may be, in part, compensatory for feared and unfulfilled needs for human warmth and companionship.

MATURITY OF THE ENTERING FRESHMEN

How maturely developed are the men's attitudes toward themselves and their personal relationships? To emphasize the consistency of the developmental relationships between the different self-structures, we examine the dimensional maturity of the men's self-concepts and personal relations within a more general context that includes their intellective skills and values as well.

Most of the evidence about the personality of the entering freshman is based on reflective self-reports that come from different types of tests. The reports are quite consistent and make psychological sense, suggesting that he may have considerable self-understanding. The definiteness of his values and interests suggests he is quite well aware, at one level of understanding, of what he wants and wants to be. But if dreams do disguise, and if sexual preoccupations do screen, the unconscious conflicts about emotional isolation and loneliness, and hence a deeply buried need both to love and to be loved, then the freshmen have much yet to learn about themselves as human beings, not at the level of intellectual but at the level of organismic emotional understanding.

The history of the freshman's achievement, the logicality of his thought processes, and his realistic orientation suggest a well-developed intellectual allocentricism. But the increased aesthetic orientation, combined with the trend toward narcissism and his progressive aloofness from close personal relations, suggests that his personal-social relations are still autocentrically organized. The most critical developmental problem confronting him appears to be his relationships with both men and women. If he does not emerge out of his autocentricism, will the maturing of his intellect, his values, and his image of himself remain undeveloped as well? Will the men absorb and make more their own the strong social tradition and values of the college, and will they find more adaptive ways to express them?

Certainly, his values, interests, and self-concept seem to be well integrated at one level of organization. He seems destined to become a professional intellectual. His personality also certainly seems to fit that of an intellectual who will work in some professional but distant relation with others. Yet, this integration gives the impression of being forced and premature, because it seems to be at the price of forming a stable identity not marked by self-doubt and rigid constriction. If our impressions have merit, then the contemporary student is faced by the major task of first accepting and then integrating his needs for giving and receiving affection and love into his concept of himself as a professional intellectual. He has yet to learn how to form integrative and stable personal relationships.

The entering freshman seems to be quite stable for his age. Although his intellectual control and high level of achievement suggest that his intellectual skills are very stable, the increasing inner tension, constrictive control of his impulses, and use of passive intrapsychic releasers like dreaming indicate that he has yet to find more adaptive and aggressive ways to meet his social world. He may fool others by his cool calmness, but it is just such an apparent stability that hinders the development of more stable and mature personal relationships. He may need to go through some disorganizing periods to become as educable as his talents deserve and personal needs require.

Finally, the freshman also seems to be quite autonomous, if only because of his self-sufficiency in his personal relationships, though it is just such independence and control that may hinder further maturing in his relationsships. He rates low on indices of dependency, preferring to figure things out for himself. He is dedicated to being an individual and he has the resources to sustain loneliness. His narcissistic potential means that his self-image is probably quite autonomous and that he may resist those educative effects of the college that are contingent on a more modest view of himself and his own importance. When this "front" does give way, considerable instability and self-doubt about his own competence may occur.

To answer one question of the chapter, the men are more maturely developed in their intellectual skills and perhaps their values than they are in their personal relationships with others and in their attitudes toward themselves. They had formed in secondary school a stable and autonomous equilibrium, centered pervasively around their intellectual capabilities and a concept of themselves as intellectuals. But if they are to develop more allocentrically in their relations with others and form a more integrative self-concept, they will have to become more unstable and open to the influence of the college. If the college is really liberally educating, it will help its freshmen become more disorganized. It will heighten and develop their reflective capacity to understand their instability and how to search for a more stable identity. It will also provide values and expectations that will support and guide the men as they form a more mature adaptation to the demands of the college and of their own structure.

DETERMINANTS OF PERSONALITY CHANGE

Why is the freshman apparently becoming more intellectualized, inhibited, and interpersonally autocentric than the freshman of even a decade ago? Do such trends reflect only changes in local admission practices, or do they describe other young persons in affluent America?

The principal differences between the earlier and contemporary freshmen that might account for the personality trends are the changes in their scholastic aptitudes, type of secondary school, and religious affiliation. Neither parental education, social background, nor occupation has changed markedly during the two decades.

Statistical studies of the correlates of the SAT verbal and quantitative aptitudes of the entering freshmen do not compellingly suggest they account for much of the total pattern of personality change. Very limited data suggest high quantitative aptitude scores may be directly associated with poorer personal integration, perhaps because of overcontrol and restraint in impulse expression as well as of retarded allocentric and socially assertive development.

The changing ratio of students from private (primarily Quaker) and public secondary schools does not seem to account for much of the change either. The direction and magnitude of most of the changes for the private school men were so similar that they constituted a replication of the principal trends. However, the private school men did differ from their classes in some respects. They were much less conventional in their religious beliefs and practices and had a heightened sense of moral responsibility. Their more sensitive consciences seemed to be associated with stronger inhibitions over the expression of aggression, which was internalized and converted into demanding ideals and ethical concerns rather than externalized into active aggressive involvement in political or intellectual issues. The autocentric interpersonal trends described in Table 3.1 were much less clear. The private school men were more sociable, cooperative, gentle, trusting, and acceptant of others.

Nor does the changing ratio of Quaker to Jewish students account for the trends found in the specific classes studied. However, other extensive studies of larger randomly selected samples suggest that the relation between personality type and religious affiliation might profitably be studied more systematically, particularly if associated variables like urban residence could be controlled. As the college draws more of its students from the large metropolitan areas of the East Coast, the trends might very well become more accentuated.

That any single determinant is responsible for the pattern of personality change is doubtful. Our hypothesis is that the trends describe a characterological change in American white young adults from suburban and urban middle and upper classes. Other educators familiar with the results confirm their accuracy in describing their own students—both men and women.

If the changes are more general, then what may be producing them? Such a question takes us into larger issues for which we have only meager data. The families of the men, particularly their fathers, do not appear to be a principal contemporary source of pressure for the majority of freshmen. Since the mid-forties, some 50 per cent of the freshmen report that they have been quite independent of family control. There has been a 25 per cent increase in the number reporting that they feel free to argue with their parents. Only one out of ten reported that his family found fault with him unnecessarily. A steadily growing number (from 80 to 90 per cent) report that no older man had ever been strict with them when they were younger. Interestingly, there has been a small but increasing number, now 60 per cent, who report that their conduct is influenced by the customs of society, even in a group as individualistically inclined and jealous of its autonomy as the Haverford one.

Do these self-reports suggest that the entering freshmen have been raised permissively, that their fathers have not had a decisively direct influence on their development, and that in the absence of a strong determining male, the influence of peer, school, and societal values has become psychologically more important over the years? The classes of the sixties, the post-Sputnik youngsters, have experienced increasing pressures to achieve, radical curricular changes in mathematics and physics, psychological pressure induced by advanced placement and other accelerated, frequently competitive, programs, dramatically increased academic work loads in both private and public schools, the "panic" competition for admission to the so-called "good" colleges, fear of the College Board examinations, expectations of many long professional years of training, and many other strains and pressures. Such demands and expectations must inevitably work their effects on growing youngsters, but it remains a moot question whether such pressures—or opportunities—make contemporary students any more educable and mature (Heath, 1966, 1968a).

CHANGING STUDENT AND CHANGING COLLEGE

It is now time to draw the analyses of the college and the student together and to assess how the character of both may affect the test of the theory of maturing.

A comparison between the students' view of the college and of their ideal college suggested that the college was not satisfying the students' social and emotional needs. If the students could change the college, they would make it, in order of decreasing importance, more relaxed, well-rounded (less "eggheadish"), friendly, public, exciting, sociable, easygoing, fun-loving, warm, flexible, artistic, and big (Pervin, 1966). It is not that the students want a "collegiate" college. They want a better balance to their academic lives.

Quite unexpectedly, neither the faculty nor administration were identified by the students to be the principal source of their dissatisfaction with the college. Generally, the students would like both to be more well-rounded, exciting, fun-loving, and flexible. It is the "other students" the men of the Pervin samples would like to change most. They would prefer students who were, in order of decreasing importance, more relaxed, well-rounded, flexible, cooperative, humane (instead of self-interested), fun-loving, friendly, and warm. A principal source of strain at the college in recent years may well be the quality of the interpersonal relations of the students. If the character of the student body continues to change in the direction suggested by the results, such strain will only become more accentuated.

The college and the student body seem to be changing in the same direction. Just as the college has become more focused, so the students have become more homogeneous. The faculty no longer requires that its students take as broad a range of liberal arts courses; the entering students are more selective in the interests to which they will commit their energies. Intellectual excellence has become an even more salient goal of the college, just as the intellectual way of life has become more valued by the entering students. The growing aesthetic interest of the students is paralleled by faculty attempts to institutionalize such interests. The demise of the college's religious tradition has been paralleled by the decline in the entering students' regard for religious values. The growing interpersonal autocentricism of the students has been accompanied by an increasing emphasis in college policy on its individualistic or anarchistic rather than social or communal traditions. More prosaically but of longer-lasting effect, the college is constructing dormitories containing bedrooms for single but not several students.

It is too soon to determine what the effects of such changes will be upon the power of the college to educate its students liberally in the future. The important questions to ask a decade from now may be questions like these: Has the early crystallization of the interests and personalities of the students led to an early specialization that has really been congruent with their identity? Does the decreased psychological variety of one's peers or the accentuation of one type of student (and perhaps of a young faculty as well) evoke more reflective adaptations and educe hidden personal qualities more readily? Does a college have as stabilizing and integrative maturing effects if it does not have a distinctive core of values and institutional forms for their expression and reinforcement that capture faculty and student allegiance and devotion?

Looking to the past decade, we may ask how may the character of the college and of its students limit the test of the theory of maturing? Our hunch is that generally the hypotheses about maturing should be adequately tested, particularly those about the maturing of the men's intellective skills and values. We are less sanguine that the hypotheses about interpersonal development will be confirmed. How the changing relation between the communal and individualistic traditions of the college and the prized self-sufficiency of the students will affect the hypotheses about allocentric and autonomous development we don't know. The hypothesis that a maturing person becomes more reflective and stable should be fairly tested. How integrative the students become depends upon how they modify their values about the expression of their emotional and social needs.

No institution speaks to all the maturing potentials of its members. The maturing of some self-structures may have to wait upon the maturing of other self-structures.

CHAPTER IV

Plan and Procedures

~~~~~~

$\mathcal{A}$ two-stage research program was designed to study the development of three randomly selected groups of students at different points in their college career and to identify the determinants of that development. Studies of alumni to discover whether the changes that occurred in college endured are reported in Chapter Six.

To study the personality change of the students, we administered a basic test battery to each person during his first week at college and readministered the same tests at the end of either his freshman or senior year. Other measures designed to test other hypotheses about maturing were given, although only one sample received every measure both on entering college and at a later time. To encourage the cooperation and frankness of the students, their replies were held in confidence, their test materials identified only by code numbers, and their reported interviews disguised.

To identify the determinants of their development, we scored, rated, and interpreted, for the types of change that had occurred, each student's coded test material. We discussed the results with each student personally, after which we used systematized rating and ranking procedures and intensive but regularized interviews to identify the determinants of the students' development in college. Each student was tested and interviewed for a total of eleven to twelve hours.

THE SAMPLES

Our samples are small. Seventy-three randomly selected students from three different classes were studied intensively: 25 per cent (twenty-four students) of each of two graduating classes, hereafter called *Senior I* and *Senior II samples,* and about 20 per cent (twenty-five students) of one entering freshman class, called the *Freshman sample.*

What defines a "class" in such studies is problematical. Seniors who had had their college careers interrupted by a leave of absence, did not matriculate with their class, were known to be married, or were on special status were excluded. Furthermore, the Senior samples were drawn from classes that had already lost about 20 per cent of their members for academic and personal reasons. Of the seniors of the two classes invited to participate, only 51 per cent and 65 per cent actually participated. The Freshman sample was randomly drawn from a larger group, representing about 80 per cent of the entering class that had earlier volunteered for the study and had completed all of the tests given it the first week of college. All invited freshmen participated in the intensive follow-up study conducted at the end of their first year to check the seniors' comments that their freshman year had been their most crucially formative one.

Of the many problems that may qualify and complicate our generalizations, two of the most troublesome concern the Senior samples. Did those who participate differ from those who didn't? How representative of their classes were those who did participate?

Deans and student judges who had no knowledge of the studies or of who did or did not participate rated the personality traits of the participators and nonparticipators on adjective checklists and judged their degree of maturity. The two groups did not differ in most traits. The participators of the Senior I sample tended to be more sociable, friendly, cooperative, self-controlled, reasonable, and to have wider interests than the nonparticipators, who were judged to be more demanding, intense, independent, self-reliant, creative, and spontaneous. The few statistically significant differences found from an analysis of extensive personality data available on the two groups as entering freshmen confirmed that the participators were more self-controlled as well as more practical and down-to-earth. The judges reported they could not reliably distinguish between the participators and nonparticipators of the Senior II sample, who also did not differ on the personality tests. Confirming previous findings (Heath, 1965), the judges tended to rate those who participated to be more mature than those who refused to participate.

The judges also said the Senior samples were generally representative of their own senior classes; this judgment was subsequently confirmed by statistical comparisons between the personality test scores secured at the matriculation of the samples and of other samples randomly selected from their own entering classes. When forced to judge the representativeness of the participating and nonparticipating groups to the Senior class as a whole, the judges unanimously agreed that the participators of the Senior II sample were representative, but they did not agree about the Senior I sample, which they judged to be too homogeneous. Statistical analyses showed that the Senior I sample was in fact more homogeneous, for it was less variable than its own class on fifty-nine of eighty-four measured personality variables. The Senior I sample also had too few men who were temperamentally congruent with men successful in the more aesthetic occupations. The Freshman sample did not differ significantly from its own class except in being less impulsive and, somewhat contradictorily, less rigid. We expect the results of the Senior II and Freshman samples to be more discriminating and valid.

MEASURES OF STUDENT DEVELOPMENT

Research on the maturing of young adults has been handicapped by the lack of basic information about personality change and by the lack of appropriate measures for detecting such change (Bloom, 1964). Researchers have relied upon established psychological tests

like the Study of Values (Allport, Vernon, & Lindzey, 1960), vari-
ants of questionnaire procedures like the Minnesota Multiphasic Personality Inventory (MMPI), or upon more diffuse procedures like
psychiatric interviews. A few researchers, like the Vassar group, have
empirically developed and cross-validated some scales, based on demonstrable personality changes, presumably maturing ones, from freshman to senior year in women (Webster, Sanford, & Freedman,
1955; Webster, Freedman, & Heist, 1962; Webster, 1956). Except for the Sanford sponsored studies, systematic or comprehensive
theories of personality or educational development have guided few
of the research efforts on student development or produced specific
tests by which to measure predicted changes (Newcomb & Feldman,
1968). As a consequence, much of the early research on personality
development in college (Jacob, 1957) is of the hit-or-miss variety,
not systematically integrable into either psychological or educational
theory.

Our more modest studies were guided primarily by the theory
of development described in Chapter Two. Generally, three types of
measures were used to test its predictions: (1) standard psychological
tests like the Study of Values and MMPI, not univocally related to
the specific predictions of the theory, and the Rorschach, for which a
novel but *not* well-validated scoring system directly applicable to the
maturity theory was available; (2) new procedures specially designed
to measure the developmental dimensions and structures that defined
the maturing person; and (3) interviews not specifically focused on
the theory of maturing that could, however, be coded for the theoretically predicted changes. The interviews also provided an opportunity to elicit information about unpredicted personality changes.
Other information about each student included aptitude scores, grade
record, judgments by peers and faculty of his maturity, and the judgments of the chairman of the department in which he majored about
his intelligence, determination, emotional stability, originality, and
personality.

STANDARD PSYCHOLOGICAL TESTS

The tests administered to all students their first week as freshmen and readministered in the same order at a later time were the
Study of Values (AVL), the Strong Vocational Interest Blank (SVIB),
and the Minnesota Multiphasic Personality Inventory (MMPI), which

have been discussed in the preceding chapter. The traditional scores of these tests were not generally used to define the dimensions of maturing,[1] although the pattern of their results permitted us to make inferences about maturing. The MMPI has proved to be helpful to other researchers who have selected from its hundreds of items questions to form new scores of more specific personality traits. Those more reliable and valid scores most appropriate to the theory of maturing were used in the studies, though the paucity of research on most of the scores meant that they might be equivocal and ambiguous measures of our specific expectations.[2] The Tolerance (To), Social Responsibility (Re-r), Social Introversion (Si), Social Poise (Sr) scales, as well as the traditional scales measuring social aloofness and withdrawal (Sc), yielded information about allocentric values and interpersonal development; the Impulsivity (Im) and Dependency (Dy) scores, and possibly the traditional psychopathic deviate scale (Pd), may be inversely related to value and interpersonal autonomy; the Repression (R) score measured inadequate awareness of oneself; the Rigidity (Rg-m) and Over-control (Eo) scores indexed too great stability or lack of integrative flexibility; and so on. The dominant psychopathological emphasis of the MMPI limited its usefulness for assessing more healthy traits, though we did use Barron's Ego Strength (Es) and the Intellectual Efficiency (Ie) scores as more general indices of maturity and capability. Previous research has demonstrated that many of these scores are related as predicted to a variety of measures of maturity (Heath, 1965). Analysis of changes in the responses of the students to the individual MMPI and SVIB items given in their freshman and subsequent years also provded more specific information about other aspects of maturing.

RORSCHACH TEST

Most researchers studying personality change have relied on self-report procedures similar to the MMPI rather than on the so-called projective tests, like the Rorschach ink blots, that reputedly measure a person's motives and conflicts of which he is less aware. The

---

[1] Subsequent statistical tests using those less theoretically relevant scores (AVL and SVIB) are evaluated at a two-tailed *p* level.

[2] The definition and validity of each special MMPI score cited may be found in Dahlstrom & Welsh (1960). The results of these theoretically relevant scores were evaluated using one-tailed *p* levels.

Rorschach administration, scoring, and interpretative procedures are so complex and difficult that it is uneconomical to use such a test with large numbers of students. Although we also relied most heavily on tests in which the students could consciously maintain control over their descriptions of themselves, our small samples permitted us to use the Rorschach, in which such control is less possible, not so much for the purpose of assessing change as to provide supplementary information and a context by which to check the consistency and psychological meaning of the self-report results.

The Rorschachs were rated for the degree of maturity and self-organization of each student and were subsequently scored using both traditional (Klopfer) and newer (Holt) scoring procedures that measured different components of the model of maturing.[3]

TESTS TO MEASURE THE THEORY

The Self-Image Questionnaire (SIQ). The maturity of a student's self-image was measured by the Self-Image Questionnaire (SIQ). A student rates himself on thirty bipolar trait scales that have been commonly cited to describe mature and immature persons. By varying the instructions and administration conditions of the SIQ, it is possible to secure measures of the dimensional maturity of a student's self-image; for example, readministration of the test following a time interval provides a measure of the stability of his self-image; comparing his self-ratings with those made of him by judges who know him well provides a measure of how accurately he symbolizes his self-image. Finally, the SIQ yields measures of a person's self-esteem and degree of maturity as judged by others. The SIQ and its scores measuring the dimensional maturity of the self-image have been quite useful. More recent research has further confirmed the validity of its dimensional and maturity measures.[4]

The Perceived Self-Questionnaire (PSQ). The Self-Image Questionnaire procedures are of only limited usefulness since they measure the dimensional maturity of only the self-image. Could not the theory generate a more powerful and fruitful measure of the di-

---

[3] *Explorations of Maturity* reports in detail the technical scores indexing the theory of maturing as well as their validity correlates.

[4] The SIQ, its scores, and their validity correlates have been previously reported (Heath, 1965).

mensional and structural complexity of the maturing person described in Chapter One? A fifty-item questionnaire was designed to measure each of the specific theoretical predictions of the theory of maturity. The test provides scores indexing the maturity of a person's values, male and female interpersonal relations, self-image, and cognitive skills, the degree of his stability, integration, allocentricism, autonomy, and symbolization, and of his maturity generally. The evidence from a variety of samples suggests the Perceived Self-Questionnaire (PSQ) total score may be measuring maturity. The dimensional and structural scores are also closely associated with other measures indexing the maturity of the same dimension or structure.[5] The results to date indicate not only that the PSQ may be useful in describing personality change but also that the theory of maturing has some power in generating new procedures and insights, thus indirectly providing further support for the theory itself.

IDENTIFYING DETERMINANTS

Five to seven weeks following the completion of the testing program for a sample, each student participated in a study to identify those factors that influenced his development in college. He completed a Personality Change Rating scale, listened to a synthesis of the results of the tests administered during the first phase of the research, and then engaged in several procedures designed to assess the effects of the college upon his development.

PERSONALITY CHANGE RATING SCALE

An important determinant of a person's image of himself, usually ignored by researchers on personality change, is his own idea of the type and rate of his own change—whether it be immaturing or maturing. Each student first described spontaneously the types of changes he noted in himself since his matriculation, the changes he regretted, and those he wished he had experienced. Using a series of line scales, he judged the degree to which he had changed in his intellectual skills, image of himself, values, male, female, and family relationships, and creativity.

[5] Appendix B describes the test and some of the results obtained with it.

INTERPRETATIVE REPORT PROCEDURE

Prior to the initiation of the second phase of the research, interpretative summaries of each student's coded test materials were made independently of any knowledge of his identity. Tentative hypotheses were formulated about how he had developed in college as well as about the direction in which he seemed to be evolving. The hypotheses were not made within the framework of the theory of maturing, about which all of the students were ignorant in any case. Instead, the analysis induced hypotheses from the student's aptitude and academic grade pattern that were then checked, refined or replaced by subsequent hypotheses formulated from a sequential analysis of the tests measuring the changes in values, interests, personality traits, self-image, and less conscious motives, defenses, and conflicts. Although the report of the analysis to each student took from sixty to ninety minutes, it did not exhaust the test information. Such thoroughness was beyond the purpose of the research and the time available. All hypotheses were presented as highly tentative. Each student was encouraged to disagree and to comment about the report and to assess its accuracy following the completion of the study. Only three of the participating students expressed serious reservations about major parts of their summaries.

To illustrate both the progressive hypothesis-forming, confirming, and disconfirming procedure used to reconstruct each student's change and the type of changes discussed with him, parts of several interviews are given later.

INTERVIEW PROCEDURES

The student was given a list of forty-six determinants that might have influenced his change while at college. The list had been compiled on the basis of the judgments of faculty, deans, and students about the important collegiate determinants of personality change. The list included such determinants as the freshman English course, nonacademic relations with the faculty, the honor systems, roommates, summer vacation, the college's intellectual atmosphere, and even the availability of a car. The student added other determinants he judged had been important in his own development. Each determinant was typed on a separate card, which the student sorted into one of five categories that defined how much influence it had had upon his general personality change since he entered college. After the cards had been preliminarily sorted, he next ordered the cards in the greater-influence piles from most to least influential. His judgments were recorded. Each person then described in detail how he had changed as a result of the determinant he had judged to be most influential. Similar self-analyses were made for the following three or four next most influential determinants. At the conclusion of this part of the interview, the same procedure was used to discover the determinants of the student's change in his values, intellectual skills, self-image, and personal relationships. The order in which these self-structures were discussed was randomized among the men. Each interview, lasting about ninety minutes, was recorded and later typed verbatim.

Since we sought to determine whether the students matured in the ways predicted in Chapter One, it was imperative that they not be aware of or be influenced by any knowledge of the theory or that the study was of maturing. They were not cued about the theory or its expectations, were asked to describe their "change" rather than their "maturing" (in order not to bias the results toward the maturing rather than immaturing effects of college), and were given identical rating instructions and interview procedures. The interviewer maintained the same noncommittal interview style for each student. He refrained from suggesting any specific changes or from influencing the student's option to report predominantly immaturing effects if the student was so disposed.

Several years after the completion of the studies, the typed, coded interviews were scored for the maturing and immaturing changes as defined by the theory of maturing. That is, the type of change reported by the student for each determinant was scored for the presence of one or more of the possible twenty-five types (personal relationships were divided into male and female categories, although the two categories were analyzed together statistically) of maturing or immaturing trends reported in Chapter One, for example, increased stability of the self-image or awareness in female personal relations; decreased integration of intellectual skills or allocentric male relationships. As a consequence, it was possible to quantify and order not only the types of personality changes spontaneously described by each student but also those specific changes, whether maturing or immaturing, induced by different determinants.[6] The interviews produced

[6] Appendix C examines the validity of the scores obtained from the analysis of the interviews.

a wealth of information about both maturing and immaturing which
will be freely quoted in subsequent chapters.

VIGNETTES OF PERSONALITY CHANGE

Allan, a freshman, and John, a senior, agreed to illustrate the
interpretative and interview procedures. We also illustrate how the
interviews were scored for the different maturing (or immaturing)
trends.

Why describe Allan and John rather than Henry or Bill? We
have not tried to select the "typical" freshman or senior, nor have we
selected Allan and John as our most dramatic, colorful, profound,
or insightful students. They aren't. Allan was selected because he was
one of several freshmen who experienced much internal confusion
during his freshman year. His interview reflects more immaturing
and disorganizing, though potentially healthy, changes than those
of most other freshmen. John was selected because his interview, more
than those of most of the other seniors, illustrated almost exclusively
maturing effects of his different college experiences. Both Allan and
John also reveal in their interviews many of the basic personality effects
produced by the college as well as many of the more frequently cited
of the college's determinants of maturity.

ANALYSIS OF ALLAN

Academic achievement. Allan's aptitudes suggest that he will
function more effectively in courses requiring quantitative and logical
skills than in courses requiring verbal abstract or discursive talents.
However, on the basis of only his first semester grades and aptitudes,
his unexpected poorer performance in his mathematics course suggests
that he may not have the abstract intelligence to do well in courses
that have little concrete, visible, or practical application. Furthermore,
the consistency and level of the rest of his academic work indicate he
may not be undergoing any profound adjustment problem or emotional interference with his skill efficiency. The pattern of his academic
choices suggests he may be interested in the social sciences.

Value pattern (AVL). Allan places a very high value on
theoretical, scholarly work. This value, in combination with a high
valuation of social and political activities, suggests an interest in the
social sciences in which power can be used to control or manipulate

the affairs of others but, given the high social value, for their benefit. Sometimes such a high valuation of power suggests a person may be concerned about his own self-control. Allan should feel comfortable in the college, with its many sociopolitical activities. (He commented he had not done much politically except to picket.) Since he entered college, he seems to have developed even stronger intellectual, theoretical, or philosophical interests. Such interests may be manifested in an increased intellectualization of his feelings, which he may now be trying to contain. Does his excessively low religious value raise a question about the depth of his ethical convictions and concerns? Or is he unwilling to allow himself to be dependent on or governed by some other person or belief? He may be opportunistic and not quite responsible in some of his relationships.

Interests (*SVIB*). Allan's pattern of motivational interests shows some incongruencies with his pattern of more consciously held values. The discrepancy suggests he may be in conflict about his own future vocational direction. Some of his more consciously expressed values may be compensatory for unconscious conflicts. His temperament does not fit those successful in more manipulative or politically oriented occupations. For example, he is not motivationally similar to men who are verbally persuasive or in positions of power and responsibility. Actually, his high similarity to men in the service professions and scientifically applied fields matches his aptitudes as well as one part of his value pattern. Although his basic motivational pattern has not changed markedly, he does seem to be moving more toward the applied scientific fields, like medicine, where he can work independently and in control of his own life and perhaps that of others. His temperament leans more strongly toward the application of scientific knowledge in personal or human areas than in impersonal or technical areas.

Personality traits (*MMPI*). Allan is not a highly introversive person. He is neither aloof nor distant from others, nor is he deeply involved in his own inner life and feelings. He is an energetically aggressive, outward-going person who probably enjoys being with and kidding around with other persons, comfortably participating in social or informal group or party activities. He seems to be less stable than when he first entered, for now he is experiencing more turmoil and inner fluctuation, both in his moods and in the control of his impulses. He has become unsettled and may feel both aggressively high and on top of the world and shortly afterward feel depressingly low, weighed down by his own burdens. Since entering college Allan seems to be increasingly trying to suppress his affectional and sexual impulses. Yet, at the same time, he may find he is more strongly tempted to be more impulsive, possibly at the expense of conventional ethical norms and standards. The conflict between the intensification of his impulses and the heightening of his efforts to control them may produce considerable inner strain, but the conflict does not seem to be too overwhelming for his resources nor to be pathological in scope.

Self-image (SIQ, PSQ). Allan thinks of himself as maturing moderately since entering college, although almost solely in his intellectual skills and in his relations with women. Intellectually, he now thinks of himself as a much more aware and reflective person. He believes his relations with women are beginning to settle down, although simultaneously he is becoming more and more unsettled about what kind of person he is. He judges himself to be what he thinks others think of him, so he is not tempted to play a role to meet other people's expectations. He probably does not feel too inhibited or self-conscious in his relationships.

Personality dynamics (Rorschach). The analysis of his Rorschachs indicates some inconsistencies between different parts of his personality. He seems to be much more emotional than the other tests suggest. He could now be very moody and depressed, perhaps because of strong guilt feelings, maybe over the consequences of impulsively acting out his needs. He tends to ignore such guilt feelings by fleeing into activity, aggressive clowning, and more self-assertive or dominating activity. There is a strong inward push to move out into the world and not back into himself. He is not a person who naturally, easily, or persistently resorts to fantasy as a substitute for action, for he is strongly impelled to act. He does not retreat into intellectualism or daydreaming. Is he strongly interested in athletics, which would be one appropriate way to channel such restless energy? (Allan said he enjoyed athletics but they took too much energy.) The record hints he has strong passions, including sadistic ones, the control of which preoccupy him. (Allan said at this point that he was very fearful of hurting others, particularly girls.)

Allan may be easily aroused heterosexually; at least, he is preoccupied by heterosexual relations, thoughts of which emerge very readily. Some of his preoccupations may not be realistic, so in combination with some ambivalence in the control of his sadism, they may not be always appropriately expressed. His sexuality may not be buffered by empathy and sympathy. He may have difficulty integrating his more tender, affectionate, or considerate feelings with his sexual impulses. A very tentative hypothesis is that Allan may relate to women primarily in terms of their sexuality rather than in terms of them as persons to love. He may be somewhat hesitant to commit himself in such relations for he may have been hurt in some way in the past when he did. Furthermore, he may have more strong unconscious dependent and passive needs to be loved than he is willing to accept about himself. Such conflicts may now be increasing. As he seeks to control his impulses more, he may start to develop a more highly differentiated inner life. There is some evidence he is beginning to inhibit his tendency to act out by developing obsessive fantasies whose content consists of compensatory masculine conceptions of himself. His more aggressive assertiveness and need to feel competent as a male may be channeled into overt activity, perhaps sexual, in which he has power and control in the situation.

Vocationally he is in flux. He is beginning to form a stable integration of his temperament and motives with his more consciously held values. Perhaps until he stabilizes control of his impulses and interpersonal relationships, he may not be able to decide whether a scientifically applied field dealing with or without people would be more compatible. Our prediction is that Allan will move to work in those more applied scientific areas where he can work independently under his own control. As he builds more intellectual defenses by which to buffer himself from his impulses or find more graduated ways by which to express them he will be able to move with less anxiety into a professional career in which he can work more closely with other persons.

ALLAN'S INTERVIEW

Following the report of this very tentative analysis, Allan scanned the list of forty-six aspects of the college that might have influenced his change in college. He included his mathematics course as a forty-seventh determinant to the list. After rating each determinant for its degree of influence on his development, he then ranked the more important determinants of his change to have been, in order, his friendships with women, the social honor system, his roommates, summer vacation, and friendships with men. To illustrate how the interviews were scored for the maturing and immaturing effects of the determinants, Allan's scores, as defined in Chapter One, are given in parentheses. Because of the length of the interviews, redundant portions are omitted.

Interviewer: In terms of *general change* since you entered college, you mention *close friendships with women* as having had considerable influence upon you. Could you say in what ways you're different as a result of these friendships from when you first came in?

Allan: I'm trying to learn to achieve some sort of a meaningful relationship with other women which I've never done before really. (Immature Allocentric Female Relations) And by not having done this, I see why what I expect in someone, why I criticize girls . . . and maybe I can overcome this which I want to do, especially now with the present girl I'm going out with. (Integration Female Relations)

Int.: How have you changed as a result?

Allan: More and more I want to find one person I could really love . . . something very meaningful with my relationships. (Allocentric Value)

Int.: Do you think you've changed in any other way as a result of your relationships with girls?

Allan: I don't think so.

Int.: Now, in what way do you feel the *social honor system* has had an effect on you?

Allan: Well, I think this whole idea of honor, this is both the social and academic, but I think the social even more . . . with what's expected of you in a room . . . relationship to women is somewhat different, I think. I do consider what I'm doing. (Aware Value) I mean . . . earlier in the past years, you know, I've taken advantage of girls. Now at least, even if I still do, I do think about it [laughs]. I think that I am doing this.

Int.: Can you think of any other kinds of effects the social honor system has had?

Allan: It's a discipline, sort of. Maybe that part of the interpretation about sexual intercourse. I mean I have thought about it with a girl in my room. "This is going to be a violation if I do this." So it has been. It might have stopped me; maybe it hasn't, but I thought about it at a certain time.[7]

Int.: Now, in what way do you feel you're different as a result of *roommates?*

Allan: Well [laughs], first semester, my roommates were quite different from me. Maybe I'm more tolerant of people. I'm generally quite tolerant, but first semester I had to be especially tolerant. And this semester, my roommate and I are much closer than I was with my other two roommates. (Allocentric Male Relations) And we discuss many things. And I think he sort of opened my eyes to certain things I sort of covered up or didn't see or want to see about school, about studying, about girls. He made me think about them and also told me a few things. (Aware Self)

Int.: You mean about yourself?

Allan: About both of us. It goes both ways. For me, it's myself.

Int.: How do you feel you've changed as a result of this?

Allan: For the first time in my life I think I've considered maybe I do have some problems. (Immature Stable Self) Maybe I should go to a psychiatrist. Maybe I should see why I don't want to study, why I do hurt girls . . . this is really . . . I've always thought I was a very happy person, but this year I am depressed. (Immature Allocentric Self) All of this has come out in discussions with my roommates.

Int.: Can you say what the effect of this has been on you?

Allan: Well, I guess it's always better to know your problems. I don't know. I haven't changed that much, I don't think.

[The sections on the effect of his *summer vacation,* that is, increased awareness of himself, and of his *close friends,* identified to be his roommates, are omitted.]

Allan next rated the degree of influence each of the forty-seven aspects of the college had upon his change in values, selecting his

[7] Statements about an effect—his increased awareness of his values—of a determinant that has already been scored for that determinant are not scored again.

friendships with women and Bryn Mawr College, his roommates and
friendships with other men, his summer vacation, and the academic
honor system to have had the most important effects.

Int.:   In your change in *values,* you mention that both *close friend-
           ships with women* and *Bryn Mawr College* have had consid-
           erable influence.

Allan: Well, I think this is almost the same. Ah, what I expect from
           a relationship with girls, why I go out with them, what I want
           to do on a date. What is the purpose? Always I've gone out to
           have fun, fool around, maybe sexual, but now I've started to
           think, "What's the purpose of this related to the whole of
           life?" (Aware Value)

           [Section omitted.]

Int.:   Do you think these relations with women have had an effect
           on any other kinds of values?

Allan: Values toward women . . . also related toward values to-
           ward everyone. You know, a sense of responsibility toward
           one girl if you're going out with her or consideration for her
           feelings. (Allocentric Value) I've always considered myself
           considerate of others, so I don't know if there's been a great
           change. But every relationship does show you a different type
           of consideration you have to show . . . more tolerance; all
           of this . . . each one adds to it.

Int.:   Now, in terms of *roommates* and *friends with other men,* how
           do you feel your values have changed as a result of these rela-
           tionships?

Allan: Well, generally with this semester's roommate, especially in dis-
           cussions with him, I've been thinking of what is the purpose of
           life altogether. Why am I here at all? What do I expect? There
           has to be something more than just going out, getting married,
           and just settling down. (Aware Value) Why do I want to
           live? For what reason? Is there a purpose? And then consider
           these things.

Int.:   Have you come to any sense of direction about this?

Allan: Academically not very much. That's a big problem. I am try-
           ing to find something now to settle down with. I don't think
           so, really, I'm still sort of, you know, the future's still a little
           hazy . . . a meaningful future. (Immature Stable Self) I

know I can go out and be a high school teacher . . . but why? Why do I want to do this? Will I enjoy it?

Int.: Do you think your roommates or good friends may have had any effects on any other kinds of values?

Allan: Ah, I don't . . . I don't . . . I discuss with my roommate my relationships with other girls, trying to tie in why I do this. (Aware Self) So all of this is discussed with him, which relates to life and all these topics. Why I study? Why I don't study? Why I watch TV? Why I don't watch TV?

Int.: Do you feel your values have changed as a result of talking about them? Do his ideas have any major influence on your beliefs?

Allan: Yes, especially his ideas about getting out hostilities, you know, and depression, and being angry at something and maybe then trying to let out these emotions. (Immature Allocentric Value) I've thought about this. Why? What I could do? I don't think I've resolved this.

Int.: How did your *summer vacation* affect your specific values or attitudes?

Allan: One would be girls.

Int.: You mean wanting to settle down?

Allan: Right . . . wanting to settle down. Two, would be finding, getting more out of life than just a repetitive meaningless existence and going out at night. Well, that's what it was. It's fun and I'd like to do it this summer again, you see. (Immature Integration Self) But I can see after three months of doing it, three months is just about the limit.

Int.: You're ready for something else, but you're not sure what.

Allan: Right, right.

Int.: Now, the *academic honor system,* how do you feel it has had an effect on your values?

Allan: Throughout high school I cheated like hell, especially in German. I mean there was an excuse. The fascinating thing I find here is I don't even think about cheating on a take-home exam, until I hand in the exam and get it back. And then I say, "You know you could have cheated." (Stable Value) And the amazing thing is that I don't even think about cheating now. It's sort of . . . you know, I take it for granted. It doesn't enter my mind anymore. All right, so people don't cheat. I don't cheat, I don't think about it or very little which I think is a tremendous thing.

[Section omitted.]

Allan identified the principal determinants of changes in his intellectual life to have been his summer vacation, his living arrangements at the college, his friendships with other men, a specific course, and lectures by distinguished visitors.

Int.: In the change in *intellectual skills* you mention the *summer vacation* to have had the greatest influence.

Allan: In two ways. First, an appreciation, more of an appreciation of what I can get out of college. Bell-hopping again, you know, is not what I want out of life. I can see I want something more. (Immature Stable Value) I still haven't, you know, convinced myself the way to do it is to work. This is a problem.

Int.: You mean to work in college?

Allan: Yeah, to study in college. But at least I think I appreciate more what it means to be an English teacher, or a doctor, or a lawyer and not a bell-hop. And the other way is sort of similar. This summer was the first time in my life I ever read during the summer for pleasure. I never really read strictly for pleasure, very rarely. This summer I did, which was different, maybe because I looked for something intellectual to overcome the bell-hopping and the girls. [Because this implied expansion of his intellectual interests is a questionable example of the integration of his intellectual skills, it was not scored.]

Int.: In what way do you feel *living arrangements* have influenced your intellectual development?

Allan: Well, Barclay is a wild place and it sort of has a negative effect. It's hurt my study habits. Whenever . . . there's always an excuse for not studying, not pursuing intellectual pursuits, or something like that. (Immature Autonomy Intellectual skills) I can just sit in my room. The guys come in. We go into someone else's room. We can sit and bull. So it's just sort of not very conducive to studying.

Int.: Any other kinds of effects on your intellectual development?

Allan: [Pause.] Well, because of not studying, and seeing that I'm not studying, it's getting worse and worse as the semester goes along. At least now I can see it's wrong, that I have to change.

(Immature Stable Self) Before, I never studied much, I just took it that way. I'd say, "Well, what the hell! I'm getting through school." But even this semester there's a chance for the first time in my life of not passing a course, and maybe this will shake me up.

[Section on effects of *close friends with men* omitted, that is, increased immature autonomy and allocentric male relations.]

Int.: Then, the next one is a *specific course*. What was the effect of this specific course on you intellectually?

Allan: Well, it's a history course. In high school more and more I was convinced I wanted to pursue one of the Social Sciences—History, Political Science. And I came into this college thinking that. I didn't take any science courses. I just took one Math course. Originally science was my interest until the sophomore or junior year in high school. Then I changed. (Aware Self) I didn't bother to take any courses. And now after being exposed to history and the amount of reading that's necessary, it's sort of changed me. (Immature Stable Self) This has been a big change that I have to go back to sciences. More of my interest lies there.

[Discussion of history course and *Outside speakers,* that is, increased stable self-concept, omitted.]

Allan ranked his friendships with women, his summer vacation, roommates and friendships with men, and Bryn Mawr College to have been the most influential determinants of his changing personal relationships.

Int.: In rating the determinants of your change in *relations with other people,* you mention your *close friendships with women* have had considerable influence on you.

Allan: I think . . . especially now, I think, for the first time I found a girl whom I really feel close to. And I think . . . this alone is a change in my relations with other girls. (Allocentric Female Relations) You know, less a need to look for girls, to go to Bryn Mawr all the time, to go out with different girls. As far as relationships with guys, I don't think it really has changed me that much.

Int.: When you say "close" to her, what are you thinking of?

Allan: Well, I don't know. I mean . . . maybe it would be love or whatever that is. It is something where I . . . I want to be with her, just as part of my life, in every way, sexually. But this time it is more than sexually, maybe for the first time. (Integration Female Relations)

Int.: When you talked earlier about the need to hurt, is this still here with her?

Allan: No, I don't think so.

Int.: Is that a change?

Allan: You see, this relationship just started. That's one thing I'm afraid of . . . that this need is going to want to come back this time. I don't want it more than any other time. I've hurt girls before but I haven't or never really liked them, never thought I loved them. But this girl . . . I love this girl. This girl I don't want to hurt, and this I am afraid of.

Int.: When you say hurt, what do you mean by that?

Allan: I always tire of girls. I go out for a while and almost always it's me who decides to break off the relationship, and in this way I hurt the girl. (Immature Aware Self) And this time I don't want to do this. I don't know why I tire of them. I don't . . . I don't . . . want it to happen this time. (Immature Stable Female Relations)

[Section on *summer vacation* omitted.]

Int.: How do you feel *roommates* and, I suppose, *close friendships with other men* have changed you in the way you get along with other people?

Allan: With guys I think it's generally the same. I haven't really changed, but with girls, my roommate and I discuss each of the girls I go out with, (Aware Female Relations) what I think of them, and just in analyzing them I think it's helped me to see why I tire of them . . . why I no longer want to go out with them, why I do hurt them. (Aware Self) I don't know if it has changed me, but at least looking at the situation from an objective point of view helps, and my roommates helped me see this through discussion.

[Section on effect of *Bryn Mawr College,* that is, increased allocentric relations with women, omitted.]

Finally Allan selected his friendships with women, his roommates, living arrangements, friendships with men, and his relationships with his parents to have influenced his ideas about himself.

Int.: In terms of change in your *self-image* you mention *close friendships with women.*

Allan: I think I see myself as being more mature because of this . . . for the first time wanting to settle down, thinking of marriage. All of this I never really thought about to any great extent. [Section omitted.] I can see myself growing up. This year I think I've had a tremendous amount of change. I feel I changed this year more than ever before; my attitude toward women, studying, maybe toward life. Just questioning.

[Section omitted.]

Int.: Now, *roommates.* How do you think differently of yourself as a result of roommates?

Allan: Well, just through discussions again, analyzing my actions. Why I do things, but also, I think, at one point my roommate may have changed my image of myself. (Aware Self) He told me what other people think of me too, which is hard to tell sometimes. And he made . . . we were talking about responsibility and having some influence on people and I thought I did. Well, he said because I don't work and because I goof off a lot, some people are not affected by my influence or they say, "Forget him." And that sort of thing. I said I didn't think that was true. I thought . . . because I am a serious person, and even if I don't study, I do think though. (Immature Integration Value) Some people goof off and just fool around all the time . . . I goof off but I am serious, and people . . . he said some people would lose respect for me. He didn't say they definitely have, but he said people can lose respect for you. And this changed my self-image. (Immature Stable Self)

Int.: You mean, you've come to accept it?

Allan: To some extent though it hasn't changed me in making me study.

Int.: You mean you goof off as much?

Allan: Yeah.

[Sections on effects of *living arrangements,* that is, increased awareness of self and lack of autonomy in male relations, and *close friends with men* are omitted.]

Int.:   How do you feel your *relationships with your parents* have had an effect on what you think of yourself?

Allan: Again, I think this is maybe maturity. I've been away from my parents before college, but now, you know, you're away for a year and only go back on vacations. I think I appreciate my folks more. (Allocentric Male Relations) And I think of myself as more than just a son, sort of the difference between my folks in age and maturity is getting less and less. (Integration Male Relations) When I go home, in discussions and in my feelings toward them I don't try to hide them, you know, like you did when you're in high school.

Int.:   Can you think of any other ways you've changed your ideas as a result of relations with your parents?

Allan: No, not really.

Int.:   Has there been anything else that's had a major influence on you that we haven't talked about but should have?

Allan: [Pause.] I don't know what has caused this or why, but I see myself changing in relation to women, in maturity. In everything, I feel changes. I don't know why, but I'm thinking more about my actions. I seem to get depressed more. I don't know why. (Immature Stable Self) I also think about the future, what the meaning of life is, why one exists at all . . . just living and eating, that's nothing. I can't take just that. (Aware Self) I'm thinking more about that. (Aware Intellectual Skills) I don't know what the cause of this is.

Int.:   You mean in the last six or seven months you've really begun to reflect about yourself in a way you hadn't done earlier?

Allan: I think so. I think I always have, but not as much as I have this year. I think maybe because of . . . maybe that's caused more depression. The more I reflect, the more I see what's wrong with me, the more I'm angry about.

Int.:   And as a result of the depression you don't do anything about it?

Allan: That's true too. [Laugh.] It doesn't bother me. I like reflecting. I mean I think you have to. It's not high school any more. Your life is not planned. It's college and that's it. That's the end. But now I have to think about a meaningful relation with women, about a future profession, about what and where I want to live. You've reached a point where you have to. You can't just glide through.

Allan's test materials and interview clearly indicate he is undergoing a crisis in identity. He is unsure of what he is, what his purpose is, and where he is going. As the tests indicated, Allan has yet to form a stable identity that integrates his aptitudes, values, temperament, personality traits, and needs. His persistent preoccupation about his relations with women, seen both in the test materials and the interview, may be the manifest problem around which the more basic problem of defining who he is is being worked out. Few other freshmen so clearly focused on heterosexual issues; again, such a focus suggests that his concern is possibly compensatory.

How is Allan growing at the college? His former impulsivity and possible ethical opportunism, whether expressed in cheating in high school, sexual or "sadistic" activity in the summer, are now becoming modified as a consequence of his growing dissatisfaction with himself, his contemporary interpersonal relationships, and the values of the college. He may be becoming more inhibited, perhaps as a consequence of his growing reflectiveness. He has now become a problem to himself, a necessary stage for organizing himself at a more mature level. Certainly, he is more introspective, more guilty about his impulses and fearful of hurting someone else. His moodiness and depression and self-preoccupation may be resulting from checking his natural aggressive assertiveness and turning some of it back onto himself. We see the development of a more allocentric conscience as he internalizes the academic and the spirit of the social honor systems, the development of new expectations of what he would like to be and not be as he comes to see he doesn't want to be a goof-off, the deepening intellectualized preoccupations of a typical freshman seeking to place himself and his values within some larger philosophical context.

Despite Allan's apparent instability and turmoil, we would say he is becoming more mature and liberally educated. In our terms, he's in that educable state of disorganization in which he's trying to free himself, though not yet successfully, from *domination* by his impulses; in which he's expanding his conception of himself as a person who should have some relation to some larger integrative meaning, though what that meaning is to be he doesn't yet know; in which he's becoming more allocentrically oriented toward others, though he's still not sure he won't hurt his girl; in which he's deepening his inner awareness and learning how to use reflectiveness for adaptive purposes, even though this developing intellectual skill has yet to manifest itself in the academic compass of his life; in which he is seeking to stabilize his relationships, his academic motives and values, though he must still ask, "Why do I want to do this?"

ANALYSIS OF JOHN

Academic achievement. John entered college with excellent quantitative aptitudes and a correspondingly excellent record of achievement in quantitative fields like mathematics. But despite these strengths, John progressively declined academically in his mathematics and natural science courses during his early years at college. The increasing stabilization of his intellectual achievement after his freshman year suggests he has been a conscientious and hard-working person. The decline in the quantitatively oriented courses may have been caused by a possible loss of motivation in response to their increasing impersonality and abstractness rather than to emotional interference with his intellectual skills. He has since concentrated heavily in the social sciences, performing very well. Except for a possible adjustment problem during his first semester at the college, when his academic achievement was below what might be expected, his increasing and consistent academic improvement suggests he is a basically stable and effectively functioning person. But how is he going to use his excellent logical, analytic, and deductive abilities in the future?

Value pattern (AVL). John's basic pattern of values as a freshman was not well differentiated; this lack of differentiation suggests that at that time he might not have had very definite ideas of what kind of person he would like to be. During his four years, the theoretical, scholarly way of life has become much less important, perhaps reflecting in part his growing disenchantment with mathematics and the sciences and a growing concern for his social and emotional relationships. The devaluation of pure scholarship as an end in itself has been accompanied by an increased valuation of more aesthetic and political forms of activity. John seems to be accepting more of his own feelings into his awareness and is increasingly more willing to use them as a basis for decisions. The concomitant high value on using power and persuasiveness to accomplish his goals helps to balance the privatism or introversive withdrawal latent in a singularly high aesthetic valuation. John could be very sensitive to political nuances and tactful in social relations involving authority and power.

Interests (*SVIB*). John's temperament and motivational interest pattern seems to fit fairly well the changes seen in his values. He has become less congruent with those men in the abstract scholarly areas like mathematics and physics, and more similar to men who control, direct, and have power in private or public types of occupations in which the welfare of others is paramount. He is moving more strongly toward the applied social and verbally persuasive fields, in which he can exercise considerable responsibility in practical decision making, than toward scholarly fields. That John consciously values the aesthetic more than the social or altruistic way of life on the Study of Values but is more motivationally congruent with men in the social than aesthetic occupations on the SVIB suggests that he may be in some conflict about how to express his social and affectional interests in others. He may not have found a way to express and gratify directly his emotional needs to give and to receive from others. Instead, such needs may be expressed vicariously in self-involving emotional experiences. John may be pointed toward a career in public administration, foreign service, law, or teaching.

Personality traits (*MMPI*). John is essentially an emotionally stable person. In his four years at the college he has become a much more emotionally sensitive young man, more open to his own feelings, as the increased aesthetic value suggests, but, interestingly, somewhat more withholding of their direct and spontaneous expression toward others. He may be more emotionally distant in his relations, perhaps to protect himself from too great emotional involvement in which he may lose some control. He seems to control himself quite strongly, but since he now is more open to his own feelings, though not yet able to express them directly and personally, he may experience much more inner strain. Why is there this increased emotional distance in his personal relations, and yet the increased temperamental similarity to those in the social service fields?

Self-image (*SIQ, PSQ*). John thinks of himself as maturing considerably since his freshman year, particularly in his intellectual skills and in his values, which have become more consistent and now serve to integrate considerable parts of himself. He also thinks of himself as feeling both more comfortable around other men as well as more autonomous of their influence. Given the suggestions of the other tests, could it be he is unaware of the full extent of his needs to become socially and emotionally involved with another person? Perhaps he may feel much more inwardly comfortable with his own feelings now, though he may actually be more distant or shy outwardly, fearing too great dependency.

Personality dynamics (Rorschach). According to the Rorschach, John seems to be a basically sound and well-controlled person who has good judgment and can accurately and realistically assess what occurs in his world. He can take the world as it is without distorting it to fit any personal preconceptions, so his judgments can be trusted to be considered and appropriate. He certainly is not unconventional or idiosyncratic. He can so control and inhibit his own desires that they should not be internally perceived to threaten his stability. He may, when first meeting new people or situations, be somewhat overly inhibited, tentative, and possibly negativistic. John may not function up to his capacity in new stressful situations, for his energetic resources are not fully utilizable under stress. His real talents and potential productivity begin to emerge only after he has stayed in a situation for some period of time.

But the way John seems to control his emotional reactions seems to be less mature. He resembles a sleeping bear just beginning to rouse itself. Do his increasing aesthetic and decreasing theoretical values portend that he is beginning to perceive an inward freeing of his emotional and impulse life? He seems to be very sensitive, reflective, and well-controlled in his emotional relations with others, but at the expense of being more emotionally spontaneous. Could it be that his strong needs and feelings for others, seen in his motivational congruity with men in the social service fields, have yet to be integrated or sublimated into his personal relationships? He may sense the growing discrepancy between his inner expanding life and its more limited outward manifestations and think of himself as less a person than he is. He may feel guilty at this time about expressing his own emotional needs, particularly when he is in dependent relationships. The estrangement from the heat of his passion and anger may make him feel at times as if he is not quite fully alive. There may be stronger but repressed needs to be exhibitionistic, to flaunt his suppressed masculinity and he may need to learn how to accept his aggressivity and sexuality, to enjoy his impulses, to take pride in them, to assert them in culturally acceptable ways, perhaps through the assumption of some responsible caring role in the community. Once he becomes more acceptant of his own masculinity and emotional needs, he should become even more productive in the future, for he has the basic control and judgment to make wise use of such freed energy. His dominant problem for the immediate future seems not to be to learn to establish intimate relations with another, which he can do; rather, it is to incorporate and to integrate his awakening impulses into his relations with others. (John made no comment about this analysis. Several years later when asked for permission to print his material, he reported the analysis to be "largely accurate." He is "pretty happy and reasonably successful" in his career and he has married the girl mentioned in the following interview.)

JOHN'S INTERVIEW

Similar interview procedures were used with John as with Allan. John identified, in order, the effect of his roommates, his friendships with other men, the social honor system, close friendships with women, academic honor system, and Bryn Mawr College to have been important influences on his general personality development while in college.

Interviewer: With respect to your *general change* from freshman to senior years, you select *roommates* to have had the most influence on your change. Could you describe more specifically how you've changed as a result of your roommates?

John: Well, my roommate situation is a bit unusual because three of us who were put together freshman year are still together. (Stable Male Relations) And we have been so for four years. Then, we picked up a fourth man last year. He's been with us all along, and so we got to know a good deal about a person in four years. We get to know what kind of a mood he's in and how to react to it. You get to know his values pretty thoroughly, how he feels about things. (Aware Male Relations) And also now I feel that some things like . . . I haven't had religion and not too much science, but just sort of rubbing elbows with religion, chemistry, and psychology majors has helped me broaden my own outlook. (Integration Intellectual skills)

Int.:   How are you different now than you were as a freshman, which might not have been the case had you not roomed with these people?

John: [Sigh.] Ah . . . that's . . . that's a little bit rough. I guess we were all pretty much the same type of people. A little bit introspective perhaps, a little shy, and we sort of grew out in each other. And if I had started out with people who were very gregarious, it probably would have taken me a while to blossom.

Int.:   So you feel that being somewhat similar helped you to become somewhat different?

John: Yes, I think so for all of us.

Int.:   How can you describe that change?

John: Well, in the first place, it was sort of, I think, a feeling of security, very quickly realizing . . . a . . . there are some other guys that are pretty much just like me, and then doing things for the first time together. (Integration Male Relations) Maybe starting with pretty much the same values, and gradually branching out through different friends that each of us had . . . meeting some guys in other dorms or other guys across the hall. So that we started pretty much three guys and gradually branched out into a circle of friends with various experiences, drawing each other in. We got interested in the same club together, that type of thing.

[Section on effect of *close male friends,* identified to be his roommates, is omitted.]

Int.:   O.K. Well, the next influence you selected is the *social honor system.* What effect has this had on your development from freshman to senior year?

John: Well, the honor system's always impressed me a good deal. I don't think when you come to Haverford you really understand it. You know what it is, but you don't know what it means to the atmosphere on the campus. Ah . . . and it's something that's pretty hard to describe, I think. But the fact that it makes the social situation, this is strictly the social honor system I'm referring to, a lot more comfortable and natural. (Integration Female Relations) Like at Princeton and other big schools, it seems to me the way that they date and entertain women is unnatural and they don't seem to me to result

in as healthy relationships. Now, I don't know whether I can
say this is a specific change in me, but I think I look at it as a
development. It could have been more difficult if I hadn't been
living under a social honor system.

Int.: Well, now, in what way do you think it could have been more
difficult?

John: Ah . . . I think I would have had a harder time meeting
. . . after meeting a girl getting into a situation to know her
at all. When I came here I was very . . . I would say . . .
socially inept and it would have been the hardest thing in the
world for me to first meet a girl, have coffee dates, or study in
the library at a big university and never get to feeling very
comfortable at all [clears throat].

Int.: Now, the next one was *close friendships with women.*

John: Ah, well, just going back to the last question, I feel I am a
good deal more socially aware and handle myself socially a
good deal better than I did freshman year. (Aware Male Relations) I . . . well, I don't know. It's been a while since
. . . I've been dating one girl steadily for almost a year and a
half, (Stable Female Relations) so I haven't had any experiences starting to date new girls, but I could without too much
trouble. (Stable Self) I mean I'd be socially capable of it and
I think probably when I was a freshman I had sort of an in-
feriority complex about. . . .

Int.: O.K. Now, the next one was the *academic honor system.*

John: This again goes back to the whole atmosphere . . . sort of integrity and honesty, putting the premium on the way I handle
things myself. (Autonomous Self) I think this more than anything develops responsibility.

Int.: Do you think its effects are different than those of the social
honor system?

John: Ah . . . there are some . . . well, basically now. I think the
overall effect is pretty complementary . . . part of the same
thing. I think the social honor system and the academic honor
system, I guess, have a little bit different effect, but as far as
the contribution to my growth, I think they have been the same
in different areas.

[Section on *Bryn Mawr College* omitted, that is, increased integrative female relationships.]

The social honor system, academic honor system, relationships
with parents, and roommates were identified by John to have markedly
influenced his change in values.

Int.:   Of your change in *values* you mentioned the *social honor system* to have had the most influence.

John: I think there's a great deal of emphasis on responsibility and
on respect . . . respect in general for the women guests and
also for your roommates, and the college community. (Allocentric Values) It all sounds like I like the honor system
[laughs].

Int.:   How do you think it's changed you?

John: I think this . . . this emphasis makes you stop and think about
what you're doing (Aware Self) and how it fits . . . how you
can . . . you say to yourself, "Well, why am I doing this," or
it makes you, I think, look . . . look at your own motives . . .
and . . . and it makes you sort of pass judgment . . . way
you feel about this in a way which I suspect it would be a lot
easier to avoid, and I suspect a lot of people did avoid it until
they were faced with it. (Aware Value) And in this way I
think . . . I think the honor system really contributed to personal growth. I don't know how it specifically contributes to
values but if nothing else it makes you stop and consider.

Int.:   Now, the *academic honor system.* How do you feel this has
affected your values?

John: Well . . . pretty much the same way, only a little more specific, perhaps. (Autonomous Self) I think it definitely emphasized the value of academic integrity. In a way . . . in high
school I figured . . . well, one is ideally academically honest.
But . . . a . . . without the emphasis on it, a little cheating
now and then is not something you consider too definitely.
When you get here, it's just accepted that academic integrity
is a basic value and when you realize what it is and what it
means to life at Haverford, it sort of becomes a major value
for everybody. (Stable Value) It is important to me. I don't
see how it is something you would be able to drop out of your
life after four years.

Int.:   Can you think of any other way it had an effect on your values?

John: [Pause.] It somehow, perhaps, defines your responsibility in
your academic work. (Autonomous Value) It sort of lets you

know that you're on your own and you realize this pretty quickly, I think. That is, "This is my problem, and I'm going to handle it, and I'm going to handle it in this way." (Stable Value) You either accept this and rely on yourself . . . or else you fold.

Int.: How have your *relationships with your parents* influenced your values in the last four years?

John: Sort of . . . this may be . . . sort of backwards way. But my parents have pretty much accepted my values and ideas as . . . as they were formulated. Ah . . . I haven't really had to . . . haven't argued with them . . . have not had to persuade them in what I wanted to do what I thought was right. They have always been very open, letting me feel the way I wanted to . . . guiding me, giving me advice and telling me when they didn't think I was considering all the factors, but never telling me what the end result should be, "Well, considering all these things, this is what you'd like to do. Go ahead."

Int.: What do you think the effect of this attitude has been?

John: Again, developing a sort of personal responsibility, a feeling of total responsibility. (Autonomous Value) If given this sort of freedom, I didn't want to abuse it. So I would stop and consider what I was doing. (Autonomous Self)

[Section on effects of *roommates* on values omitted, that is, increased awareness of values and male relationships.]

John's intellectual change was most influenced by the faculty academic expectations, type of Haverford student, intellectual atmosphere of the college, and the academic honor system.

Int.: You mention *faculty academic expectations* had the most influence on your *intellectual change*.

John: Well, the first thing . . . they let me know right away things weren't quite the way I expected them to be. I started out with a 50 in my first history exam and a 40 on my first political science exam. And this was just about it [laugh]. This let me know I was going to have to shape up. Though I thought I was a pretty bright guy, I still had a good deal to learn, a long way to go before I got the results that I was . . . expected to . . . have to get. And so I don't know. I never really did quite understand why this happened to me because I don't think I was really goofing off a great deal. And I don't know how exactly I changed but I began to economize a little more properly in my studies, to apply myself more properly. (Stable Intellectual skills) And things began sort of to . . .

Int.: What do you think the effect of that was?

John: [Pause.] Well . . . it made me realize I was in a class with just about everybody else here and that the academic part of my life was going to be a much more serious business than I thought it would be. (Stable Value) See . . . you go back to my first semester freshman year. That was a weak semester. I think you have to limit that to the first half of the semester because in the next exams I pulled the lowest grades up to the middle 70's.

[Discussion of specific courses omitted.]

Int.: Can you think of any other way in which the faculty expectations had an effect on your own intellectual development over the four years?

John: Well . . . all along, the faculty, I think, is pretty much like this . . . as long as you know what they expect. But along with this they are very willing to help you come through with what they expect . . . papers and things . . . willing to talk with you and give you directions. I haven't taken advantage of this to too great an extent, but the feeling that you are not really producing for someone who is just grading papers, but you're producing for someone who's got a genuine interest in what you're doing both intellectually and scholastically.

Int.: Now, the next one is the type of *Haverford student*. In what way do you think the kind of student here has had an effect on your intellectual development?

John: Pretty much because the type of student here is a guy who is just about as bright as you are or brighter, and in high school, maybe, you meet ten people who are like that. Then here you have them all around you . . . starting in freshman year. Well, they're flunking a few things too. But, then it's sort of a process of growth which you go through together, I think, with all your comrades discussing academic questions. And the general attitude which . . . for which intellectual and academic life is highly valued. (Stable Value) It's something, it's something I don't think you could get away from even if you wanted to.

Int.: Then, the next one is the *intellectual emphasis of the college.* In what way do you feel that this has had an influence on you?

John: I'm not sure whether . . . this is entirely positive an influence all the time. The atmosphere can be very . . . very tense, as an atmosphere in which you really have to produce or fold [pause]. Sometime or other almost every year you're in a situation where you've got to produce three papers in two weeks and then take final exams. And you look back on the semester and then think "When could I have done this?" (Stable Intellectual skills) You can really see where you could have worked a little harder, not gone out on dates Friday night, but this always seemed to me to be rather inconceivable. I don't see how anybody can really do all the assigned work, then really come down to the end of a semester with a good start on all the papers and not have to put on any more pressure toward the end than he has at the beginning.

Int.: What do you think the effect of this has been?

John: I've heard one student put this in a way which I sort of think is pretty accurate. He said Haverford makes him feel like a hothouse tomato.

Int.: Forced?

John: So you are . . . sort of forced into doing. This is . . . this is . . . very uncomfortable sometimes. I'm not saying this is always bad. If you can knock out a twenty-five page paper in two or three days on three hours' sleep and turn out a good paper, you really look back on yourself and wonder how you ever did it. And it develops . . . if you can do this . . . it really develops a little confidence, (Stable Self) if you can produce under difficult circumstances, and yet produce not merely mediocre stuff.

[Section on how *academic honor system* encourages academic motivation is omitted.]

John next ranked the determinants of the changes in his interpersonal relationships, selecting in order his roommates, friendships with other men, the social honor system, friendships with women, and student clubs and service activities to be the most influential.

Int.: Now, let's turn to your *interpersonal relationships with men and women.* In what way do you feel your relations with your *roommates* have had an effect on the quality of your relations with other people?

John: Ah . . . O.K. [laughs]. I think first of all getting to know other people. I know my roommates and maybe two or three other people now well enough to know how they react, how they feel, whether they're depressed or not, pretty much what they're depressed about. (Aware Male Relations) Then I also know how to actually get along with them.

Int.: How do you think this has changed you?

John: Well, I guess this in itself is something that has changed. I don't think when I came . . . I probably had a feeling (Aware Self) that I could get along with people if I had to . . . wanted to and needed to, but I never had to to a very great extent. (Stable Self) I'm an only child, and I didn't have very much confidence in dealing with people. I think now I have immensely more confidence, more ability in dealing with people. (Allocentric Self)

[Section omitted about integrative and allocentric effects of male relationships. Sections on the effects of *close male friend- ships* and on the integrative effects of the *social honor* system omitted also.]

Int.: Now, *close friendships with other women.* How do you feel close friendships with women have changed you?

John: [Pause.] I think that this has sort of broadened me a bit. (Allo- centric Female Relations) It's gotten me outside myself . . . concern . . . gave me a real concern for somebody else, (Aware Female Relations) somebody else's problems and more confidence in myself and my ability in handling my own prob- lems. (Stable Self)

Int.: [Pause.] Any other change?

John: It's a very nice feeling to be able to help somebody, to mean something to somebody else (Allocentric Self) on an emotional and intellectual plane, and to appreciate . . . to appreciate a female in a sense you can't or don't appreciate male friends.

Int.: Finally, *student clubs and service activities.* How do you feel these have had an effect on your personal relationships?

John: I got into the club with my roommates, I guess in the middle of my freshman year, having done very little on campus. I never will forget the first time I spoke before a group . . .

stumbling all over myself. I think generally this has given me a good deal more confidence (Stable Self) . . . not maybe expressing myself well, but without feeling self-conscious, falling over my thoughts. (Integration Self) Then I became head of the club last year. This was something of a new experience. I never really ran an organization. It required keeping track of a lot of people, getting people to do things, coordinating a lot of people and time.

Finally, John selected his summer vacation, student clubs and service activities, roommate, and friendships with women as the principal determinants of his change in his ideas about himself.

Int.: In what way do you feel your *summer vacations* changed your *ideas about yourself?*

John: I worked as a counsellor for the past three years. Well, last summer I wound up counselling boys who were fifteen and sixteen, taking them on hiking trips. We would go out for about seven days. This is sort of a circumstance where you've got to have pretty much confidence in feeling you're going to know how to handle this. (Stable Self) I know this is . . . this is something I wouldn't have wanted to do the summer before. But I felt I was going to try it. This involves handling difficult, tough kids pretty much all by myself. And throughout the summer 80 per cent of the kids that I had were bigger than I was. And there are occasionally some pretty rough situations. This thing involves commanding respect and working, working well in groups with people, guiding them and it also involves physical skills, hiking and outdoor skills in general. There are some things I never felt I was really strong enough in, but as I progressed through these summers, I felt more and more confident. I sort of looked on this as sort of supplementary to my academic skills and intellectual interest, (Integration Self) which I always had sort of taken for granted and felt were there although there were times when I had a little bit of trouble. But it was . . . this is a part, a part of myself I always felt was there, where the outdoor skills I felt weren't.

[Sections omitted on effect of *student clubs,* that is, increased awareness of male relations, *roommates,* that is, increased awareness of self and values, and of *friendships with women,* that is, stabilized self-confidence.]

Int.:   Is there anything else that has happened to you in the last four years that we should have discussed that we didn't?

[Section omitted in which John discusses how he learned that he did not want to compete in academic research and decided to go into the foreign service instead.]

OBSERVATIONS ABOUT JOHN

John is not an Allan and the challenge to the college is to educate each individual in the way he needs to become more mature. Allan had to learn to accommodate to a way of life that valued irresponsible impulse expression less and ethically considered spontaneous emotional relationships more. He was a more vigorously assertive and outwardly going person who had not yet found, by the end of his freshman year, constructive ways to accommodate to the academic demands of the college. Allan experienced, we might infer, more inner confusion and turmoil than did John at the same point in his college career.

John, on the other hand, temperamentally seems to have been more congruent with the academic and ethical demands of the college. He had better control over his own intellectual talents to use them more advantageously earlier in his academic career. John's growth was more quiet and steady, gradually moving from the security of similar roommates to other persons and activities of the college. Whereas Allan had to find some more stable inward center from which to grow academically, John's good control, judgment, and solid academic achievement gave him that stabilizing center from which to become more receptive to his own impulse life and emotional needs for others. Faculty judgments of John agreed that he was very emotionally stable, determined and personable but not creative, perhaps because he was only just beginning to tap into his own emotional life.

How have John's college experiences matured or liberally educated him? His greatest change has been the formation of a stable identity or conception of what kind of person he is and is to become. This progressive stabilization may come easier to a John than to an Allan, given their temperamental differences. While Allan may face the potential of persistent inner chaos associated with strong impulses,

John may confront the possibility of too great stability that inhibits the legitimate experiencing of such chaos and impulse. John has also become a much more integrated person, particularly in his growing capacity for close friendships with increasingly different men and with his girl. He is already a person whose intellectual skills have developed allocentrically, for he is realistic and his judgments are appropriate. His strong temperamental affinity for the more socially allocentric occupations suggests he has the potential to become an even more socially-oriented and caring person. His values are more autonomously held, furthered in part by judicious parents. Finally, John, like Allan, experienced his greatest change in the expansion of his awareness of himself and, in addition, of his relations with other persons; he became more "socially aware." A quiet maturity and judiciousness pervades John's life. Allan as a senior will most likely be manifestly quite different from John as a senior, but they will have experienced in common many of the same underlying liberally educating effects of the college.

Before closing this discussion, we need to reflect at greater length about our methods and their implications for the chapters to follow. The dilemma that educators face when asked to defend their practices or institutions as maturing is that while they believe their students do become more mature and liberally educated they can cite no supporting evidence for their belief, other than their own opinions, impressions of their students, or, in attempts to be more "objective," comparative grades, nationally awarded honors, or even subsequent salary earnings. Few will dispute these types of evidence to be subjective, imprecise, or even irrelevant to the rich and variegated connotations inspired by the phrase *to become liberally educated*. In describing the process of maturing in college we also seek to clarify what becoming liberally educated means. But we too have no assurance that some of the particular methods we prefer to use, while more objective, precise, and even reasonably valid measures of maturing, will be more illuminating or relevant. We may have too facilely assimilated becoming liberally educated with maturing. To keep our sights clearer, we need to review briefly the limitations of our methods as measures of becoming liberally educated.

Our methods do not measure directly some widely accepted definitions of a liberal education. We have not catalogued a person's acquired knowledge to determine whether a liberally educated person has a wider and more differentiated store of cultural information or has developed an ordering set of intellectual principles and generalizations that have brought clarity, focus, and understanding to his information. Nor do we have measures of a liberally educated person's generalizing skills, his ability to penetrate through irrelevancies to grasp the essential, to identify similarities and distinguish differences, to hypothesize judiciously and to test with integrity. And certainly our measures do not comprehend the realms of virtue and value. We have, for example, no objective measures of moral integrity, honesty, or trustworthiness or of the philosophical and value assumptions a student has developed about nature or man himself.

We have preferred, instead, to concentrate on measuring the quality of a liberally educated person's adaptation, anticipating that such measures will indirectly tap his knowledge, particularly that about himself, his skills, and his values. Although the network of earlier and recent results associated with our methods suggests they may yield some valid information about the quality of a person's adaptation they remain, perhaps, too restrictive and focused in meaning. To free ourselves from such restrictions, we must rely heavily on our more wideranging interview procedures to enrich and extend our understanding of maturing and becoming liberally educated.

CHAPTER V

The Maturing Student

$\mathbb{D}$o students change—hopefully, mature—in college? Do they mature more in some areas of their personalities than in others? Do their intellectual skills, values, concepts of themselves, and interpersonal relationships become more stable, integrated, allocentric, autonomous, and symbolized? Or do students develop in ways other than the theory of maturing predicts? These are the questions of this chapter.

Two types of distinctions must be made immediately when analyzing how students change. First, we must make clear when we compare the Freshman with the Senior samples in contrast to when we compare each sample with its own previous base-level when it entered college. Secondly, we will distinguish between what students *be-*

lieve and *report* about their change and what the more objective test data show that change to have been longitudinally. The men believe they changed much more than their test data reveal. Other studies of development, based primarily on objective test data, report that relatively little fundamental personality change occurs in college (King, 1967). We will comment later about discrepancies between the judgments of students about their development and measures of those changes by psychological tests.

PRINCIPAL DEVELOPMENTAL CHANGES

Three generalizations emerge from the data:

1. The objective measures of change suggest that seniors may be more mature than freshmen and that they may have matured beyond where they themselves were as freshmen. Neither the freshmen nor the seniors are less mature than when they matriculated.

2. Seniors *believe* they matured more in college than the freshmen judge themselves to have matured.

3. The rate of maturing varies in different sectors of the personality. The process of maturing is essentially that predicted by the theory of maturing.

MATURITY OF THE SENIORS

Although the seniors do not describe themselves to be more mature (PSQ), to have more self-esteem (SIQ), or are judged to function more maturely (Rorschach) than the entering freshmen, yet, the trends in the data suggest the seniors were indeed more mature. On the MMPI, the seniors tended to be more healthy and stable than the freshmen both at the time of the latter's matriculation (MMPI: Tot. trend) and after the freshmen had been at the college eight months (MMPI: Tot., .10, .10).[1]

Independent judgments of the maturity of the men were also secured. Judges who had known each person well since his entrance to college rated him on thirty different traits (SIQ) that defined ma-

[1] When differences between the scores of the seniors and the freshmen are due to differences between the samples when they entered college rather than to intervening changes in the seniors, the results are not reported.

turity, once as they knew him as an entering freshman and once as they knew him later.[2] Not only were both the freshmen and the seniors rated to have matured on these different traits (.05, .001, .001),[3] but the seniors were rated to be more mature than the freshmen (.01, .001) and to have matured more since being at college than the freshmen had (.05, .05).

In contrast to the findings of other researchers (Nichols, 1967; Stewart, 1964; Webster, 1956), no evidence was found that either the freshmen or the seniors became less socially mature or more pathologically disturbed or unhealthy over time.

THE SENIORS' BELIEFS

The objective tests do not compellingly confirm that the seniors matured appreciably. On the other hand, the seniors are convinced they matured considerably while in college. Although both the freshmen and seniors made significantly more statements in their interviews about maturing than immaturing (.001, .001),[4] the seniors made significantly more statements about maturing than did the freshmen (.05). When asked to rate the amount of their *change* since their matriculation, the seniors as well as the freshmen rated themselves to have matured rather than to have become less mature. But the sen-

---

[2] The judges knew nothing of the study or its purposes. Their judgments of the men at Time 1 and at Time 2 were randomized within the samples and were made on different days to reduce contamination of their second by their first judgments, which they didn't know they would have to make.

[3] Statistically significant findings are followed in parentheses by their *p* values. *p* values of .05 and .01 mean the odds are less than five and one out of a hundred the results were due to chance. Occasionally nonsignificant findings that confirm a trend are mentioned, though their *p* values are generally not cited. When comparisons involve more than one sample, the *p* values for each are included. One-tailed *p* values are reported for scores selected to test the hypotheses of the study. All other *p* values are two-tailed, including those for individual MMPI and SVIB item differences.

[4] Only the statistical results of the interviews of the Freshman and the Senior II samples are given here because the interview of the Senior I sample was not exactly comparable. Similar reportorial practices are used when test forms and procedures of the samples were not identical, that is, Senior I's Personality Change Rating Scale and Senior II's Rorschach procedures differed from those of the Freshman sample.

iors tended to rate themselves to have matured more than the freshmen rated themselves to have (Personality Change Rating Scale: .10). Finally, the seniors rated themselves to have matured more in the ways predicted by the theory of maturing than the freshmen rated themselves to have matured (PSQ: .001, .10).

But how can this be? The seniors rated themselves on the PSQ to be no more mature than the freshmen rated themselves to be when they entered college. Yet, the seniors report they matured more than the freshmen judge themselves to have matured. The answer is that the seniors rated themselves retrospectively on the PSQ to have been consistently and occasionally significantly less mature when they entered college than the Freshman sample rated itself when it matriculated. However, other evidence suggests the seniors were not less mature as entering freshmen than the Freshman sample was. The inconsistency is due more to the limitations of rating scales than invalid judgments of the seniors. Self-ratings are relative, not absolute, judgments. They are influenced by the type of reference group to which one compares oneself as well as to one's knowledge of how one has changed over time. Entering freshmen may compare themselves to their high school friends and rate themselves to be very mature. Eight months later they may compare themselves to their college classmates and so rate themselves to be less mature than they rated themselves earlier. Seniors may compare themselves to other seniors and rate themselves to be less mature and so appear, when compared to the entering freshmen, not to have changed in college. These and other technical limitations of rating scales do not necessarily limit the other uses to which we later put them.

Other data do suggest the seniors matured considerably but the specific ways in which they matured were obscured by the summative types of objective scores we had been using.

DEVELOPMENTS THAT DEFINE MATURING

The question, "Do students mature in college?" should be stated, "In what ways do students mature in college?" This latter question does not mean we are abandoning the assumption that maturing is an organismic process. Individuals develop more in one sector of their personality than in another at different times, depending upon the demands of the environment and their readiness to respond to those demands. But the systemic assumption does imply that overdevelopment of one dimension will eventually inhibit further maturing of that dimension and accentuate the need for growth in other ways. A person may become too stable or rigid and closed to the modifying effects of other experiences. He may become too self-sufficient in his autonomy, too conformist in his allocentricism, or too obsessional in his symbolizations. We must keep the organismic context of maturing in mind when analyzing the data about specific dimensions.

The results provoke some general observations. First, the men of the Freshman and the two Senior samples agreed remarkably well about the types of maturing and immaturing effects their college experience had upon them (.001). Table 5.1 gives the percentage of statements made by the Freshman and the Senior samples in their interviews about their maturing and immaturing changes. Most of the personality changes the seniors describe began in the freshman year. The consistency of the pattern of both maturing and immaturing changes among the samples strongly supports the reliability of the students' self-assessments.

Second, this impressive consensus among the students agrees with more objective test measures of their change, like the PSQ—the only test for which exactly comparable scores were available (.05). Combining the interview with the PSQ scores produced the results reported in Table 5.2, which orders the types of personality change that occurred in all three samples.

Third, a heightened need to mature in one self-structure accentuates the phenomenal importance of that type of growth. As Table 5.1 indicates, the samples reported that they matured most in their attitudes about themselves, interpersonal relations, and values, and least in their cognitive-intellective skills. But Table 5.1 also indicates that the principal immaturing effects of the college occurred, in order, in their interpersonal relations, attitudes toward themselves, and values, and least in their cognitive-intellective skills. This pattern of immaturing effects is confirmed by the students' spontaneous replies to the question on the Personality Change Rating Scale, "I wish I had changed more in. . . ." Thirty-six per cent of the total number of scorable replies given to this question mentioned interpersonal relationships, particularly their integrative and allocentric dimensions: 30 per cent referred to their self-concepts, almost exclusively their stability; 19 per cent to their cognitive-intellective skills, primarily their stability; and 15 per cent to their values, also their stability. Inferentially, the

TABLE 5.1
Percentages of Maturing Effects as Scored from Interviews

Personality structure	Sample	Developmental Dimensions					% Tot
		Stability	Integration	Allocen-tricism	Autonomy	Symboli-zation	
Intellectual skills	Fresh	2.5	7.1	5.8	1.6	4.4	21.4
	Sr I	1.8	7.1	6.1	1.8	4.4	21.2
	Sr II	3.0	6.0	4.0	1.2	2.4	16.6
	Combined	2.5	6.6	5.1	1.5	3.6	19.3
Values	Fresh	5.1	4.0	3.7	3.2	5.3	21.3
	Sr I	3.4	3.8	4.8	3.4	4.3	19.7
	Sr II	4.7	2.8	4.5	3.6	3.6	19.2
	Combined	4.6	3.5	4.3	3.4	4.4	20.2
Self-concept	Fresh	9.0	4.5	2.4	5.0	13.6	34.5
	Sr I	5.4	4.4	2.8	4.8	12.8	30.2
	Sr II	9.5	7.7	2.4	5.2	13.0	37.8
	Combined	8.4	5.9	2.5	5.0	13.0	34.8

					Personal relations
Fresh	1.5	4.0	11.1	0.0	5.7	22.3
Sr I	2.6	5.4	12.8	1.4	6.5	28.7
Sr II	2.5	6.0	9.5	1.0	7.1	26.1
Combined	2.1	5.2	10.8	1.0	6.4	25.5
Total %	17.6	21.2	22.7	10.9	27.4	

TABLE 5.1 (*Cont.*)

Percentages of Immaturing Effects as Scored from Interviews

Intellectual skills	15%	Stability	24%
Values	17%	Integration	21%
Self-concept	31%	Allocentricism	18%
Personal relations	37%	Autonomy	28%
		Symbolization	9%

students may be saying that they are most content with the effects the college had upon their intellectual skills and values. The discontent of a third of the sample about their interpersonal relations and the type of person they felt they were can be understood better in terms of their answers to the question, "I wish I had *not* changed in the way

TABLE 5.2

Comparative Importance of Personality Change in College[a]

Type of Change	Rank of Maturing Effect	Order[b] of Immaturing Effect
Integration of intellectual skills	1	16.5
Symbolization of self-concept	2	15
Integration in interpersonal relations	3	5
Symbolization of interpersonal relations	4	18.5
Allocentric interpersonal relations	5	1
Stabilization of self-concept	6	2
Allocentric intellectual skills	7	20
Integration of self	8	3
Integration of values	9	12
Allocentric values	10	18.5
Autonomous values	11	6
Symbolization of intellectual skills	12	11
Autonomous self-concept	13	8
Stabilization of interpersonal relations	14	9
Stabilization of values	15.5	10
Symbolization of values	15.5	13.5
Autonomous intellectual skills	17	7
Stabilization of intellectual skills	18	13.5
Allocentric self-concept	19	16.5
Autonomous interpersonal relations	20	4

[a] Based on combined rank of degree of change measured by PSQ and Interview. The correlation between the degree of change measured by each was .42, p < .05.

[b] The term "Order" is used throughout the text to distinguish maturing (Rank) from immaturing (Order) effects.

I have in. . . ." The students talked primarily about changes they had experienced in their personal relations and self-concepts. Some felt they had become less open and spontaneous, more defensively suspicious, less tolerant and responsible, more self-sufficient, self-centered, and detached. In their attitudes toward themselves, some felt they had become less confident, assured, and natural.

What sense do these strands make? Obviously, not all students matured similarly. The modal pattern of change may not accurately describe about one-third of the sample who, for example, were dissatisfied with their interpersonal maturing. But the results of Chapter Three suggest another interpretation as well. The entering freshmen were most underdeveloped in their interpersonal skills and, inferentially, overdeveloped in their intellectual, narcissistic, and "cool" attitudes toward themselves. These two areas psychologically demanded the greatest change. They therefore were the most important areas in which to mature. Happily, many seniors had grown considerably in their interpersonal relationships and attitudes toward themselves. They made more statements in their interviews about maturing in these areas than did the freshmen (.05, .05).

INCREASED SYMBOLIC REPRESENTATION

Two generalizations are merited by the data: (1) Both the seniors and freshmen matured in their capacity to symbolize their experience. The seniors matured more than the freshmen. (2) The increasing ability of both the freshmen and seniors to symbolize their experience is most evident in their expanding awareness of themselves.

The growing capacity for reflection, for internalizing and representing experience symbolically, and the consequent inner enrichment of the men was not adequately measured by the psychological tests,[5] which failed to reveal the full extent of the men's reflectiveness and perceptiveness as they were displayed in the interviews. One of the Senior samples (PSQ: .001, trend), supported by the Freshman samples (PSQ: .10), became more aware and reflective since its entrance to college.

The development of the *intellectual skill* to symbolize and monitor one's own thought processes was a moderately important effect of becoming liberally educated (Rank 12, Table 5.2), using our objective measures. However, the quality of the reflectiveness shown in the interviews leads us to judge the development of the ability to reflect to be one of the most important effects of a liberal education. All of

---

[5] The PSQ items, for example, measuring this dimension were not found to intercorrelate with other items as highly as expected in some samples. The items have since been revised and subsequent studies with them indicate they are now more reliable. Psychology has no measures that assess objectively and validly the accuracy of a person's representations of his experience.

the samples reported an increased ability to reflect, though only one Senior sample reported it to have improved significantly (PSQ: .01, trend). The seniors, supported by the freshmen, also reported they had matured in their ability to recall more readily facts necessary for analyzing and solving intellectual problems (PSQ: .05, .01); fewer seniors judged that they had fewer novel ideas than other persons (SVIB: .01, 25 to 9 per cent).[6] Perhaps an indirect measure of the greater reflectiveness of the seniors compared to that of the freshmen was the larger number of maturing statements made in their interviews (.05).

The freshmen also tended to develop a more imaginal and enriched inner life (Rorschach: M%, .10; #R, .001). While the freshmen seemed to become more imaginally productive than the seniors (Rorschach: #P, .05; #R, .05, two-tailed), the difference may be more parsimoniously accounted for by the qualitative differences in their thought processes. The seniors were significantly more integrative, relating their percepts into larger syntheses (Rorschach: W%, .002) and so gave fewer responses, while the freshmen more passively organized the blots according to their easier, more perceptually dominant, isolated (Rorschach: D%, .001; d%, .05) and conventional forms (Rorschach: #P, .05). The growing awareness of the freshmen was mirrored in their comments about their intellectual change:

> I think I've changed quite a bit here. I can truthfully say I wasn't aware. This is one of the things I can say that Haverford has done for me most. It made me look beyond the way things are, to look behind them. I was never aware of things behind. I lived, acted, did things. I had relations with people. I did not reflect beyond that to find out the causes, why I did them.

and

> I think I'm more reflective when I approach a problem. I think I consider. I think, "Here, I'll go off half-cocked." I take a more intellectual approach because this is the example I've been given.

[6] The percentage change from Time 1 to Time 2 will be cited when the number to whom the statement applies, although statistically significant, does *not* describe the majority of the sample.

Becoming more immature in one's capacity to reflect, indexed, for example, by increased repression, provoked only a moderate number of citations in the interviews (Order 11).

We encounter a similar measurement problem when analyzing how the men matured in their awareness of their *values*. Although development of an awareness of one's values was not objectively determined to be one of the more important effects of maturing in college (Rank 15.5) or one in which failure to develop was reported very frequently (Order 13.5), our hunch is that our methods again underestimated its salience. The seniors tended to agree that they found it easier to reflect about their motives and values and to understand the reasons for their behavior than they did as freshmen (PSQ: .01, trend). The freshmen show no change—a result contradicted by the interview results, which may more accurately illustrate their development. Speaking of the effects of the college's social honor code, one freshman said,

> This certainly helped me review my own values and moral code, and I think, developed a stable moral code. As I said before, basically I'm the same person, but I don't think I ever would have thought that much about it.

Speaking of the effects of a faculty member upon him, a senior said,

> Well, he has compelled me by the force of his personality, the dynamics of our relationship, to reexamine my goals, my attitudes towards what I want out of life.

The second most important maturing development of all of their changes for both the freshmen and the seniors was an increased awareness and understanding of themselves (Rank 2), the development of a more conscious *self-concept*. Few students said they became less aware or understanding of themselves (Order 15). Both Senior samples and the Freshman sample reported that they matured considerably in their self-awareness (PSQ: .05, .05, .10); they felt they could accurately describe themselves to someone else if asked to do so (PSQ: .01, trend, .05). However, the self-concepts of the seniors were no more accurate at the end of four years than those of the freshmen at the end of their eight months when measured differently (SIQ).

One independent test of the accuracy of the self-concepts of the men is the extent of their disagreement with the summary analyses of their individual test protocols, if we make the improbable assumption that all of the interpretive syntheses were correct. Whereas many clinicians, on the basis of extensive experience with neurotics but very limited experience with healthy persons, believe that the Rorschach taps "deeply" repressed fantasies and wishes, which the person would reject if they were verbalized to him, our experience based on interpreting Rorschachs to hundreds of college men suggests an alternative hypothesis. Accessibility to and acceptance in awareness of traditionally "in-depth" Rorschach interpretations are directly related to the maturity of the person. The Rorschach has consistently and powerfully illuminated the "meaning" of a student's more objective test scores because it portrays the dynamics of the person, not because it reflects forces of which he is *necessarily* unaware and could not emotionally accept or assimilate if verbalized. From this hypothesis it follows that defensiveness and rejection of the test analyses may indicate inadequate symbolization of interior experience and, therefore, less mature development. All such disagreements were noted on the written test analyses, and when the analyses were reviewed, we found only one senior and two freshmen who disagreed seriously with their analyses. Generally, most of the seniors and many of the freshmen remarked with surprise about the accuracy of the analyses and spontaneously extended the interpretations into their own lives by citing personal examples. Our impression was that the seniors were more insightful and facile than the freshmen in assimilating the interpretations to their personal experience. The freshmen had become quite aware of their inner feelings and motives, but their new symbolizations had not yet been as well integrated with their memories of the past or into their conceptions of themselves and their futures.

More objective indices of the increasing ability of the men to symbolize their experience confirmed the Rorschach observations. The seniors, but not the freshmen, had become less repressed since entering college (MMPI: R, .05, trend), perhaps illustrated by the larger number who as seniors admitted into their awareness less socially acceptable types of activities in which they had participated when children: stealing (MMPI: .01, 25 to 42 per cent), "playing sick" to get out of something (MMPI: .01), or liking hopscotch (MMPI: .01, 29 to 48 per cent). Although fewer seniors reported they preferred to plan their long-term futures (SVIB: .05, 29 to 13 per cent) or their current work in detail (SVIB: .05, 46 to 29 per cent), these changes may represent more their decreased compulsive control than any decrease in their capacity to symbolize immediate or future possibilities. More freshmen, but not seniors, believed they should try to understand their dreams and be guided by them (MMPI: .05, 20 to 44 per cent).

Yet, it is the interviews that not only revealed their more mature self-insight but highlighted the importance of their increased self-awareness for their overall development since they graduated from high school. One senior said,

> I've become more aware of the depth one can experience another person. In other words, each girl friend makes me aware of another level of depth to which I can reach and to which I can open up myself with a person. . . . Among other things, it's made me realize there is much more in me than I thought before to be gotten to.

And another described his efforts after self-understanding this way:

> Well, any sort of criticism, even if somebody curses me out, calls me a dogmatic bastard, which happened recently, I think about it. You see, I try and see why am I really a dogmatic bastard.

The seniors are saying that much of their increased understanding of themselves was initiated by their relationships with others, in difficulties that also led to greater understanding of other people. Increased awareness about their *relationships* with others and their motives was one of the moderately important effects of the men's college experience (Rank 4); few students reported that they had failed to increase in such understanding (Order 18.5). The objective summary measures *seemingly* suggest that the men matured in their understanding of women (PSQ: .05, .05, .05) more than they did of other men. The Freshman sample and one Senior sample agreed that their feelings about earlier girl friends now came more readily into awareness (PSQ: .01, .05). The seniors, though not the freshmen, believe they improved in how to understand why they had disagreements with their girls (PSQ: .001, .001). Given the more pressing heterosexual impulses and concerns of the seniors (Rorschach), it is not surprising they were more preoccupied in the interviews than the freshmen in trying to understand women and their relations with them. One rather puzzled senior said, "In a sense, you get to know a little more how a woman thinks . . . I guess that's going to be a long long road before I ever know what a woman thinks."

The interview data, however, suggest the men developed a much more genuine understanding of other men than of women. Eighty-five per cent of their statements about their expanding awareness of other persons were about understanding other men. Excerpts from the interviews of two seniors illustrate the significance of this change:

> When I was in high school . . . I never got to know their insides. Here, I'd see guys getting drunk, having trouble with their girls, problems with their parents. I learned an awful lot about human beings. I was just completely isolated from them before.

> I don't think I was aware before of the different levels you can take people on, you must take people on: how serious you have to be with them, how much of yourself you divulge to them; how much you go out of your way to adjust to them like doing small things for them; how much you see them as means; how much you use them as ends.

Such expanded understanding of others and of their more private feelings may have caused the decrease in the number of seniors who felt that other persons exaggerated their misfortunes to get sympathy and help from others (MMPI: .05, 61 to 44 per cent).

AN ALLOCENTRIC PERSONALITY

We can make two generalizations about the allocentric development of the students: (1) The seniors were more allocentrically developed than the freshmen, though not as consistently so in their values. (2) The extent of allocentric development varied in the different sectors of the personality, seemingly lagging in the development of the men's self-concepts.

The Senior samples reported they matured more allocentrically (PSQ: .001, .01) than the freshmen rated themselves to have matured (PSQ: .10). All of the men, especially the seniors, reported their *cognitive-intellective skills* had become more logical and realistic since entering college (PSQ: trend, .05, .01), which was one of the more important effects of becoming liberally educated (Rank 7). Failure to develop more allocentric cognitive skills was not a problem to either the freshmen or seniors (Order 20), perhaps because those who did not show much development had already dropped out or had been asked to leave the college. The data suggest that the Senior samples may have matured more in their intellectual efficiency (MMPI: Ie, .05, no change) since their matriculation than the Freshman sample did. More seniors increased in their ability to write concise and well-organized reports (SVIB: .01) and make more appropriate judgments (SVIB: .01), which ability may have contributed in part to their higher academic achievement. But the interview data are clear that much of this development took place in the freshman year.

> Haverford has had a broadening effect. I can see people's points of view. I can see things in the light of what I feel; I can analyze them both ways. I can probably deal with little more intricate problems than I have before.

Speaking of his English course, another freshman said,

> . . . it does affect one's skill if only to fertilize your ability to type! It literally trains you to think clearly, to think clearly in a hurry and get it down on paper in an organized coherent manner that conforms to certain grammatical rules.

The students' increased intellectual allocentricism was not confirmed by the Rorschach. Neither did the freshmen improve during the year nor were the seniors better than the freshmen in their reality testing or their ability to accommodate themselves to external demands (Rorschach: modified F+%). Nor was the thought organization of either the freshmen or seniors characterized by fewer condensations or other dreamlike processes.

Turning to the development of more allocentric *values* and *self-concepts* (ranked tenth and nineteenth in importance), we encounter the first major challenge to our hypotheses. Some of the test data are equivocal, inconsistent, and tend to contradict other test results and the interviews of the seniors.

The Senior samples showed no change in tolerance (MMPI: To) and tended to think of themselves as less socially responsible than they thought of themselves when freshmen (MMPI: Re-R, .05, trend, two-tailed). The freshmen, on the other hand, became more socially responsible (MMPI: Re-R, .05) and tolerant (MMPI: To, .05), though they still tended to be less tolerant at the end of eight months than the seniors were after four years (MMPI: To, .10, trend). Even though the samples did not differ in their valuation of a social, loving way of life initially, it was the freshmen and not the seniors who tended to become even more appreciative of this attitude toward others (AVL: .10, two-tailed). They valued social altruism even more highly than both the Senior samples (AVL: .05, .05), who, for example and for some unaccountable reason, increased in their dislike for the crippled (SVIB: .05, 25 to 35 per cent), and sick (SVIB: 23 to 36 per cent) and less liked people who were elderly (SVIB: .05, 23 to 10 per cent). Finally, the self-concepts of the seniors were no more allocentric than those of the freshmen when measured by the SIQ. The allocentric dimension was the one dimension on which all of the samples showed the greatest lag in the development of their self-concept. The PSQ results tended to confirm this negative finding, for none of the samples reported it matured much in the allocentricism of its self-concept.

The evidence that *confirms* the hypothesis is more varied. To illustrate the tenor of some of the interviews of the seniors, several examples are cited, first of allocentric value development.

> Did I want to go into medicine for social standing or did I want to go into medicine because I wanted to help people? It turns out right now my only motive for medicine is that I will be helping people, inspiring confidence in them. If I didn't have that, I wouldn't go into medicine.

Another, speaking of his relation to society, developed this deeply allocentric view of himself:

> I think that perhaps the whole idea of what you work for and what you gain from society is really not all your own, that you are only part of a long continuing process and what you have accomplished is, in part, a result of your own endeavor but also, in part, a result of the people who have gone before you. So that any claims that society may make on what you have done or accomplished, I think, are valid claims.

Others talk more directly about themselves:

I've become more sensitive to others, other people's wants. I've come out of myself. I am not as egocentric as I was when I came here.

I think I'm a warmer person, more sensitive, more spontaneous.

In tests like the PSQ, the seniors more than the freshmen reported that their values and beliefs had become more allocentric (PSQ: .01, .01), centered more around the lives and needs of other people than just their own (PSQ: .05, .05); they said such beliefs and values had become more realistic and practical (PSQ: .01, .05). These reported changes also appear in the increased desire of the seniors, though less frequently in those of the freshmen, to serve in socially altruistic activities. More seniors, as well as freshmen, expressed interests in teaching adults (SVIB: .01, .05). More seniors said they would like to teach children (SVIB: .01), meet and direct people (SVIB: .01), or take on more responsibility (SVIB: .05), like trying to solve the difficulties of others (SVIB: .01). Many of the Freshman sample already opted for these activities. The seniors became more sympathetic to teachers (SVIB: .01) and social workers (SVIB: .05). Their declining interest in competitive interpersonal activities like political and athletic races (SVIB: .05, 56 to 40 per cent) was reflected in their increased dislike for conventions (SVIB: .05, 31 to 50 per cent), and (including the freshmen as well) the use of power to gain political influence and control of others (AVL: .01, trend, trend). Finally, data from a new scale designed to measure democratic, liberal, and socially responsible attitudes given to several freshmen classes, including that of our sample, confirmed that the increasing allocentricism of the Freshman sample was representative of its class. However, the change could not be replicated with a second freshman class, perhaps because of intervening special situational events at the college (Perloe, 1967).

The inconsistency in the results was not expected. The college's historic religious tradition strongly values allocentric, liberal, and democratic causes and the Pervin findings in Chapter Three showed Haverford students to be more liberal and socially concerned than many other college students. It is tempting to say the test scales were not adequate, but our other research in America and abroad has strongly and consistently confirmed that the MMPI To and Re-R and AVL Social scales are predictive of the maturity of a person. That both the freshmen and seniors apparently did not think of themselves as becoming more autocentric in their values and self-concepts (Order 18.5 and 16.5 respectively for the number of such statements made in their interviews) suggests that the freshmen and seniors were *not* developing dissimilarly. An explanation may lie in the fact that the inconsistencies were in the data of the seniors and not of the freshmen. Could the inconsistency be a manifestation of the acute negative identity crisis that occurred for many seniors the latter part of their senior year? They vociferously rejected the college and its traditions, frequently in tumultuous and recriminating ways. Their futures were more settled. They had been accepted in graduate and professional schools. The college was no longer "useful" to them. They began to break their very strong dependency ties to the college by unconsciously devaluing, even destroying, much about it they had previously valued. It is easier to separate from that you think you no longer love. This hypothesis has some merit, for the same seniors, when questioned within two to three years after their graduation about the more enduring effects of their college experience, extolled its virtues and claimed, as we shall see later, that they did not realize how liberally and socially concerned persons they had become during their four years. In this context, perhaps the inconsistent findings reflect the temporary ambivalence of the seniors. Somewhat wistfully, we would like to think this explanation makes the inconsistencies more supportive of the theory.

But there is no dispute that the development of a more allocentric self-concept was not as salient in the students as were other types of development. The students' overemphasis on their own individuality and uniqueness may have limited for many the development of the allocentric perspective of the seniors we quoted.

One of the more important developments of the men was an increased social feeling for others and stronger needs for close friends (Rank 5). The failure to mature allocentrically in their *interpersonal relations* was the most persistent and widespread source of concern in the interviews (Order 1), which may account for some inconsistencies in the objective test results. Only one senior group developed allocentrically in its relations with men and women (PSQ: .05, .05). The freshmen showed no change in their relations with men but matured allocentrically in their relations with women (PSQ: .05).

The increased interest in being with others, already shown in some of the changed social values of the men, most clearly occurred in the seniors. Compared to their freshman days, more of them enjoyed parties (MMPI: .05, 36 to 50 per cent), though more preferred to pair off than to be part of the crowd (MMPI: .05, 31 to 46 per cent) and to flirt (MMPI: .01). They preferred jobs for the congeniality of their co-workers (SVIB: .01, 17 to 47 per cent) rather than just for their salaries (SVIB: .05, 33 to 17 per cent). They implied they were less tactless (MMPI: .05, 57 to 42 per cent), felt they were better able to criticize others without giving offense (SVIB: .01) and to get others to do what they wanted (SVIB: .01). More seniors were becoming more interested in people. More said they could remember the faces and names of other persons (SVIB: .05, 17 to 29 per cent). And we have already seen that as seniors they enjoyed meeting and helping people more. More freshmen reported they also felt increasingly sympathetic about other people who were in trouble (MMPI: .05).

The interviews revealed that the most meaningful allocentric development for both the freshmen and seniors occurred in the acceptance of their needs for others and in learning to care for others.

> It isn't just a matter of putting up with what they have to say about the situation so I can tell them about my situation. And, I don't know. You get interested in a couple of other guys . . . They become part of you . . . I mean little things seem to become part of the other . . . I guess in one sense I have a greater dependence or greater need for other people than I ever did before.

> I think that I care more about other people's feelings than I did before.

> Well, I guess I've learned to appreciate people much more.

PERSONALITY INTEGRATION

The principal generalizations that can be made are these: (1) The seniors were more integrated than the freshmen, who were beginning to show some of the same pattern of integrative changes as the seniors. (2) The progressive integration of both the seniors and freshmen was the most important maturational change in college. It affected all sectors of the students' personalities in different but important ways. (3) The increasing integration was facilitated by a change in the type of controls used to master impulses.

Generally, the seniors were more integrated than they had been as freshmen (PSQ: .001, .01). In their interviews, they also made more statements scored for increased integration than the freshmen made in their interviews (.05). While the freshmen developed similarly, the magnitude of their change rarely approached that of the seniors.

The most prominent characteristic of becoming liberally educated for all of the samples was an increasing integration of their *cognitive-intellective skills* (Rank 1). Whether after only eight months or four years of college, the students agreed that their thinking had become more consistent, differentiated, and detailed (PSQ: .05, .05, .001). They more frequently took into account the full complexity of problems (PSQ: trend, .01, .05) as well as sought to relate and integrate intellectual ideas and facts to form more comprehensive and meaningful patterns (PSQ: .05, trend, .001). The effect of the freshmen's first year at college was to make them more attentive to detail, to analyze and differentiate the more from the less obvious (Rorschach: D%, .001; d%, .05) rather than to increase their synthetic constructive capacities. The seniors more actively searched to make relationships and syntheses than the freshmen (Rorschach: W%, .001). One senior said most simply, "I always see things in perspective as a result." Another said of the effects of a faculty member upon him that he

> . . . gave me a feeling that what I should do later on must have a thickness and a breadth to it. Should not be highly specialized. That a person can only make a substantial contribution when he can see the interrelation . . . when he can see the playing of one idea, one process, on another, and that a high degree of specialization or a highly narrow professional field is not the most advantageous one; that the Renaissance man can still make a very substantial and valuable contribution to society. . . .

Failure to become more intellectually integrative did not concern the students (Order 16.5), possibly because so many felt they had matured in their capacity to think relationally. But there was one facet of relational or integrative thinking that may have remained underdeveloped. A distant index of integration may be a person's originality or ability to form novel relationships. The seniors tended to rate themselves (Personality Change Rating Scale) to have matured least in their creativity. The academic chairmen agreed with these self-judgments. Of the traits the chairmen rated for each senior, originality was rated to be only average—their least developed trait, according to the faculty.

Since, as the alumni will tell us later, one's values and priorities become an increasingly central organizing focus around which one's self-concept or identity becomes shaped, we will move back and forth between the two in our discussion of them. The growing integration of the students' *values* and of their *self-concepts* was one of the more important effects of their college experience (Ranks 9 and 8), particularly for the seniors. They had begun to develop a way of life that brought together their values and desires and that gave them a sense of direction (PSQ: .01, .05). They neither felt as torn and divided by conflicting values and desires (PSQ: .05, trend) nor as inconsistent and contradictory, uncertain of their direction (PSQ: .05, .05). Because of this greater value-self integrity, the seniors felt fewer inner contradictions between what they knew themselves to be (PSQ: .05, trend) and what they believed other people thought them to be (PSQ: .05, trend). Hence, they could be more spontaneous because of the growing identity of their private and more social selves. Such increased self-integration was not, however, confirmed by the SIQ on which the freshmen and the seniors did not differ.

Integration and internal harmony may occur at different levels of complexity. Maturing means becoming *progressively* more integrated; that is, becoming more differentiated and complex a person. One index of greater integration, then, is an increasingly differentiated pattern of motivational interests. Interests become more dominant and crystallized, which is what happened to the seniors. Both Senior samples changed significantly in sixteen of their interests compared to the Freshman sample's change in only three (SVIB: the range of initial scores was the same for the samples). The seniors changed more in 35 per cent of their measured interests than the freshmen did in the interest in which they changed the most. With maturing, the pattern of interests does not change qualitatively as much as it does quantitatively. The men as seniors still were more professionally and scholarly than economically and technically inclined—only significantly more so (SVIB: Occup. level, .05, .001), and were more so than the Freshman sample was at its admission to college (.05, trend).

How did this growing value-self integration come about? In subsequent chapters we will identify the environmental factors that stimulated the change. The test data illuminate the mediating determinants. The dominant maturing change manifested in the tests was a freeing of suppressed impulses, the "humanization" of conscience, an opening to a wider range of internal experiences, a greater receptiveness in attitude toward one's self and others. It was the welling up of new feelings (recall the freshmen said they felt more intensely than others) and the environmental challenge for new adaptations that created the impetus for new integrative efforts.

Chapter Three described the entering freshmen to be increasingly inhibited, over-controlled, compulsively constricted, emotionally "tight" persons who had learned to use their gifted intellectual powers, in part, defensively to maintain their "cool." The emotional compass of their lives was quite circumscribed. It takes more than eight months to change this style of control. The lives of the freshmen revealed confusion and stress more than any significant change in their modes of control. The lives of the seniors demonstrated more clearly the specific types of integrative changes that occurred in their consciences and modes of control.

What are the data? One impressionistic index of the internal confusion and lack of inner clarity and integration in the freshmen was our difficulty in making psychological sense of their tests and Rorschachs when we synthesized them for the student interviews. The protocols of 48 per cent of the freshmen and of only 6 per cent of the seniors were explicitly noted "not to come together at all." Such comments as these were made about their records: "need his help in interpreting this," "he could well reject all of this," "some discrepancies between his judgments and mine," "complex; may not want to talk too much about his private life." After a decade of synthesizing and interpreting the test materials of upperclassmen for vocational, therapeutic, and research purposes, the most difficult of all records to interpret were many of those of the Freshman sample. It is impossible to find some integrative meaning in the record of a freshman who says of himself, "I feel I am being torn apart in one thousand directions." The senior records, however, even those less integrated ones, were still psychologically understandable and much less defensive.

The more objective test data support these clinical impressions. The pattern of the changes of the freshmen was less consistent than that of the seniors. We will note later that, paradoxically, the freshmen seemed inwardly more confused and disturbed but consciously less worried and anxious. They matured in their ability to concentrate their energies on intellectual work (MMPI: Ie, .05) and to take a more assertive, aggressive attitude (MMPI: Do, .001), which our previous research indicates are characteristic of maturing persons. But on the other hand, in eight months there was no reduction in their over-control and repression. In fact, the freshmen tended to become more constricted; more became less willing, for example, to let themselves get caught up in a good idea (MMPI: .05, 48 to 24 per cent) or to daydream (MMPI: .05). More freshmen became less comfortable around quick-tempered people (SVIB: .01), more resistant to working under pressure (MMPI: .05), less responsive to events that might counteract feelings of depression (MMPI: .05, 72 to 44 per cent); more freshmen were dissatisfied with their sexual lives (MMPI: .05, 20 to 44 per cent). Could it be that the freshmen had moved to a more "mature" level of instability, a heightened inner looseness and chaos, to which they responded with the same types of controls? To meet the immediate intellectual demands of the college required the mobilization of more energy and its more aggressive active use in their academic work. They therefore became more intellectually efficient and assertive but also more constricted in the amount of energy available for less pressing but competing activities, like "dating," or for meeting increased stresses.

It is the pattern of change of the seniors that suggests how the heightened educable potential of the freshmen will be realized and become more integrated into their personalities. Their controls had become more integrative since their freshman year and had matured more than those of the Freshman sample. Both Senior samples became less compulsively controlling of their impulses (MMPI: Eo, .05, .05) and more open to their impulses (MMPI: Im, .01, trend, two-tailed). They became less repressed (MMPI: R, .05, trend). One sample tended to become less rigid (MMPI: Rgm, .10). The seniors bound their energies less by physical complaints and somatic symptoms (MMPI: Hs, trend, .05). They externalized and projected them more into overt aggressive behavior (MMPI: Ma, .05, trend, two-tailed). Simultaneously with their expanding inner emotional lives, the seniors developed a greater *conscious* control of their impulses (MMPI: Es, trend, .05). Perhaps for this reason, their behavior was no more anti-social or irresponsible than it was when they were freshmen. In fact, the behavior of the seniors was more socially responsible than that of the Freshman sample, which had yet to experience the loosening of its inhibitions (MMPI: Pd, .05, trend).

How did the seniors express their increased spontaneity and responsiveness to their more immediate feelings? They were no longer as tied to convention, routine, and ritual. Fewer seniors were as inter-ested in their appearance (MMPI: .01, 67 to 38 per cent) to the dismay of alumni, saving money (SVIB: .01; freshmen, .05), work-ing regular hours (SVIB: .01, 33 to 19 per cent; freshmen, .05, 36 to 20 per cent), having steady and permanent work (SVIB: .01, 26 to 2 per cent), and participating in any vocational activity that required long hours of monotonous, repetitive, or impersonal work (SVIB: .05). They became even more disinterested in bookkeepers, account-ants, chemists, lab technicians, astronomers, statisticians, pharmacists, and librarians (SVIB: at least .05). Reflecting, perhaps, their own increasing emotional freedom and expressiveness, more seniors became attracted to people who were emotional (SVIB: .01, 25 to 48 per cent) and less rejecting of those who were talkative (SVIB: .05, 21 to 6 per cent). Their dislike for more constricted people like pessimists (SVIB: .01) and those who talked slowly (SVIB: .05, 23 to 42 per cent) increased. More seniors enjoyed the excitement of being in a crowd (MMPI: .05); sought out thrills (MMPI: .01), read detective and mystery stories (MMPI: .05), and newspaper articles on crime (MMPI: .05).

The consciences of the seniors became less moralistic. They were not as narrowly proscribed as when they were freshmen. The following Rorschach excerpt of one freshman serves as an illustrative contrast:

> The main theme throughout is strong guilt—an overdevel-oped conscience—about the expression of his impulses, par-ticularly hostile, even sadistic, wishes. The arousal of anger feelings makes him quite anxious and may lead to a vague, undifferentiated kind of thinking in a rather passive way. He may become gentle and preoccupied about religious or ethical issues. He probably is quite introspective and hence has good control over his behavior. But the persistent pre-

occupation about the rightness and wrongness of his impulses and desires may make him feel he is not quite mature in his personal relationships.

The seniors were more acceptant of their foibles and weaknesses. Fewer seniors found they thought of things too bad to talk about (MMPI: .01, 44 to 25 per cent)—not because their thoughts were more saintly (for the Rorschach showed them not to be)—but because they were no longer as condemnatory of parts of themselves. More seniors would probably enter a movie without paying if they could get away with it (MMPI: .05, 19 to 33 per cent); more didn't view the law as sacrosanct and unbending (MMPI: .01); fewer felt guilty if they were "cross and grouchy" toward someone else (MMPI: .05). The seniors became more open to and acceptant of their sexual needs. They learned in the four years to enjoy flirting more (MMPI: .01), talking about sex (MMPI: .01), seeing movie love scenes (MMPI: .01), and permitting sexual fantasies to preoccupy their consciousness (Rorschach: content). As the seniors and freshmen became less condemnatory of their own desires, they discovered that other persons weren't as sexually immoral as they had once thought (MMPI: .01, 27 to 6 per cent; .05, 40 to 16 per cent). The following excerpt of one senior's comments is illustrative of some of these changes in the attitudes of the seniors toward their sexuality.

He [his roommate] gave me a much broader viewpoint on sexual morals. In other words, I was sort of feeling guilty about doing certain things. That didn't stop me from doing them. I was just feeling guilty about them. . . . But I changed my viewpoint to a certain extent [so] that I didn't feel guilty about them any more.

One of the more insistent and important changes that the seniors experienced as a result of their disinhibition and humanization of their consciences was the emergence of their masculine, assertive, and aggressive impulses—at least into conscious fantasy, though perhaps not yet into overt behavior. More seniors claimed, in contrast to when they were freshmen, they felt like smashing things at times (MMPI: .01). They became interested in more masculine and adventurous activities. Exploring, auto racing, ranching, working with horses, operating machinery, or somewhat facetiously, chewing tobacco and pursuing bandits in a sheriff's posse were now less unattractive to them than such activities had been when they entered college (SVIB: at least .05; percentages of changes not listed).

The increasingly aggressive thrust of the fantasies of the seniors was also manifested in their Rorschachs. The analyses, made independently of any knowledge of the types of changes just noted, noted the loosened control of many of the seniors as well as their frequent expression of assertive, even sadistic, images. Yet, few of the men were judged to have integrated their emerging masculine and assertive energies satisfactorily into their ideas of themselves as well as into their heterosexual relationships. As a consequence, the men were not described to have stabilized either their images of themselves as competent and effective masculine men or their heterosexual relationships, about which they remained in conflict. The Rorschach analysis of one senior illustrated some of these changes. He

> . . . seems to allow his sexual impulses into his image of himself but not his aggressive assertiveness, about which he is more ambivalent and perhaps in conflict. When he feels like becoming angry or hostile, his emotional reactions are somewhat forced; he may become submissive, rather than outwardly aggressive. Under stress, rather than actively cope, he may withdraw and become more passive and dependent. The consequence is that he may not think of himself as the vigorous and masculine male that he seems to be. He does not sustain the attack under stress. He tends to flee. The result is a failure to stabilize his heterosexuality and a flight into other kinds of sexual preoccupations that may be compensatory and should not be taken at their face value.

As other researchers have also consistently reported (Arsenian, 1943; Huntley, 1967; Newcomb & Feldman, 1968), both the freshmen and seniors developed a much wider and more differentiated range of cultural and aesthetic interests. They highly valued channeling aroused feelings and sensitivities into various forms of artistic and creative expression (AVL: .01, .001, .05). By the time they were seniors, they had become more interested in architecture, art, art galleries, cartoons, museums, literature, symphony concerts, sculpture, dramatics, theater, and even antique furniture and cabinet making (SVIB: all .01; percentages of changes not cited). The increased aesthetic interests not only enriched their lives but probably also provided a stable and integrative type of sublimation for their emotional sensitivity and what some would call their more feminine needs, which, while predominant when they were entering freshmen, became even more so during college (MMPI: Mf, trend, .01, trend). The aesthetic is the route most frequently selected by contemporary students to integrate their overdeveloped intellectualism with their underdeveloped emotional and social needs. The data suggest that this type of integration is more maturing for a senior than for a freshman. Chapter Three suggested that too strong an intellectual-aesthetic commitment in a freshman might limit his social or allocentric development.

Failure to develop a more integrative self-identity (Order 3) was more anxiety-arousing to the men than failure to develop a consistent value system (Order 12). Two types of possible immaturing effects accompanied the integrative changes we've described. When intellectualization and intellectual achievement were primarily defensively and compulsively motivated, thereby being nonintegrative, reduction in the inhibitions required to maintain their earlier academic achievement led to a motivational crisis for many freshmen that continued for some through their college years. Some lost interest in academic work. They found it tedious, boring, and joyless. For many, "academic" became a bad word and some anti-intellectual attitudes developed. Fewer seniors reported they enjoyed reading (SVIB: 46 to 21 per cent), looking at educational movies (SVIB: .01, 69 to 46 per cent), or being as interested in planning their work in detail (SVIB: 46 to 29 per cent) than they had as freshmen. One senior's interview reflected some of these trends:

> Well, it [academic work] saturated me. There are just so many clever puzzles that could keep your interest. . . . I place a higher value in reading an English book and just enjoying it, taking it for the experience, rather than sitting down and looking for the intricate metaphors and symbols.

Although many men developed more stable and genuine intellectual interests, the intensity of their academic life made the men more aware of their less developed emotional lives. One senior talked of the relation between his intellectual and emotional needs this way:

> Well, as a result of being so deeply involved in purely intellectual abstract concerns, the nonintellectual personal emo-

tional needs that I have have been accentuated, I suppose,
and when I feel a need for that kind of personal emotional
involvement, it's a good deal stronger than it would have
been if I simply had been floating along, not being terribly
wrapped up in impersonal mental problems.

The second immaturing effect occurred when the aesthetic way
of life was itself a defensive integrative solution that closed off to the
person other feelings and needs. The Rorschach analysis of two seniors
illustrates how such a partial integration may have immaturing consequences:

But this love affair with the child within is retarding his
maturing and does not sustain his heterosexual maturing.
Tends to keep him within an egocentric grip and when
more "serious," "for-keep" impulses emerge, when more
frankly aggressive, assertive, and sexual ones come into
awareness, he tends to play with them by retreating into
philosophy, aesthetics, myth. The aesthetic way of life is integrative but it is not releasing and maturing. So he may
not have sensed, as his other tests also reveal, any great inner growth in his relationships with others in the past several years.

Or he

. . . may assume the sophistication of the aesthete to mask
the intensity of his feelings. He has considerable humor and
a sense of the delightful to get away with it, [but] his feeling
life gets very quickly super-refined, involuted, and convo-
luted into an abstract aesthetic humanism. . . . Does he
play the role of the "cool intellect, the refined aesthete" at
the expense of the very vigorous and vital part of his personality, namely, a strongly competitive masculine assertiveness?

The seniors felt an opposition between intellectual and emotional development and their temporary satiation with the intellectual
demands of the college was most clearly manifested in an interesting
nonintegrative way. The proportion of seniors and freshmen whose
more consciously held values (AVL) were discrepant in some way
from their less consciously developed motivational interests (SVIB), as

tabulated from their interpretive summaries, was similar. The discrepancies of the freshmen were due primarily to inadequate differentiation of their basic interests. But those of the seniors were due to an exaggerated devaluation (the AVL Theoretical) of their own basic intellectual identity (SVIB professional pattern), compensated for by an overvaluation of more expressive personal and feeling attitudes (AVL Aesthetic) not that clearly demonstrated in their more basic motivational interests (SVIB: Artist, Architect, Author).

Much of the same integrative development describes the maturing of the *personal relationships* of many of the seniors with both men (PSQ: .05, .05) and women (PSQ: .01, .05), one of the more important characteristics of maturing in college (Rank 3). They report they became more sensitive to new feelings and developed new interests as a result of their female relationships (PSQ: .05, trend). The seniors but not the freshmen increasingly felt they could be more themselves with a girl friend, that there was little they held back of themselves in such relationships (PSQ: .001, .05), a feeling increasingly shared by the freshmen (PSQ: .10). But just how integrative the interpersonal changes of the freshmen were is not clear from the data. Most of the test items suggest the average freshman was only beginning to mature in this area, perhaps because not having learned how to open himself to his own feelings and impulses, he was not yet able to establish more open and trustful relationships with others. It was an increasing number of freshmen, not seniors, who said they had been disappointed in their love relationships (MMPI: .05). However, the interview data suggest that a considerable number of the freshmen had formed such trusting relationships with other men, as illustrated by one of them:

> He was the first person that I've been really able to be open and quite frank with. Because he's been really open himself, I found it much more easy to say things that I wouldn't to other people before this. . . . I think it's helped me to be open with other people as well. . . . It's helped me to be more self-confident. . . . I think self-confidence and self-assertiveness go along with this being open.

Not to have formed such open and trusting relationships with someone was considered to be one of the more important immaturing experiences in college (Order 5).

PERSONALITY STABILIZATION

Briefly, two principal generalizations can be made: (1) The seniors were consistently more stable than the freshmen, who appeared to be developing in the same way the seniors had. (2) The rate of stabilization varied in the different sectors of the personality. The freshmen, in particular, became more stable in their intellectual skills and values than in their concepts of themselves or their relationships with others. The seniors also seemed to have matured less in their interpersonal relations than in the other areas of their personality.

The seniors reported they had become more stable during their four years (PSQ: .001, .05). In their interviews, they also made more statements about becoming more stable than the freshmen did (.05).

Both the freshmen and the seniors became more stable in their *cognitive-intellective skills,* though the seniors reported significantly more stabilization occurred (PSQ: trend, .01). This change, however, was not one of the major developments for the students (Rank 18), though the inability to use their intellectual talents effectively was a moderate source of concern (Order 13.5). The Freshman and one of the Senior samples increased in their intellectual efficiency (MMPI: Ie, .05, .05), but the seniors as a group were more intellectually efficient than the freshmen. Their better intellectual efficiency was reflected in their higher academic achievement (.05, .05) as well as in their consistent academic improvement over the four years (.01, .001).

The ability to use one's intellective skills efficiently is affected by the degree to which inner disturbance and emotional upset intrude into their operation. More seniors but not freshmen report that they had learned since entering college how to retain their intellectual control even when they reasoned with personally disturbing information (PSQ: .01, .05). The freshmen, more emotionally unstable and confused than when they entered (Rorschach: m%, .05; Sum DD, .001), had yet to develop more stable means of intellectual control. More freshmen at the end of the year reported that they were unable to concentrate as well (MMPI: .05) and that they had periods when their "mind seem[ed] to work more slowly than usual" (MMPI: .05). Sixty-four per cent of the freshmen but only 31 per cent of the seniors accepted the latter as true for them.

The seniors developed more stable beliefs and *values* since their freshman year (PSQ: .01, .10). The freshmen had not yet formed a more stable value system by the end of their first year. If their ideas were challenged, the freshmen, but not the seniors (PSQ: .01, trend), became more uncertain about their beliefs. To illustrate how much more crystallized the beliefs of the seniors were, we compare the changes in their religious beliefs with those of the freshmen. Of the eleven items in the MMPI dealing with religious attitudes and behaviors, the seniors changed significantly on six and the freshmen on none, although more freshmen had begun to become less conservative in their beliefs and less formally religious in their behavior. In other words, the freshmen had changed in the same direction the seniors had but they had not yet changed as much. Fewer seniors agreed with each of the following items:

| | Agreement (Per Cent) | | Per Cent Change since Matriculation | | |
	Freshmen Time 2	Seniors	Freshmen	Seniors	p
I believe there is a God	64	52	—4	—15	.05
I believe there is a Devil and a Hell in afterlife	16	4	—4	—17	.01
I believe in a life hereafter	32	27	—12	—23	.01
I believe in the second coming of Christ	16	13	0	—13	.05
I pray several times every week	36	9	+4	—14	.05
I go to church almost every week	16	9	—16	—41	.01

The motivational interest pattern of the freshmen also began to become like that of the seniors (SVIB). Whereas the Freshman sample differed significantly in thirteen of its interests from the freshmen interests of the seniors (SVIB), by the end of their first year, the Freshman sample differed significantly in only two of its interests from those of the seniors.

Although the development of more persistent and stable values was not rated by the samples to have been one of their more important changes (Rank 15.5), many freshmen developed early a more intrinsic and stable appreciation for the intellectual life. We shall see later that alumni retrospectively rated the development of a genuine interest in intellectual activities to have been one of the more important enduring effects of their liberal education. The freshmen say, "Well, on the one hand it [the intellectual tradition of the college] has increased my desire to be an intellectual in most fields. . . ." or "I have more of an appreciation for scholarship. I certainly respect it more than I did before." And a senior said,

> I have come to feel that . . . the essential role in life is the role of the mind and the use of the mind. I couldn't exist without it. I feel that the mind is more important than anything else. And I feel that in being able to use my mind I not only do what I want to do but also what I should be doing as the most important thing.

Not to develop such intrinsic intellectual motivation early in college was perceived by twice as many freshmen as seniors to be symptomatic of not maturing.

The stabilization of the *self-concept* was an important index of becoming more mature (Rank 6). Although the Senior samples did not differ from the Freshman sample in the stability of their self-image as measured by the SIQ, the seniors did describe their self-concepts to have become consistently (PSQ: .01, .10) more stable since their freshman year. The self-concepts of the freshmen tended to become less stable. The seniors claimed that since they entered college they had become more resistant to changing, when challenged by someone else, their opinions of what kind of persons they fundamentally were (PSQ: .001, .10). Over the four years, a greater number of seniors (but not freshmen) became more sure of themselves (SVIB: .05). More freshmen and seniors no longer gave excuses when caught making a mistake (SVIB: .05; .05). More seniors became more able to meet emergencies quickly and effectively (SVIB: .01). Finally the seniors were less tense and confused than the freshmen (Rorschach: m%, .05), although they did not differ in inner tension from the Freshman sample when it matriculated. A typical remark of one senior was,

I'm much more relaxed now. I can talk to other people
without worrying what they think of me. And just say the
hell with it . . . I guess more confidence in my own self
as a person. Now that I'm able to relate to other people
. . . I have more faith in myself as a person.

The chairmen of the academic departments in which the seniors majored agreed with their self-assessments. They rated the emotional stability of the seniors to have been between good and excellent, one of
their highest rated traits. Finally, a more objective measure of the senior's increasingly stable identity came from the blind clinical analyses
made of each man's test materials and Rorschach. I had made explicit
comments that they might well postpone making a vocational choice
in the written analyses for 52 per cent of the freshmen but for only
10 per cent of the seniors. The data indicated their identities were still
so diffuse and unstable that no clear direction had yet emerged.

Interestingly, the increased stabilization in the attitudes of the
seniors toward themselves was paralleled by an increased stabilization
in their attitudes toward their bodies. The Freshman sample did not
show the same magnitude of change. An increased number of seniors
reported on the MMPI that:

they seldom worried about their health (.05);
they were not worried about catching diseases (.01);
they were neither gaining nor losing weight (.01);
they had no difficulty in starting or holding their bowel
movements (.01);
they could read a long while without tiring their eyes (.01);
their eyesight was as good as it had been for years (.01);
they were not bothered by pains over the heart (.05);
their speech was the same as always (.05, both seniors and
freshmen);
they had never been paralyzed or had had any unusual
weaknesses of their muscles (.01).

The only sign that the seniors may have become more physiologically
unstable was the increase from 25 to 42 per cent in the number reporting they became restless if they sat too long (MMPI: .05).

Not to know what to believe about oneself and what one is to
become and do is one of the more worrisome and unsettling experiences for any student (Order 2). The interview material suggested
that this crisis reached its zenith for most freshmen sometime within
their first six to eight weeks of college. They now faced so many possi-

bilities and alternatives that they had become less decisive and more confused (MMPI: .05). One freshman said,

> I've become a lot more scatterbrained, very digressive. I can't finish things on time. I can't always read things perfectly because there's just not enough time. I'm forced to be a little haphazard some of the time. What causes this is the intellectual pressure, all the work that has to be done. . . . It forces me not to learn everything perfectly. [Interviewer: When you say "scatterbrained" what do you mean?] Completely disorganized. I can't believe in myself. Deflated my ego, and knocked the chip off my block; probably made me more livable.

The Rorschach confirmed these changes in the freshmen. They had become more emotionally uncertain and confused since their entrance (Rorschach: m%, .05). They experienced in awareness the press of stronger drives and desires (Rorschach: Sum DD%, .001). More freshmen reported they felt more intensely than most other people did (MMPI: .05). Whereas 72 per cent of the freshmen made that statement after their first academic year, only 40 per cent of the seniors did after their four years.

Yet, paradoxically, although they were more inwardly tense and upset, fewer freshmen felt they were less happy than other persons seemed to be (MMPI: .05, 40 to 20 per cent), worried as much about possible misfortunes (MMPI: .05, 40 to 16 per cent), and felt at odds with themselves as much (MMPI: .05, 76 to 44 per cent). Fewer reported being as physiologically upset, like having diarrhea as frequently (MMPI: .05, 24 to 4 per cent). Apparently, once the freshmen knew where they stood and what was ahead of them for the next three years, they learned to adapt their attitudes about themselves to living at a higher level of inner tension and instability. Happiness may well not mean the absence of tension, confusion, and even pain. Happiness may mean feeling alive, living intensely, and being emotionally aroused.

Less adequate objective evidence is available about the stabilization of the men's *interpersonal relationships*, which were not considered to have been a salient growth experience (Rank 14). Generally, the seniors described themselves to have become significantly more stable in their personal relationships, particularly with women (PSQ: .01, trend). But, as we have already seen, the Rorschach analyses of

the seniors quite consistently mentioned that the men had yet to stabilize their heterosexual relationships, which seemed to be marked by
considerable ambivalence and guilt.

The more interesting finding is what did not occur, namely,
the development of more stable and enduring friendships with other
men. The failure to establish and keep close friends was one of the
more immaturing effects of their college career (Order 9). Thirty per
cent of the seniors, for example, spontaneously mentioned in their interviews that they regretted never having formed a close male friendship while in college. The seniors, but not the freshmen, reported that
their close male relationships had persisted for longer periods of time,
however (PSQ: .05, trend).

Why did not more of the men develop more stable relationships? The Rorschach analyses suggested that few freshmen were ready
to form more stable intimate relationships because of conflicts about
expressing their affectional needs for others. Instead, they withdrew
into impersonal intellectual activity and became more emotionally detached and aloof. This common problem of the freshmen is illustrated
by this excerpt from one Rorschach analysis.

[He has] very strong needs for close affectional and physical
contact with others, perhaps in playful ways, but he feels
guilty . . . [about] his needs for others. So while he yearns
for closer contact, he tends to keep himself aloof, at a distance. He may be suspicious of the motives of other people
as well as defensive about others who want to involve him
emotionally. If he ever got drunk, such affectionate needs
should emerge though he might react with a forced kind of
aggressiveness or hostility. He seems to be quite an emotionally responsive person who is not quite at home with his
feelings for others or with his need to allow himself to be
more dependent on others.

The affectional and dependency needs of the seniors were more
clearly assimilated to their strongly emerging sexual needs, about which
many were preoccupied in a way the freshmen were not. Whereas intimacy for the freshman was still relatively sexless or more sublimated,
for the senior, intimacy was fused quite blatantly with sexuality. Too
close relations with other men provoked fears about their masculinity
and potency. The freshman remained aloof because, as we saw in
Chapter Three, of his fear about losing his "cool," about appearing

emotional and needing others; the senior remained aloof because of his fears of becoming too strongly sexually involved. But for the senior, in contrast to the freshman, retreat into intellectualism to provide a compensatory sense of competence and power was increasingly felt to have immaturing effects on his development. The Rorschach analysis of one senior, confirming what he claimed he already knew about himself, was, in part, that he

> . . . may inwardly sense some strong [sexual] temptations against which his intellectualized ideas have stood as a defense in the past. In some way, his impulsive life is viewed as a potential threat to him and his reaction has been to use intellectual control as a means to guard himself from such inner "destruction." But such intellectual control may have been at the expense of full emotional-social development.

One cannot develop stable interpersonal relationships if one is ambivalent in his feelings toward others. One senior colorfully described the negative side of his ambivalence toward women this way:

> I've discovered that most women are snakes. I've discovered not to trust them. Unfortunately, that goes against every natural biological law that's ever been made and so I find myself with rather a problem.

AUTONOMY

Three generalizations can be made with reasonable confidence about the hypothesis that maturing involves increasing autonomy: (1) The seniors became more autonomous and more so than the freshmen. (2) The freshmen became less autonomous and seemed to be in more conflict about growth on this dimension. (3) Increasing autonomy was not judged to be one of the more important dimensions of growth; in particular, its relevance to the maturing of one's interpersonal relationships was ambiguous.

The Senior samples reported that they became more autonomous since their freshman year (PSQ: .01, .01), while the freshmen tended to become less autonomous. The seniors also reported that they changed more than the freshmen actually changed in autonomy (PSQ: .01, .01). Furthermore, the seniors reported in their interviews more instances of becoming more autonomous than did the freshmen (.05).

The evidence is scanty and not consistent that the *cognitive-*

intellective skills of the seniors became more autonomous, a development ranked seventeenth in order of its occurrence. Whereas both Senior samples agreed that their intellectual judgments had become more their own and less influenced by the opinions of others (PSQ: .01, .10), only one sample asserted it had learned to restrain its desires and values from affecting its judgment about intellectual issues (PSQ: .05). An illustration of the growing independence of their judgments is this comment by one senior describing a faculty member's effect on his intellectual autonomy:

> Ah, I think he taught me the value of honesty in an intellectual endeavor, in an intellectual occupation. . . . Saying and doing honestly what you really think in a situation [is most important]. This person was not at all ashamed to say, "I believe," or "I think," or "It has been my experience." . . . I've followed his example, feeling less constrained, feeling I can go more freely against tradition and the ordinary ways of looking at things.

The Rorschach did not detect any maturing in the degree to which the thought processes of either freshmen or seniors became less frequently organized by unconscious wishes or fantasies. That a number of students reported in their interviews that they had not been able to maintain or grow in their intellectual autonomy (Order 7) was supported by a number of interpretive comments of their Rorschachs. The analysis, in part, of one freshman was this:

> He needs to constantly check his ideas with those of others— not those like himself, but the "general other," for his emotions may come to dominate his thinking, leading to unrealistic or inappropriate conclusions. Trouble is that he will believe what judgments he comes to are correct and so he may become uneducable.

And of a senior, the analysis was that he

> . . . has opened himself too much to the inner world of the unconscious and is dominated by a good deal of primary process (dreamlike) fantasies that take obsessional forms. Too many feelings remain unintegrated and not sublimated into more productive forms in the outside world. He is stuck in a morass of inner feelings; introspectiveness has not

yet brought a meaningful synthesis. . . . [This] inner pre-occupation severely limits his intellectual efficiency and productivity at this time. If he is in the natural sciences (which he was) where he can maintain his intellectualism in formal impersonal types of courses, his academic work may reflect [only] minimal impairment (which was not the case).

But the following senior disagreed with this analysis:

Enormously emotional with a wide range of emotional re-actions available, ranging from severe depressions, moodi-ness, feelings of self-depreciation and guilt to great sensitivity toward and affectionate feelings for others. Looks as if he doesn't protect himself enough both from external and in-ternal stimulation, for he is an easily moved person, and when moved, there is a reduction in the quality of his think-ing and judgment. . . . Since he is so easily stimulated, increasing interest in more impersonal, practical types of ac-tivities may help to control such emotionality by eliminating or reducng the external cues [that set off] his feelings.

One of the important values of the college is that its students should develop their own values and ideas about themselves so that they will have the courage to dissent and act according to their con-victions. Developing more autonomous *values* and *self-concepts* was only a moderately important maturing change (Rank 11 and 13). The seniors reported that they became more autonomous in their val-ues (PSQ: .001, .001). Their ideas about themselves became more distinctively their own (PSQ: .01, .01), and were no longer as easily influenced by the opinions of their friends and family (PSQ: .05, .05). One source of this increased autonomy for the seniors was the belief their values (PSQ: .01, .05) and self-concepts had become psychologi-cally contemporary or autonomous of childhood and parental influ-ences. Such independence contributed to a more mature concept of themselves. One senior said,

. . . but now I accept them (parents) more as people be-cause I don't depend on them as a source of security any more, I guess. And it's much more satisfying. [Interviewer: How do you feel this has changed you?] In a sense, I feel more mature, more sound.

And another senior said,

> In my freshman and sophomore years, my dependence on them changed a lot. Now, I'm part of the family again, but I'm also an adult in my own right.

Seniors alleged they became more immune to external and internal challenges to their images of themselves and self-control. More seniors were no longer as bothered by being made fun of by others (MMPI: .05), by having someone observe them while they worked (MMPI: .01), by having their sleep bothered by thoughts or ideas (MMPI: .05), or by interrupting a task they had begun (MMPI: .05). However, when their self-concepts were directly challenged and contradicted in an experimental session, the seniors were no better able than the freshmen to resist changing their concepts of themselves (SIQ).

Conflict about developing more independent values and self-concepts was one of the important immaturing experiences at the college (Order 6 and 8). The freshmen seemingly became less autonomous in both their values and ideas about themselves. Perhaps because of their greater awareness of the sources of their own values, the freshmen felt their values were still being influenced by their childhood experiences and parents (PSQ: .05, two-tailed).

The hypothesis that a maturing person becomes more autonomous in his *interpersonal relations* was confirmed for the men's relations with their parents but not for their relations with their peers. More seniors became more desirous of leaving home (MMPI: .05, 32 to 48 per cent) and more, in fact, 62 per cent, did report they had become increasingly independent and free of the control of their parents (MMPI: .05). In contrast, 42 per cent of the freshmen claimed they had become more independent. Both the freshmen and seniors tended to become less identified with their families. For example, more would not feel, so they report, "nervous" if members of their family got into trouble with the law (MMPI: .05, 12 to 40 per cent; .05, 23 to 36 per cent). The growing independence of the seniors from their families was perceived to be very maturing, as one senior commented:

> Well, when it became apparent to me that I was no longer dependent and that . . . I even had a responsibility to them, more than the other way around, I guess [I became]

more mature and confident of my relationships with other
people.

Is increasing interpersonal autonomy really maturing? This is
a more complicated question than our theory describes it to be when
we consider the young men's affectional and love relationships with
their peers. Neither the freshmen nor the seniors reported any consistent maturing in this area (PSQ), nor did they become less dependent
generally (MMPI: Dy). The following excerpts from the interviews
of three seniors help clarify the problem:

> I don't feel as dependent on my really close friends as I did
> . . . if I'm in trouble . . . I still go to my close friends,
> but the fact that I'll be leaving most of my close friends at
> the end of this year doesn't scare me as much as it did at
> the end of high school. I'm sorry about it and I'm going to
> miss a lot of these men, but it's not as if I don't know what
> I'm going to do without them.

A second said,

> Yes, as a freshman, I thought I was far more independent,
> far less apt to feel a need for other people, and I realize
> now that is not at all true. In fact, I've a very great desire
> for . . . other people.

And a third said,

> Before coming here I felt very insecure . . . about being
> able to be a man, being able to have some sort of relation-
> ship with women. So I was very happy and surprised when
> someone responded to me and this set up a very dependent
> relationship on my part, since I've never felt that I, on my
> own, that I needed this affection too much.

Autonomy, defined as independence of the emotional influence
or control of another, is an index of maturing that depends upon the
level of maturity at which it is being assessed. The autonomy of the
first senior is mature because his need for others is not preventing his
further development as a fuller person. Using a narrow definition of
autonomy, the statements of the second and third seniors might be
considered immature expressions of autonomy. Yet, given the evidence
from Chapter Three that the entering freshmen were emotionally aloof

and too self-sufficient individualists, the experience of becoming more emotionally dependent upon others may have been a crucial necessary condition for their further maturing. Such an interpretation of the maturing effects of becoming more dependent in affectional relationships was also made independently in the Rorschach analyses of the men. A number of the men were described to be alienated from their dependent needs, and, therefore, unaware of how much they needed others. They were not expected to develop much further until they literally learned how to "fall in love." For example, he has

> strong needs for physical affectional contact with other people and needs to be dependent on others which may not be completely in awareness. . . . They haven't been satisfied. . . . He remains emotionally self-sufficient. His reaction to the arousal of his affectional needs is their repression, possibly some hostility and their sublimation into compulsive hard work. . . . May have to allow himself to become more disorganized and upset in order to sense how strongly he needs other people and thereby learn how to love.

We can now understand why the development of more autonomous personal relationships was the least demonstrable maturational change in the men (Rank 20), and why "failure" to so develop was one of the most frequently mentioned statements in the interviews (Order 4). The statements made in the interviews about becoming more dependent on others were not scored within the larger meaning that such dependency had to each person. They were mis-scored as evidence of immaturing rather than as transitional steps toward potentially greater maturity.

UNPREDICTED CHANGES

In what other ways did the students change that have not yet been described? What data remain unmentioned that may challenge the comprehensiveness and adequacy of the theory of maturing for organizing the developmental process? The more general adequacy of the theory will be discussed in Chapter Nine, after we have examined more data.

A systematic review of all of the material available for each person suggested that it was the interview and the Rorschach and not the more objective test data that have not been adequately summarized. We could make no meaningful interpretation of the following statistically significant but unmentioned test findings (findings similar to those already described are not listed).

Senior changes:

1. Increased number who sometimes vote for men at election about whom they know very little (MMPI: .01).
2. Increased number who do not make wagers (SVIB: .05, 23 to 38 per cent) and a decreased number who deny they have ever loaned money to acquaintances (SVIB: .01, 25 to 6 per cent).
3. Increased number who would enjoy developing business systems (SVIB: .05, 38 to 54 per cent).
4. Increased number who would like to live in the city (SVIB: .05, 38 to 54 per cent).

Freshman changes:

1. Increased number who sometimes vote for men at election about whom they know very little (MMPI: .01).
2. Decreased number who have felt strangers were looking at them critically (MMPI: .05, 52 to 32 per cent).
3. Decreased number who report resenting being taken in so cleverly by someone else that they would have to admit that "it was one" on them (MMPI: .05, 44 to 20 per cent).
4. Decreased number who, when taking a new job, said they would like to be "tipped off on who should be gotten next to" (MMPI: .05, 40 to 24 per cent).
5. Decreased number who said they would like to hunt lions in Africa (MMPI: .05, 52 to 28 per cent).
6. Decreased number who often have taken orders from someone who they believed did not know as much as they did (MMPI: .05, 44 to 24 per cent).
7. Decreased number who dislike people who always agree with them (MMPI: .05, 60 to 36 per cent).

The impression both the interview and Rorschach gave is not that other, very different types of changes that have not been mentioned occurred, but that more change occurred in some sectors of the students' lives than we have described. Our test data do not adequately indicate the magnitude of the motivational or dynamic changes in the men and their effects on the men's conceptions of themselves. Whereas the freshmen seemed turned back into themselves, the seniors seemed to be on the verge of making a major decisive thrust into action. As one senior said of his growth, "The effect [of college] has been to make me spend several years introspectively, growing inwardly instead of outwardly."

The seniors do seem to be on the edge of becoming much more active, coping, aggressive, and assertive men. They are psychologically ready to move outwardly to test the strength and direction of their inward growth. A number of seniors sensed the discrepancy between their felt readiness for action and the felt passivity of their academicism. This discrepancy prevented the stabilization of a conception of themselves as vigorous effective men. The Rorschach suggested the men had become much more virile, aggressive, intrusive—in short, masculine—than they had yet to accept about themselves. Perhaps not until the world beyond the confines of the college tests the seniors' heightened potential for action will they resolve their doubts about their potency and stabilize a conception of themselves as the masculine and highly competent men the data suggest they were becoming.

In answer to our question at the beginning of this chapter— Yes, students did change. They became more mature, more in some sectors of their personalities than in others. The pattern of the freshman's subsequent growth in college is largely set during his first months at the college. Much of his later growth represents a further stabilization and integration of that growth rather than the development of new types of changes. The process of maturing in college involves primarily a progressive integration, an expanding capacity for symbolization, particularly of oneself, and a developing allocentricism. Although a student also becomes more stable, particularly in his self-concept, and autonomous, such developments, while both necessary and important, do not seem to be the central and most distinctive maturing experiences in college.

How contingent these particular developments are on the personality of the entering freshmen we do not yet know. Certainly the trends for contemporary freshmen to be more inhibited, over-controlled, and intellectually narcissistic can be reversed in a powerful liberally educating setting. The freshmen in time do become more spontaneous, their consciences more humanized, and their intellectualism tempered and integrated within a larger perspective. But the transformation of the contemporary freshman's interpersonal autocentricism remains unrealized; the real growing edge of the seniors remained the development of even more allocentric interpersonal skills, values, and concepts of themselves.

Adequate objective tests measuring the range and types of changes that students experience while maturing are not yet available. Our impression is that it is not that students do not change and mature in college, as some studies might suggest, but that the methods used to detect change may not assess the types of actual change that occur or, if they do, may not adequately discriminate the amount of change that does occur. Of course, some colleges may not have much effect on their students.

Two important tasks now confront us. The first is to determine what the most *enduring* maturing effects of the college experience were (Chapter Six). The second is to study the relation of the college environment to the maturing process—first from the viewpoint of the college itself, and second, from the viewpoint of the theory of maturing. We ask first, "What characteristics of the college had the most pervasive maturing effects on the students?" (Chapter Seven), and second, "What are the principal determinants influencing growth in *each* sector of the personality; for example, what caused the maturation of the students' values?" (Chapter Eight).

CHAPTER VI

Alumni Experiences

How enduring are the maturing effects of the college experience? This question has seldom been assayed (Freedman, 1962, 1967; Newcomb & Feldman, 1968; Newcomb, Koenig, Flacks, & Warwick, 1967). Yet, for what purpose is it to demonstrate that students mature in college if such changes do not continue and persist into the post-college years? A cynic might argue very cogently that the personality changes we have just described are only temporary adaptations to a peculiar type of psychological environment. When under the persuasive control of the more typical practical, everyday world, the men will regress to their freshman selves or, in competitive settings, actually develop in ways contrary to those manifested in college. If the men have not really stabilized their maturing changes and have not become more autonomous of the influence of the environment, the two dimensions we concluded to have been least represented in the men's development, then such post-college regression is even more certain. Another critic might assert that the pattern of maturing effects we described does not accurately portray the development of the men. Conceivably, the men may have matured in other ways that can be detected only when evoked and tested after they leave college. This chapter seeks to determine the more enduring effects of the college experience. It is unabashedly exploratory. Its findings are neither secured by large samples nor disciplined by objective test data.

How does one test the power of a college experience to induce changes that persist into adult life? Certainly, graduate school and professional performance, status and income are not very useful indices. The only test we know is to ask alumni about the persistent effects of their college years as they recall them. And that is just what we did. In contrast to those who distrust retrospective reports, we have learned to respect and listen to the opinions of men who value, above all else, to be honest with themselves and with others. But in interpreting such reports, we do have to remember that what is reported to have occurred may not have occurred and what is not reported to have occurred may have, in fact, occurred. The alumni may have changed less than they report—or more. We had no *practicable* way by which to check the accuracy of their self-reports.

MATURING OF ALUMNI

We sought to determine whether the effects of the college experience persisted for at least two decades. The sample representing primarily the classes of the 1940's (including some from earlier and later classes) was composed of twenty-five alumni (called the Alumni Council) who had been elected by their peers to govern their affairs at the college. Fifty-five per cent of the Alumni Council participated. The decade of the 1950's was represented primarily by our principal sample (called Alumni sample). It consisted of thirty-nine alumni whose classes were described as entering freshmen in Chapter Three. It represented 48 per cent of those who had been randomly invited to participate. Follow-up letters to the men of both samples who did not participate resulted in securing information on 80 per cent of all who were initially invited to participate. The decade of the 1960's was represented by the two Senior samples (called Alumni Senior sample), whose development in college Chapter Five described. These men were canvassed two to three years following their graduation.

How representative of their classes were the alumni of the Alumni sample? We discuss this sample's results in detail, since it had been out of college long enough to establish itself vocationally, but not out long enough to have lost as much contact with its college experience as older alumni. Occupationally, it, like the Alumni Council, was fairly representative of Haverford alumni. Twenty-five per cent of the Alumni sample were teachers, scholars, and research scientists; 24 per cent were physicians; 23 per cent were presidents and vice-presidents of businesses or held similarly responsible positions in foundations or other institutions, like hospitals; 14 per cent held other executive positions of considerable responsibility; 7 per cent were editors and 5 per cent were lawyers. Both alumni samples were similar occupationally, except the Alumni Council had more teachers and the Alumni sample more business executives.

Religiously, the Alumni sample seemed to be reasonably representative of the Haverford alumni of the 1950's, except that the sample contained more Jews and fewer Quakers. The original random sample was representative of the religious composition of the classes, but the Jewish alumni had the highest and the Quaker alumni the lowest rate of participation in the studies.

More importantly, did the respondents differ psychologically from the nonrespondents? We compared the measures of personality, temperament, and adjustment secured from both groups when they entered college, their aptitude and college achievement records, and their departmental chairmen's evaluations of them as graduating seniors. The respondents of the Alumni sample differed significantly from the nonrespondents on only six of the ninety-three measures, a number barely exceeding that expected by chance. If we dare to interpret what may be chance differences, the respondents as freshmen may have been less inhibited and defensive, more impulsive, dependent, perhaps more biased in their opinions, and may have had more mercurial interpersonal relationships. As seniors, they were judged to be less determined and original than those alumni who didn't respond.

The information from the nonrespondents, secured from the follow-up letters, also confirmed that in terms of their college experience and the reasons for their development at the college they did not so differ from the respondents to make us question the validity of the larger outline of the results of the Alumni samples.

The Alumni Council and Alumni samples completed a twelve-page questionnaire that was modeled on the studies used with the undergraduates reported in Chapter Four. Each alumnus first described how he had changed while at college. No reference was made to either maturing or immaturing types of changes so as not to influence the type of change reported. He next identified the principal determinants of that change by sorting each of forty-six cards, on which were printed the same determinants used in the undergraduate studies, into one of five categories that indicated the degree of its influence upon his change. After next ranking the more important determinants, he described in detail on successive pages of the questionnaire the effects that each of the five more important determinants had had upon his development in college. He was then asked to assess the relevance of the college's size, intellectual tradition, and Quaker history and atmosphere for the education of a contemporary student. These organizing categories were selected because they had been cited by a former president to be the distinctively "liberally educating" qualities of the college and because we had used these categories for our own analysis of the college in Chapter Two. The remaining questions asked him to state his current religious preference, the effect of his college experiences on his subsequent religious-ethical development, on his occupational competence and satisfaction, on his participation in community activities, and, finally, on his philosophy and way of life.

As more than one alumnus, in typical Haverfordian fashion, either drily or sharply pointed out, the questionnaire was not an easy one to complete. It demanded of many alumni much more than the suggested one hour, and it assumed that they could separate the effects of their college years from those of subsequent events. Given their heavy responsibilities, it was gratifying that so many alumni found the time to complete the lengthy and demanding questionnaire. Seventy-five per cent of those who did not return a questionnaire claimed that their lack of time, not disinterest in the study or the college, was the principal reason for their failure to participate.

The completed questionnaires were coded in the same way that the undergraduate interviews were scored, so that direct comparisons of personality maturing and immaturing could be made between the different samples.

The Alumni Senior sample, previously discussed in Chapter Five, rated and ranked the determinants of their change similarly, described changes they experienced in college of which they weren't aware at the time, and reassessed the principal effects of the college as well as the relevance of its size and intellectual and Quaker traditions to the education of a contemporary student.

COLLEGE IN RETROSPECT

The replies of the Alumni and Alumni Council samples are discussed together because of the similarity in the pattern of their replies.[1] The replies of the nonrespondents of these samples and of the Alumni Senior sample will be cited where relevant.

What was the tenor of the replies of the alumni and what general impressions emerged from their spontaneous descriptions of their "change" at the college? For the most part, the alumni assessments of themselves were very searching, thoughtful, and impressively open. They did not seem to magnify themselves or their achievements, to praise the college, or to slant their replies to fit any preconception they may have had about the study whose theory and expectations were unknown to them.

Several dominant and recurring themes marked the self-assessments of the alumni. From their perspective of at least two to almost fifty years of post-college experience, the men viewed their college experience as an integral and continuous part of their lives. Most did not report any break in the felt continuity of themselves as persons from what they were both before and after their college experience. Thus, the effect of the college was not to "change," as any number of very discriminating alumni noted, but to "crystallize," to "consolidate," to further develop, to clarify an underlying direction in their growth, which they may not have been aware of at the time of matriculation as freshmen. As one alumnus said, ". . . during my four years at

---

[1] Roughly similar percentages of both samples spontaneously reported the college affected them to the same degree. More objectively, the *pattern* of maturing effects reported by the Alumni sample was significantly similar to that reported by the Alumni Council, that is, rho was .67, $p < .001$, indicating that irrespective of when they were at college, the men report experiencing very similar personality changes.

Haverford, I evolved, but did not radically change." Another said, "Haverford *developed* me—but it didn't change me. . . . The question above seems to indicate that Haverford is *all-important*. Come on now; it's only four years in a lifetime of experience!"

But for others—12 per cent of the alumni, in fact—those four years "produced a profound change," a change that may always demarcate a significant turning point in their lives. As one alumnus wrote,

> I changed thoroughly during my four years at the College; everything about me underwent either formation or transformation; nothing was the same before and after but my basic personal traits. Even of these, some particularities were no doubt fundamentally altered.

To secure some quantitative measures about their change in college, the alumni's general statements about their development were coded for the *implied* amount of maturing or immaturing experienced in college. Almost universally, the men reported they matured in college. Only one of the sixty-four alumni reported no movement at all; only one reported the college produced predominantly immaturing effects upon him.[2] Forty-seven per cent of the respondents (21 per cent of the nonrespondents) reported some maturing, usually within some limited aspect of their personality. Thirty-three per cent (24 per cent of the nonrespondents) reported considerable maturing, while 12 per cent (48 per cent of the nonrespondents) explicitly claimed the college experience had had very important formative and maturing influences on their lives. Interestingly, several alumni reported they were not aware of how they were maturing while in college.

> It was not until I had been out of Haverford for a few years that I began to understand what Haverford had done for

[2] The nonrespondents, who were asked to rate *explicitly* the maturing effects of the college upon them, agreed. Only two of the nonrespondents said the college produced immaturing effects upon them, thus confirming again that our responding alumni were not unrepresentative of the larger population. The discrepancies between the respondents and nonrespondents mentioned in the rest of the text are more likely due to differences in the methods used to determine the college's effects than to "real" differences. Figures cited in this chapter should be interpreted to indicate only the *relative* importance of one category to another.

me—without my knowledge, and, I often think, against my will. Haverford had given me a *basis* for thinking—independent, intelligent thinking.

Others claimed, somewhat paradoxically, that the college actually did not begin to affect them until they had left its shadow.

I didn't change very much as a person while at college—the major change took place during three years in the army after the four years at Haverford. But the ideas, attitudes, faculty, and friends at Haverford were major influential factors in the changes which took place after leaving Haverford.

Could it be that young men rebelling against a college's influence may not be aware of how much of its values they are internalizing until they encounter the world outside, the world in which their developing identities must now be tested? To check this observation, the Alumni Senior men who, as seniors, had been asked to describe their change in college were asked several years later, as alumni, to report any changes that had occurred in college of which they had been unaware as seniors. Less than a third of the respondents reported recalling any new changes. Of those few changes mentioned, increased self-confidence, greater tolerance of others, and improved social skills were most frequent.

A final impression was more intriguing. Most of the alumni, regardless of their ages, described the effects of their college experience in very similar terms. For three to four decades until the mid-sixties, there was apparently a very real continuity in the psychological experience of becoming educated at Haverford. Why? One obvious reason is that the men may be describing a universal maturational process that all humans go through when freed and encouraged to do so. A college experience of a particular type may primarily stimulate and encourage growth trends already in process. But many of the alumni attribute such change to their "Haverford experience," claiming it was the college itself that "caused" such development. We return later to the alleged determinants of that continuity of effects.

What were the specific maturing changes reported by the alumni during their years at the college? Too few *immaturing* effects were tabulated to be reported. Of the total 843 statements about maturing that were spontaneously reported by the alumni, 36 per cent[8] concerned their own development as persons, their own attitudes toward themselves; 31 per cent were about the maturation of their values; 19 per cent, the development of their cognitive or intellectual skills; and 14 per cent, the maturation of their interpersonal relations with men and women. Or, to analyze the results from the viewpoint of the dimensions that define maturing, 30 per cent of the alumni statements concerned the stabilization, in particular, of their identities and values; 25 per cent, the integration, primarily, of themselves, their values, and cognitive skills; 19 per cent, the developing allocentricism, particularly, in their personal relationships, intellectual skills, and values; 16 per cent, the expanding awareness, again, primarily of themselves and their values; and 10 per cent, their growing autonomy, especially in their own decisions and values.

We highlight only the principal specific changes about which there was most agreement. The foremost change reported was the resolution of the identity crisis and the stabilization of self-concepts (accounted for by 12 per cent of the 843 statements). The alumni reported they emerged from college much more confident about themselves and their talents, a self-confidence immeasurably enhanced once they encountered the greater diversity in talent and effectiveness that is more typical of the world outside of the college.

This process of stabilizing and consolidating themselves did not seem to have been organized around, as we would have predicted, choosing and preparing for their future occupations as much as it was organized around forming central, determining, and integrating values. Except for 12 per cent of the alumni, primarily the physicians and the writers, their college experiences were not viewed as preparatory or directly related to their future occupation. Instead, the college prepared them as human beings, in terms of (1) "strength of character which makes me a good teacher and leads to profound satisfaction," (2) "confidence and the ability to approach and complete any given assignment," (3) "value(s), problem solving, and breadth of thinking which are essential in running a modern business," (4) "giving me the desire to exert my best effort and to employ critical thinking. This

---

[3] We must emphasize once more that the percentage figures reported in this chapter are cited *only* to give comparative information about the magnitude of the different effects.

is a broad basis from which greater competence and satisfaction could be achieved, irrespective of occupation," and (5) "showing me a way of living. I have much satisfaction, now, in my life; and I think I owe Haverford a good deal of it."

For the alumni of the mid-sixties, as well, the college's most important effect was not narrowly academic or professional but humanistic and self-fulfilling. The college need not apologize to the alumni for not being vocationally or professionally oriented. Many would urge resisting the encroachment of too great specialization in the curriculum.

Actually, as the above alumni comments suggest, it is quite artificial to separate out for analysis the maturation of the alumni's conceptions of themselves from the development of their values. Most alumni are very clear that the central core of their college experience was the development of their motives, values, and conceptions of themselves as ethical persons who learned to "choose what is right as opposed to what is easiest." It is therefore not surprising that the second most frequently cited effect of the college was the stabilization of their motives and values (11 per cent of the 843 statements of maturing).[4]

It is also not surprising that the consolidation of a basic value system or, more broadly, a philosophy of life, while in college had enduring effects that persisted many years after graduation from college. To the question, "Did your college experience contribute to your attitudes, philosophy, enjoyment, and satisfaction about the way of life you are now living?" 87 per cent of the alumni answered affirmatively —many strongly affirmatively: "very great effect on my life," "major contribution to my way of life," "a major factor in determining my present way of life," "of course." The college had such effects as these on their way of life: "taught me to be honest to myself"; "help[ed] me to learn contentment while avoiding smugness"; "tended to make me emphasize the intellectual and cultural aspects of daily living; it made me skeptical, sensitive, yet unemotional, cynical but appreciative of human talent and wit. It has been the predominant influence on my attitudes"; "made me less provincial intellectually and socially. I also learned to be involved with *principles* and became somewhat less pragmatic in my thinking about political and social issues."

---

[4] Cox, in an independent study of Byrn Mawr, Haverford, and Swarthmore alumni of the early fifties, also noted that the Haverford men's identities were more prominently organized around ethical-religious values and concerns (1968).

Two themes define the more specific type of value development for the alumni. One important effect of their college experience was the development of an ideal of excellence and the value of persistence in achieving that ideal. The alumni learned to be "dissatisfied with half-hearted effort," to value "stretching" themselves, to realize "that excellence in work makes a personal difference, that pursuing the truth of a matter in any field of endeavor is a liberating experience." One after another of the alumni reported that they learned to value—even to enjoy—work, hard work, no matter how "distasteful." To some, the college encouraged "at least a *partial* desire to really study and try for something besides 'just passing.' " It taught others "the meaning of hard work as a foundation for any kind of achievement," out of which developed an "increased pleasure and excitement in learning" and a "life-long intellectual curiosity."

But the value of excellence and its pursuit is not limited only to activities in the visible and tangible world. A second and more widely reported theme is that the college reinforced and inspired a standard of personal conduct, of ethical excellence, that served as a "cornerstone," a "stable frame of reference," that has "stood up to later reexamination and experience."

What is the content of these standards of moral excellence many alumni identify to be at the core of their identities? The alumni, like the undergraduates of the previous chapter, speak of becoming more liberal, but do not identify their changed values in terms of specific political or economic doctrines or beliefs. While many alumni reported that the college increased their interest in political affairs, not one alumnus reported that it made him a radical or doctrinaire, left- or right-wing, socialist or conservative. Rather, they talk of developing persistent social and ethical-religious values that integrated their conceptions of themselves (of the 843 statements about maturing, 10 and 7 per cent were about the integrating effects of the college upon, respectively, themselves and their values).

Certainly, one very central substantive value change that the college seemed to work in many alumni was to sensitize and deepen their sense of social responsibility and concern for other human beings (7 per cent of the statements of maturing). Coordinate with the development of such a value was a parallel change in the allocentric quality of their actual personal relationships with others (7 per cent of the statements of maturing). In describing such allocentric value and interpersonal development, the alumni spoke of learning compassion, social consciousness, acceptance of others, and, more frequently than any other value, respect and tolerance for others and their opinions. One alumnus spoke for many when he said, "I learned to respect and enjoy the friendship of many persons whom I might have avoided prior to exposure at Haverford."

Given the preoccupation by the undergraduate samples about their personal relationships, it is interesting to note that some alumni did not come to understand how allocentric their values and personal relationships had become while they were in college:

I have become aware of how much Haverford taught me to respect and care for other people. I do not think I was conscious of this during college. This is perhaps the single most important effect of the college.

Haverford taught me to listen to others, to respect them for what they are, to be tolerant and, in the Christian sense (this alumnus reported no religious preference), to love them. . . . I do not think I realized that I had learned this, for each year I am more keenly aware of the value I placed on the standards of personal fidelity and tolerance I learned at college.

The alumni don't just talk about such allocentric values. Many act on such concerns. Among colleges, Haverford has one of the higher rates of volunteers for the Peace Corps, Vista, and the Quaker VISA service programs. Others report they learned to "feel deeply about social injustices and speak out against them even when it's unpopular to do so because of the examples . . . [they] saw and heard about during college."

Closely allied to such allocentric value maturation is the more frequently reported ethical-philosophical-religious development of the alumni. The alumni are very clear that this type of development was the central integrating fact of their lives at the college. The men express this experience in different ways. Some say the college made them aware of a "center of integrity." "The emphasis on personal integrity . . . was a profound influence." In this or in other ways, the alumni expressed their conviction that the college helped them to become more honest persons. By insisting they examine their own consciences and then act responsibly on the basis of what they found, the college set high expectations of what a mature young man was to be like. The consequence for one alumnus was, "I became an engaged and committed individual"; for another, "I learned to adopt a set of standards more internally oriented"; and another, "I had to make decisions alone plus stand by my decisions after they were made."

Another related facet of the ethical-philosophical-religious maturation was the development of a value by many alumni of forming a way of life that was integrative for them. That is, self-realization itself became a value. Such a value opened up many alumni to the broader cultural opportunities of the college.

> Perhaps the most important initial influence Haverford had on me was exposing me to new ideas and simultaneously giving me the opportunity to explore and examine them with this "openness."

Others talked of a "general enlargement of intellectual . . . interests and knowledge, especially in areas of philosophic values," and "a more balanced appreciation of various facets of life in general."

Since a religious orientation may provide a stable and integrative direction to one's life, we must examine the persisting effects the college was alleged to have had on the subsequent religious life of the alumni. Recall that the religious preferences of the Alumni sample who completed the questionnaire were, when they were freshmen, similar to those of the student body in general, except that more Jews and fewer Quaker students were represented in the sample than in the student body. No data were available about the religious preferences of the Alumni Council as freshmen, whose expressed religious preferences as alumni are overweighted by Quakers (33 per cent of the sample); but almost half of them became Friends as a result of their college experience.

The principal effect the college had upon the men's religious lives was to develop a meaningful ethical humanism divorced from formal religious doctrines or an identification with the traditional institutional churches. Apparently, the rejection by the undergraduates of more *conventional* religious beliefs and practices, described earlier, persists for many years after college. If we examine just the Alumni sample, 21 per cent said they became agnostics or atheists as a result of their college experience. This change occurred primarily in the Protestants and Jews. The number of Catholic preferences did not change; the number of Quaker ones increased. More importantly, 54 per cent of the sample spontaneously said their Haverford experience either initiated or strengthened their interest in religious and ethical issues, while an additional 13 per cent mentioned only the development of ethical concerns. The replies of the Alumni Council were similar. Clearly, the alumni's college experiences had primarily constructive effects on their intrinsic ethical and spiritual development. Only a small number (four of the sixty-four alumni) reported the college had primarily destructive effects on their religious and ethical beliefs.

We have seen that the principal effect of the college was to stabilize and integrate the alumni's identities around a core of meaningful values, the allocentric nature of which was also manifested in their personal relationships. But the reader may be perplexed, as we were. Given the college's strong intellectual tradition and the obvious scholarly accomplishments of so many of its alumni, why didn't the college's *intellectual* maturing effects emerge more saliently in the spontaneous reports of the alumni? The two most frequently mentioned intellective effects, the allocentric and integrative ones, when combined account for only 10 per cent of the total number of maturing statements cited. Even some of those alumni in our sample who graduated near the top of their classes, with college honors, failed to mention the intellective maturing effects as frequently as the other effects we have described. And as we have already noted, the great bulk of the alumni reported that their academic work at the college was not specifically relevant to their subsequent occupational competence or satisfaction.

Apart from numerous methodological artifacts of the study that may account for this unexpected finding, our own hunch is that it is difficult to reflect and report about one's own intellectual changes, and that the failure to do so does not mean such changes have not occurred. What lingers in memory are the more deeply emotional and motivational experiences that have more immediate and direct effects upon one's decisions and actions. For example, we have already noted the development of a motive to excel, which, in part, is manifested in intellectual achievement.

But lest we give the false impression that, for the alumni, the intellectual maturing effects were not notable, we must examine just what effects did occur. As one alumnus said, his college experience taught him to "observe, assess, analyze, criticize, construct, formulate, act." The alumni describe the development of allocentric skills like critical thinking, critical reading, critical evaluation more than the development of creative or synthetic or constructive types of skills. They learned to approach problems from many different points of view, to maintain "an openness of mind, capable of examining and reexamining, searching and challenging," "to go beyond the words and to concentrate on the thoughts being expressed." The college had just as powerful integrative intellectual effects for a number of alumni; they not only gained "an enormous variety of knowledge" that broadened them, but also learned to apply their intellectual skills to a range of problems wider than just the academic.

> The most significant development in my character at Haverford might be described as a process of intellectual and spiritual integration, which changed me from a responsible but often work-a-day student to a responsive questioning aspirant to the title "intellectual."

Other less prominent types of maturing effects reported by the alumni are not described, since most of them are similar to those reported by the undergraduates.

PERSISTENCE OF EXPERIENCES

The alumni data warrant several tentative generalizations about the enduring effects of a liberally educating experience. True, the validity of the generalizations must be tempered by the limitations of retrospective judgments that are frequently unconsciously distorted to justify and give meaning to one's past decisions. However, while agreement does not ensure validity, it does engender more confidence in the results. And the men of the different samples did significantly agree about the persisting maturing effects of their college experience.

1. The maturing effects of the college are judged to persist and may become even more evident following college.
2. The pattern of maturing effects of college is somewhat different for the alumni than for the undergraduates. Specifically, the maturing of one's values becomes retrospectively more salient and that of one's interpersonal relationships less. The maturing effects of college become more stabilized and crystallized around a more integrated self-concept.

3. The model of maturing adequately encompasses and orders personality development in adults, but its adequacy cannot be fully evaluated except longitudinally. Development occurs differentially in the various sectors of the personality. There may be a sequential dimensional response to new situations that cannot be adequately described at a single point in time.

First, the alumni described the persisting effects of their college years in terms remarkably similar to those used by the undergraduates. Although the pattern of maturing effects of the alumni and undergraduates was significantly similar, $p < .05$, no statistic can convey the impression the reports give of the continuity and consistency in the effects the college experience had for the different generations.

That a number of alumni reported they had matured in ways of which they were unaware when in college is not surprising. Self-assessments of change are comparative judgments based, in part, on knowledge of other persons. To know what one has become, one must test oneself in different situations. The tests of the homogeneous college world are palpably different from those of the heterogeneous noncollegiate world. The judgments of the alumni may be more valid because they have been more broadly tested. As an example, the alumni reported they matured more in their values in college than the undergraduates suggested. Perhaps not until the men were confronted by "real-life" opposing values, by decisions for which they would be held accountable, did they become aware of what their more central values and priorities really were.

Secondly, alumni differ from the undergraduates about the more important maturing effects of college that persisted. Table 6.1 lists the ranked salience for the undergraduates of the principal maturing experiences mentioned by the alumni.

In contrast to the undergraduates, who were more preoccupied about the maturation of their self-concepts and interpersonal relationships, the alumni reported their college experience contributed more to the stabilization and integration of more allocentric values about which, as we have seen, their self-concepts had become stabilized. The change in the pattern of the effects reflects probably the different adaptational problems of the generations. The contemporary undergraduates, even more than their predecessors, are "hung up" by preoccupa-

TABLE 6.1

Principal Alumni Maturing Experiences

Type of Effect	Alumni Interview Rank	Undergraduate Interview Rank
Stability of self-concept	1	3
Stability of values	2	10
Integration of self-concept	3	5
Integration of values	4	14
Allocentric values	5	12
Allocentric personal relations	6	2

tions about their relations with their peers. The effects of the college tend to become judged by and assimilated to this dominant preoccupation. But the alumni have stabilized their heterosexual, familial, and social patterns. They are more preoccupied by occupational and community tasks that require responsible decisions and actions. What they value is more important. The alumni did not say that interpersonal and other forms of maturing had been unimportant. They did assert, instead, that the college's vision of a liberally humanistic and ethical way of life exercised a central and more enduring influence on their subsequent development.

Thirdly, the alumni data support more fully the model of maturity. They report more clearly than the undergraduates the centrality of the stabilization (but not the autonomy) dimension and the interrelationship of self-structures like the self-concept and values. To avoid overemphasizing transitional changes and underemphasizing delayed but more enduring effects, studies of the effects of college must study a longer time span than just the college years themselves.

Is there an orderly sequential development to the maturing process in young adults? Our hunch is that there may be, and that it is initiated by induced instability, to which the person responds with increased awareness and more allocentric and integrative adaptive attempts. Eventually, an adaptive solution is evolved that stabilizes and begins to function more autonomously. This sequence occurs at different rates in the different sectors of the personality. The developmental process is "completed" first in the maturation of intellective-cognitive skills, next in the same-sex and then opposite-sex personal relationships. The maturing of a person's values tends to follow the stabilization of his personal relationships. The maturing of the self-concept takes longer and goes through more transitional stages, eventuating in a stable integration with the person's values.

Let us try to sketch an overall synthesis of the above inductions. The freshman is "shocked" by the demands of the college. He becomes unstable and disorganized, though, in a "good" college that provides adequate supports, not enough to regress seriously or withdraw. That is, a good college helps its students to remain "educable." Disorganization and confusion are painful; without them, students may never make efforts to understand. The freshman becomes more aware of his own inadequacies, questions his competence and values, and despairs. He finds his greatest support from his relations with his peers, toward whom he now turns. But to survive in college, he must learn to concentrate his intellectual energies for academic purposes. His intellectual skills, never severely disorganized, mature rapidly during his first year; they become more stable and autonomous. Most of his intellectual growth is completed, we would hazard, within his first two years at a demanding college. He has meanwhile attended to other aspects of his development. He becomes much more preoccupied about his personal relationships and interpersonal values, particularly heterosexual ones. He searches religion, philosophy, and aesthetics for some meaningful answer and synthesis. In the meantime, his male relationships begin to stabilize, freeing him for more growth heterosexually. By the end of his freshman year, his self-concept has shifted from being "God's gift to humanity" to being a person of little value. The sophomore "slump" is a consequence of his argument with himself about what his direction in life is to be. A transitional stabilization of his self-concept occurs when he thinks he knows what his vocation is to be, but he never does develop a genuinely felt sense of worth until he tests his competence as an alumnus.

The junior year is probably the most psychologically quiet time in college, when much consolidation occurs. By the time he is a senior, he has tested his preliminary vocational identity as well as begun to form a stable heterosexual relationship. His values are becoming more integrative, though they are still self-serving and not yet stabilized. He is eager, though apprehensive, to test himself more assertively. His unfulfilled developmental tasks for his existing level of developmental organization upon graduation are the stabilization of his heterosexual relationships, the integration and eventual stabilization of his values and self-concept, and the development of their increased autonomy. Not until his heterosexual competence is tested in a sustained marriage relationship and his occupational identity confirmed by demonstrated competence and satisfaction does he begin to identify himself with a way of life allocentrically organized around the lives of others. Hypothetically, his more stable self-value identity results in the development of a mature autonomy that is neither rebellious nor narcissistic. The effect of the college experience for many alumni was that it provided a model of value as the core around which their growing integrity was organized.

If these inductions are correct, then the adequacy of the model of maturing cannot be simply determined by cross-sectional or segmental studies. The data force us to reassert an assumption of the theory. Development is an organismic process that must be studied over a time span sufficient to illuminate the complexity of the interactive dimensions that define maturing.

CHAPTER VII

Principal Effects
of the College

၊ၯ၊ၯ၊ၯ၊ၯ၊ၯ၊ၯ၊ၯ၊ၯ၊ၯ၊ၯ၊ၯ၊ၯ၊ၯ၊ၯ၊ၯ

W‌hy did the students change in the
ways they did? What caused their expanding awareness and deepening
tolerance and trust in others, their more socialized intellectual skills
and stabilized self-concepts and values? This and the next chapter
identify the determinants that produced such growth. This chapter
asks, "What are the principal maturing and immaturing *effects* that
collegiate experiences have upon young adults?" It illustrates how the
specific psychological effects of different social-institutional arrangements can be assessed. Our hope is to offer a model and method by

which to examine the relation between personality change and institutional practices.

We must modify our immodest hopes immediately. Personality change is the product of many interwoven determinants. The collegiate experience is only one type of several that interact to produce change. As we begin to analyze and trace how a college works its effects, we must inevitably prune and simplify and so risk failing to grasp the principal determinant of all the changes we have observed— the pattern, the context, of influences that reinforces and makes more decisive the effects of any particular determinant.

To remind ourselves of the complexity of the factors that produce change, we briefly review those we do not discuss. Certainly, some part of the changes Chapter Five described may be accounted for by physiological maturation. Kinsey (1948) said that the sexual impulses of the male are most imperious in the early twenties. Surely, much of the seniors' more dominant heterosexual preoccupations are related to their increased physiological calls. Sexual desire does impel action, calls out more assertive masculine behavior, and so transforms reality. The neighboring woman's college is no longer the thousand miles away for most seniors that it is for many freshmen.

The men's increased independence of their parents is the product not only of physical emancipation from daily parental supervision and control, but of cultural expectations of the behavior appropriate for a young male. Americans value independence, self-sufficiency, and "making a go of it" by the age of eighteen in a way that, for example, Turks and Italians do not. This societal expectation is so deeply internalized that few American males escape the guilt and sense of inadequacy that come from prolonged dependence upon their families. To go to college sharply symbolizes such a leap into maturity.

Certainly, becoming involved in some responsible work, whether it be academic, manual, or white-collar, induces manifold effects upon a person's maturing. Almost nothing is known about the effects of work on personal development. So we do not know if many of the maturing effects observed in the students may have been due primarily to their involvement in disciplined sustained work per se rather than to any particular characteristics of the college setting.

Obviously, the magnitude and patterning of personality change must be related to the type of student admitted to the college. Would not young men of high intelligence and emotional restraint be more responsive to the reflective emphasis of the college than other types of young men? A person's educability also depends upon the situation in which it is brought to test. It is provoking to ask if either Allan or John might have been as educable in a different type of college.

Given the magnitude and types of personality change observed in Chapter Five, we can hardly account for much of that change solely in terms of physiological maturation, departure from home, involvement in work, or temperament. As much academic folklore and some research suggests (Eddy, 1959; Newcomb, 1943; Sutherland *et al.*, 1962), we must look to the specific setting in which maturing occurs for a more profound and detailed understanding of why a person develops in particular ways. Such an exploration may place the important determinants of change in perspective.

DETERMINANTS OF PERSONALITY CHANGE

How can those collegiate determinants most potent in producing development be identified? Recall that all of the samples, including the alumni, rated the determinants on a five-point scale and then ranked the degree to which each of forty-six determinants influenced them as well as their intellectual skills, values, self-concepts, and personal relationships. Following each set of ratings and rankings, the men were interviewed about the effects of the determinants they judged to be most influential in their development. The interviews were subsequently scored for maturing and immaturing indices of change.

Such a procedure generates four different indices of the importance of a determinant for development: (1) The *ratings* assigned to each determinant were averaged for each sample so that they could be ordered in terms of their rated importance. (2) The *frequency* with which each determinant was selected by the sample to have been one of the five most important influences on its development provided another measure. For example, roommates were identified by 52 per cent but faculty expectations by only 16 per cent of the freshmen to have been one of the five most important determinants of their overall development in college. (3) The *number of statements* made in their interviews by the sample about the effects of a particular determinant was assumed to index the psychological importance of that determinant to the sample. For example, of the total 1,392 maturing statements made by the two senior samples, 15 per cent were about the effects of their relations with women. (4) The *range of effects* attributed by a sample in its interview to a particular determinant was also assumed to index its power and psychological importance. That is, the seniors claimed their roommates induced a total of twenty-one, but their natural science courses only seven different types of maturing effects. That roommates had a wider range of maturing effects does not mean that the natural science courses were less effective. In specific sectors of the personality, like intellectual skills, the courses were reported to have produced more maturing effects than roommates.

The determinants were then ordered on each index. One summary rank of a determinant's importance was secured by averaging its ranked position on each index. Reliance on multiple criteria to identify the important determinants—including criteria like three and four, which summarized actual behavioral incidents and effects—mitigates the potential unreliability of using only verbal ratings. The thirteen highest ranking determinants of the undergraduate samples were identified to be the most powerful determinants of personality change. They are listed in Table 7.1. Although the alumni samples were considered representative of their classes, we did not know whether they judged their college experiences differently. To check this possibility, we asked those alumni who did not complete the questionnaire to rank-order the first ten of the twenty-four most frequently selected determinants in terms of their importance to their own development in college. Table 7.1 also lists these less reliable data, that is, the data only of the rating index of the Nonrespondent Alumni sample.

In analyzing the effects of the principal collegiate determinants, we will draw more heavily upon the freshman and senior interviews, which were more extensive than the alumni questionnaires. Several generalizations can be made from Table 7.1 and the interviews.

First, just as the alumni described the effects of their college experience in terms similar to those used by the undergraduates, so Table 7.1 indicates the alumni and undergraduate samples agreed more than they disagreed about the important influences upon their development. Given the reduced reliability of the judgments of the Non-respondent Alumni sample, its rankings agreed surprisingly well with the rankings of the other alumni samples. Seven of the thirteen determinants identified as highly influential for the freshmen were also similarly indexed for the seniors *and* Alumni sample, suggesting that throughout the college years a small set of determinants exercised a

TABLE 7.1

Importance of Collegiate and Noncollegiate Determinants of Maturing

Determinant	Freshmen 1960's	Seniors I & II 1960's	Alumni[a] Seniors 1960's	Alumni Sample 1950's	Alumni[b] Nonrespondents 1950's	Alumni Council 1940's–30's
Interpersonal						
Roommates	1	2	6	1	5.5	3
Type of student	4	7	4	9	10	—[c]
Close male friends	3	3	3	4	12	10
Close female friends	5	1	2	11.5	—	—
Intellectual-academic						
Intellectual atmosphere	2	4	1	2	1	1
Faculty academic expectations	8	13	7	6.5	5.5	—
Specific course	7	11.5	10	—	11	—
Specific faculty	—	5	5	6.5	2	2
The Quaker tradition						
Religious-ethical	—	—	9	5	4	5
Academic honor system	6	—	—	3	7	4
Social honor system	12	11.5	—	8	—	13
Noncollegiate experiences						
Summer vacation	9	6	—	—	—	—
Parental relations	13	9	13	—	—	—

[a] The Alumni Senior sample combines the Seniors I and II samples, who were canvassed two to three years following their graduation.
[b] Includes 57 per cent of the nonrespondents to the Alumni and Alumni Council studies.
[c] Ranks above 13 were not considered as reliable and so were not included in table.

continuing and pervasive effect upon the men. Again, consistency does not guarantee that the identified determinants were really the more powerful ones—but it does encourage us to believe they are.

As will be illustrated later, the psychological consequences of some determinants change in time. The same determinant has different effects depending upon which point in the maturing process we are looking at. Furthermore, the importance of a determinant also changes in time. For example, the freshmen rated only three, but the seniors thirteen, of the forty-six determinants to have had a considerable influence upon them. The impress of some of the determinants on the freshmen will be carved even deeper during the next several years.

Second, the four indices of a determinant's importance were generally closely related to each other. For example, the seniors rated the intellectual atmosphere of the college to be one of the more important determinants of their change. A majority of them selected it to be one of the five most influential determinants. It also produced both a large number and wide range of maturing effects in the men.

Third, the collegiate determinants produced many more maturing (four and a half times more for the seniors and three and a half times more for the freshmen) than immaturing effects on the men. Although no determinant had predominantly negative effects, the data suggest that as the power of a determinant to produce maturing effects increases, its power to produce immaturing effects also increases. While roommates impressively stimulated maturing in many, they also created conflict and immaturing in others. This observation might be phrased somewhat differently: the more a determinant monopolizes the psychological life space of a person, the greater the likelihood it may create conflict or immaturing if a person cannot respond to its demands. We document this observation later.

Fourth, thirteen of the forty-six determinants accounted for over 75 per cent of the total number of maturing and immaturing statements made by the freshmen and seniors. This, of course, does not deny that other determinants may be more influential at other points in the developmental process. For example, Table 7.1 indicates that it was the alumni, including the seniors several years after graduation, but not the undergraduates who identified the religious-ethical tradition of the college to be a central determinant of their maturing. Furthermore, the data are clear that while a determinant may be relatively unimportant for most students, it may have been just the one whose touch brought a young man into fuller command of his talents.

Fifth, an institutional determinant produces multiple personality effects and a particular personality change can be produced by a variety of determinants. A specific faculty member, for example, produces a range of different effects, like an increased awareness of one's values. But such increased awareness is also the product of many other determinants as well. The data confirm other findings (Thorndike, 1924; Webster, Freedman, & Heist, 1962) that no particular course or faculty member has a hegemony over the development of any specific maturing effect.

PRINCIPAL DETERMINANTS

What are the psychological effects of the determinants that had decisive maturing and immaturing influences on their development? To avoid misunderstanding, we must be very clear. We are *not* making a statistical survey of our too few students to determine quantitatively how many changed in each of the ways mapped by the model of maturing for each determinant. Where the data permit, a small quantitative step or two will be ventured beyond the qualitative analysis. We wish to illustrate how a model and method may be applied to illuminate the potential maturing or liberally educating effects of different aspects of the college experience.

Chapter Five demonstrated that the basic pattern of maturing that describes the senior was etched, though not as deeply, in his freshman year. The interviews suggest that the freshman is most educable in his first semester, during which the college has its greatest liberally educating effect. It is remarkably successful not only in shocking and disorganizing (or challenging) its proud freshmen into "humility," as several labeled the effect, but also in providing the institutional and personal supports that eventually direct and transform their confusion and instability into more stable and mature forms of expression. By the end of the examinations of the first semester, when most freshmen find they will be able to make it after all, almost all of the growth trends noted in the seniors are clearly recognizable to the freshmen themselves. The educative influences producing such instability as well as the direction for its resolution are primarily *interpersonal* determinants, like the men's roommates, friends, and the students surrounding them, *intellectual and academic* determinants, like the college's intellectual atmosphere, faculty demands, certain courses and faculty, the *ethical* orientation of the college, like the academic and social honor systems and its religious tradition, and finally certain *noncollegiate* experiences, like summer vacations and relations with parents.

INTERPERSONAL DETERMINANTS

Roommates. To live in close physical intimacy with a roommate was judged to be one of the more important determinants of both maturing and immaturing by the undergraduate and alumni samples. More statements about becoming unstable and immature were assigned to the effects of roommates (20 per cent of the freshmen and 15 per cent of the senior statements were about immaturing) than to any other determinant. The effects of roommates differ during the four years, perhaps because only the freshman cannot choose the person with whom he must live. The freshmen emphasized that their roommates challenged their confidence and understanding of themselves (Unstable, Sym–SC),[1,2] forced them to become more tolerant and acceptant (Al–MR), as well as to learn to express themselves more clearly and sharply (Al–IS). The upperclassmen also reported similar effects, but emphasized instead the allocentric and integrative effects their roommates had upon their self-concepts (Al, I–SC) and values (I–V) as well as on the formation of more enduring, integrative, and autonomous relationships (S, I, Au–MR).

What do the freshmen actually say about the changes their roommates stimulated?

He's a living example of everything I tried not to be ever in my entire life. We spend hours and hours from time to time looking at one another, taking a look into our personalities, comparing ourselves to each other. I guess we delight in see-

----

[1] To facilitate the identification of the scored changes, the following abbreviations will be used: *S,* stability; *I,* integration; *Al,* allocentricism; *Au,* autonomy; *Sym,* symbolization; *IS,* intellectual skills; *SC,* self-concept; *V,* values; *MR,* male relations; *FR,* female relations; for example, *S–SC* means stable self-concept. An immaturing effect will not be abbreviated, for example, *Unstable SC.*

[2] The collegiate determinants varied in the number of psychological effects attributed to them. We cite only those three or four effects that were most consistently mentioned by the samples.

ing one who's the opposite of us, is perfectly contented with the situation and has arguments for it. It's stretched my mind an awful lot . . . I'm sure it's stretched my roommate's and it's made me think about a lot of my beliefs, mainly my religious beliefs and such things as faith, duty, obligations to society, nation, man.

The explosion in self-awareness that the encounter with another person evokes encourages a number of other changes. Suddenly, much of what was formerly certain and stable, like one's most cherished and private ideas about oneself, is challenged, frequently by unassailable logic. The freshman, not knowing what to think, begins to "change a lot back and forth" and re-evaluates his worth.

To live so closely with another person also forces the freshmen to communicate and thereby to listen, to understand, which, in turn, teaches them to tolerate, and then to accept much about persons they never thought it possible to accept before. They begin to grow out of their egocentric shells, to open themselves to the thoughts and lives of others.

I was really self-centered . . . just thought of myself. Always before I never wanted to say anything, keep it to myself. Then he talks about girl friends. He asks me questions. I'm almost forced into answering them.

I've become . . . less distant to other people, become more open to my friends, not only here but to friends I had before. I'm able to express myself more fully. And so I think by being open with a few people has made me a lot more friendly with other people.

The challenge of a roommate's thought may also provoke more allocentric intellectual development.

I like to make generalizations. He's continually shoving me down. He's made me much more conscious of this. He's also made me resent him a lot of times, but by and large it's been very good and it's forced me to be very careful about my generalizations.

Well, through discussions it's sharpened my ability to argue. . . . It forces you to formulate your ideas more clearly and exactly.

During his college years, a student becomes increasingly less concerned about himself, finds that others are more acceptant of him, even of those parts of himself he still doesn't accept, and becomes freer of himself to grow more allocentrically.

> They conditioned me to the fact that what I'm doing is actually normal, what I like to think of as being normal, for the people on the outside.

> Just that I think much more of myself as a person, accepted by others, less feeling that I'm different from everybody. I don't mind being different from everybody; in fact, I'm as good as everybody else; but it's nice to belong.

As their images of themselves become more allocentric, the seniors become more genuinely interested and respectful of others, their boundaries become more permeable, open to a variety of assimilative and integrative effects. For one thing, the men may model themselves after their roommates, expanding the range of their adaptive possibilities.

> . . . and if you respect a person you pick up some of his ways of going about things.

> Well, I've adopted their attitudes to a certain extent. I can think of ways in which I've imitated the gregariousness of one . . . the intellectual approach of another . . . the sexual principles [of another].

For another, the men learn to value being a whole person that has integrity.

> Well, I think roommates have sharpened my sense of responsibility to being honest with others, not giving false impressions, making only promises I can fulfill. It's sharpened the importance of sticking to my word, not to say anything unless I was sure of what I wanted to say.

But to act out of wholeness one must know what one wants and values and must have some consistent view of life. Roommates stimulate such value integration.

> He made me think about [my values] on my own in order to justify [them] against what he held. So, in other words,

he made me think about [them] more and develop my own coherent theory by being sort of a wall to bound [them] off on and express what I say.

To see someone act on his convictions makes one want to do the same.

One test of such integrative self and value maturing is how such maturing is worked out in one's personal relationships. Relationships with others become more stable and relaxed. The seniors feel more spontaneous and secure not just with one or two other like-minded persons but with others different from themselves. They have reached a new level of interpersonal equilibrium in which they can maintain their integrity and autonomy, and yet, respecting the differences of others, feel at home with them.

I tended pretty consistently to regard myself as a loner, but this is becoming less so. I still put a very high value on my independence and my ability to do things without worrying about what other people think about things. But at least my ability to get along with other people, to act in cooperation with them, has grown.

Type of student. Whereas the undergraduates and alumni agreed for several decades about the influence of their roommates on their development, the different generations did not agree about the extent of the influence the typical student had upon them. Chapter Three clearly demonstrated that the character of the student body had been changing as well as becoming more homogeneous in the past two decades. Parallel with this change, as Table 7.1 shows, the type of student with whom the men lived became an increasingly more important determinant of their development.

How is the "typical" student described in the interviews, and what are the psychological effects of living with such a person? Both the freshmen and seniors agreed in describing other students to be serious, abstract individuals who lived "in little clouds," highly motivated to achieve academically but socially "inert" and uncommitted. Wrapped in their own egocentricism, the other students were perceived at first to be unconcerned about and inconsiderate toward others, as well as indifferent about appearing to be more manly and aggressive. This composite summary fits very well the objective test data described in Chapter Three.

An impressive 37 per cent of the freshmen and 35 per cent of the seniors *spontaneously* described themselves in the interviews to have been similar to the composite portrait when in high school. Student after student commented about his isolation and loneliness in the typical suburban high school world of sports, sport cars, girls, rock and roll, academic cheating and disparagement of intellectual accomplishment. The men felt set apart by their high intelligence and intellectual interests and values. They considered themselves to be "brainy" but socially inept loners and said others thought them to be superior, conceited, diffident, and vain.

The encounter with such students produced in the freshmen a strongly ambivalent reaction. The freshmen became more autocentric as well as allocentric in their relations (Autocentric, Al–MR), and more aware of and certain about what kind of persons they were (Sym, S–SC). The seniors were affected similarly. They also matured more in their awareness about other persons (Sym–MR) and in the integration of their self-concepts (I–SC). The seniors were not as ambivalent about or rejecting of the modal type of student.

The freshmen were quite conflicted about the "typical" student with whom they lived. On the one hand, their discovery of other young men who had similar intellectual interests and with whom they could have more serious and personal relationships released many from a long-felt opposition to the more typical adolescent American peer culture that had led some to think they were abnormal or queer. For the first time, many freshmen felt they belonged to a community of like-minded persons whose identities included intellectual and aesthetic values. They felt more accepted and confident about themselves. One perceptive freshman expressed his stronger sense of individuality but also his growing allocentric identification with the community this way:

> I think you could say that each one is an individual. Once you understand and accept individuality in other people, I think you are on the first step in respecting your own individuality and accepting yourself. I guess it works the other way too. You learn that you're part of a community. I guess it's pretty much true in another college. You're placed in a relatively closely knit group, more closely knit than in a town or anything like that. You think of yourself as part of a group. It is paradoxical that at Haverford you recognize you're part of a group, but at the same time you recognize your own individuality within the group.

On the other hand, the freshman also saw his own identity reflected in others, whose overinflated intellectualism, frequently in competition with his own, he saw to be costly to his emotional and social development. While the freshman valued and vigorously defended his individuality, he frequently resented offending instances of individuality in others, who seemed to be inconsiderate, narcissistic, and emotionally immature. His greater awareness of the personal consequences of his own intellectualism occasionally induced resentment toward other students as well as a strong negative identity reaction.

The most predominant type has, if anything, caused me to make sure that I don't want to become that predominant type (though this freshman was one of the most intellectualized members of his class). Life is more than bedroom, bathroom, dining room, and classroom, and I hope it continues to be so; it's that simple.

I'm still in the process of examining myself and trying to evaluate why I feel about the things the way I do. But I can say this. I don't like the students' detachment, well, I shouldn't say that, uncommitment to anything.

By the time the men are seniors they are more aware of the emotional and social needs of other men. One wonders if the discovery of the humanness in their peers is not an accompaniment of their discovery of their own needs for others and the consequent growing integration into their ideas of themselves of the wider range of impulsive and emotional needs described in Chapter Five. The seniors find they can develop emotional relationships with other self-defined intellectuals. The "typical" student

. . . has given me a new dimension to my existence. I began to think about other people a little bit more. I began to come out of myself, and in coming out of myself, I ran into an awful lot of problems. I learned a lot about people. [Interviewer: You mean the guys around here allowed you to become more of what you couldn't become in high school?] Well, I just didn't have the opportunity. I couldn't make friends in high school. It was difficult because I had different interests.

What I'm most happy about is that when I came I thought there would be mostly academic kind of people, hard-nosed, in books all the time. But I saw they are also humans so that's made me say, "You, too, can be human, John."

Close male friends. The samples also agreed that their close friendships with other men were one of the most important influences upon their development while in college. All of the samples described very similar effects of such friendships. They became much more aware of themselves (Sym–SC), allocentric and integrative in their personal relationships (Al, I–MR), and more mature generally in their values. In addition to these changes, the seniors reported their friendships increased their reflective ability (Sym–IS), made them more insightful about other persons (Sym–MR), and led to more integrative and autonomous concepts of themselves (I, Au–SC).

As Chapter Four reported, in the past decades an increasing number of entering freshmen seem to be more closed to others. The extent of their isolation and loneliness magnifies, perhaps, the importance of friendships in college. The word most frequently used by contemporary students to express both their need for and their ideal relationship with another, and with themselves, is "openness," which means being all of themselves with another person. The college's ethos also values openness and honesty about oneself. The seniors said of their peers, "Everybody is pretty open about themselves; they admit their faults" and "are honest or fairly honest in their opinions and feelings." The reflective challenging atmosphere of the college also affects the kinds of relationships the students have with each other. A close friend tells you what he thinks of you.

> I've had others tell me point-blank what they think of me, and where they think I'm lacking in certain respects and where I'm not lacking in others, and where they have confidence in me, and where they don't have confidence in me.

Such openness and frankness increase a person's awareness and understanding not only of himself but also, as the seniors said, of other people as well.

> . . . I don't remember having very close relationships with male persons before coming here. It's made me much more aware of their emotions and what they are looking for. . . .

> I'm different because I'm more aware of other things . . .

more aware of other people's concerns . . . whole different worlds have opened up.

As therapists know so well, to talk intimately and openly with another strengthens the allocentric and integrative characteristics of a relationship. Both the freshmen and seniors became more desirous of friendships, e.g., "Well, I find I want to be with people more," as well as less exclusive in their friendships. They opened themselves to a wider range of people—"I can share friendships with certain people who I wouldn't be friendly with before"—and learned to relate to others more integratively:

> If you are good friends with someone you can reach, you can get to a certain level where you understand each other; you begin to have each other's thoughts, this sort of thing.

The openness to the influence of intellectual friends in a setting that demands reflection about one's values and goals leads to considerable maturing in one's values. A freshman said,

> Well . . . having your own personal convictions challenged every day by someone who is your best friend, and for whom you have a lot of respect, ah, can make you stop thinking that he's completely crazy and start checking your own values.

The seniors also report that they grew in their capacity to reflect about issues, both intellectual and ethical, as a result of the probings and confrontations of their friends. Eventually, out of the mutual personal and intellectual exploration evolved a more consistent and integrated conception of the kind of persons they were; and this conception gave them an increased sense of independence of other persons' opinions.

> He made me feel more willing to be isolated by those things that made me different than I would have been otherwise. Sort of more confidence in the things that made me an individual.

Close female friends.   The samples of the past decade report that their women friends had an increasingly important influence upon them. Their effects don't really become too prominent until after the first several years at college, so we rely heavily on the interviews of the seniors. The rule that the power of a determinant to produce maturing effects is also an index of its power to produce immaturing effects also applies to the effects of women on the men. Nine and fifteen per cent of all of the immaturing effects reported by the freshmen and the seniors respectively resulted from such relationships. The most salient immaturing effects the women had upon the men were to block the further integration of their ideas about themselves (Nonintegration SC) and postpone the development of more stable and autonomous relationships (Unstable, Lack autonomy FR). But such a host of maturing effects were reported that we will have to ignore many about which we would otherwise comment. The young women work their magic primarily on the men's self-image (Sym, Al, S–SC) and, of course, on the men's relations with them (I, Al, Sym–FR). The mysteries of their girls also affect the men's values and intellectual skills.

Many of the effects of a man's women friends are indistinguishable from those of his close male friends, although their psychological meaning may differ because of the forces that push the students toward the neighboring women. The men's heightened sexual restlessness tells only a small part of the story. One of the principal dynamic changes that their roommates and close friends work in the underclassmen is the release and cultivation of their social allocentricism and need for other persons. The expression of interest and love in another becomes its own incentive to further expression. When such a movement is accompanied by the growing security that comes from temporarily stabilizing one's self-concept, particularly when the vocational decision is made, a young man feels more ready to explore the mystery of someone he believes to be really quite different from himself—a young woman. A close friendship with a woman does uniquely test a man's image of himself as a man. Few contemporary students achieve an inner certainty about their powers until they know they are potent males capable of loving heterosexually.

Other forces pushed the students toward the nearby women. Some men sought the appreciation and warmth they could not find among their own male peers—for example, dating provided a "redirection of a sort of frustrated affection, putting it bluntly." Other men used women unconsciously as a means to reestablish their self-confidence.

I had a lot of self-confidence when I came here but it was destroyed in freshman year. It left me. My self-confidence came back to me through my relationships with women, and now it's coming back to me in my relationships with my academic . . . discipline. . . . Maybe you could say women served as a vehicle.

Much risk is involved in learning to resolve one's ambivalences, to love, to recover from being "shot down," especially for the man whose interpersonal allocentric development is less mature. To be able to love requires a person to be mature, just as to love another makes a person more mature. To risk loving is to risk discovering parts of oneself not yet accepted and integrated into one's self-concept. Two seniors frankly discussed how they closed themselves to their girls:

As the relationships got a little more serious, I think the feeling of getting hurt has made me feel more repressive of my emotions. . . . A primary concern of mine is to avoid getting into situations where I can be hurt . . . there are certain features of me that I just don't like at all.

I used to have some deceptive ideas about being a very tender and interested person. I began to see actually how defensive I am in lots of ways when I think I'm being got to or when I think emotion is expected of me. And [I see] how easily those tendencies are aroused [and I] close up myself.

Other men refuse to risk developing too stable an emotional relationship with a woman by retreating, like the following freshman, into work and the greater security of his male friendships:

I mean I don't have any means of expressing any sexual desire . . . so this may explain some sort of aggressiveness in work . . . Since there are just men everywhere . . . I was open to homosexuality . . . perhaps forming more stable relationships with men.

Others confine their heterosexual relations to casual contacts.

As far as the girl I broke with freshman year, I'm actually less responsive to girls. I let myself get involved a lot less. I don't enter relationships with romantic possibilities the way

I did before. It's sort of something that's going to entertain
me for a while and then I go on to something else. I suppose
I haven't given many people a chance.

The last principal immaturing effect that a close female friendship can provoke is to accentuate a man's conflict about his own autonomy and independence. Some men fear the dependency and loss of
control that such friendships induce. A senior unable to say "no" to
his girl's sexual demands of him, said

> This is probably what makes me so defensive with girls. I
> became completely dependent on her and I absolutely swore
> that I would never do that again.

Most of the seniors did risk closer relations with women, even
when the first love turned out not to be the last, to become more mature, particularly in their awareness of themselves.

> When she shot me down, it just completely shattered my
> image of myself. I had to start evaluating what could be
> wrong with me. I was perfectly satisfied with the way I was
> and I could see no reason why another person shouldn't
> love me as I love me, so I started to investigate what was
> the situation within myself. I became much more critical
> of myself.

The men became aware not only of their shortcomings but
also of their capability of loving like men. This awareness pulled them
even further out of their egocentricism and resulted in the formation
of an allocentric image of themselves as attractive, loving, and lovable
persons whom others wanted to be near and on whom others wanted
to depend.

> It has made me aware, as this girl has said, "You are lova-
> ble because you can love." It has made me aware of having
> the ability of being able to love. It's made me aware of be-
> ing able to work and play and philosophize with the same
> person, and develop a very sound pattern of living with
> other people.

To know that one is capable of loving and of being loved produces inner confidence and certainty. This is a crucial psychological event to contemporary students whose intellectualism and "cool" make more difficult the assimilation and integration into their self-concepts of their sexual and tender as well as assertive passions.

> The girls have been very accepting of me, which has made me more accepting of myself.

> I have more confidence in my masculinity than I did. . . . I don't feel quite the necessity to make myself appear masculine now.

> I feel that I'm more rounded, a fuller person maybe, and I have achieved in this area so that I don't feel as if I were a failure.

The maturing of their self-concepts tends to foreshadow, though of course it partly is the result of, actual changes in their relationships with women. Most of the men are only just beginning to develop the capacity to love and be devoted to another and will not form more stable enduring relationships for several years. The senior still asks, "Am I in love?" which, of course, nobody who is in love need ask.

The men begin to form more integrative relations with women. When they first felt the security of acceptance by their roommates and male friends, they felt they were expressing all of themselves. But in their deepening relations with women they discover more of themselves. The freeing of their impulse life described in Chapter Five is one consequence of such relationships.

> It's made me a lot more willing to do things more or less impulsively because they're for her than I would have otherwise. I think it's sort of freed my inhibitions about conversations, sex, and this kind of thing.

> I've become more at ease with people. I think when a person realizes there is something within him which other people like, admire, enjoy, he becomes more secure in himself and is able to let even more people enjoy and like and admire whatever is in him which is good. And it also made me more aware of what there is in other people. And I think I enjoy, like, and admire more of them. . . .

"I think I enjoy, like, and admire" other persons more. This very powerful allocentric effect begins to take precedence over the men's own selfish needs. The men do learn it is blessed to give.

> Yeah, the ability to do little or big things for other people. The ability to give of one's self. These friendships have made me more aware of what I can give, have made me able to give it, and in so doing have made me have more to give to people. It's a spiral process.

The urgency to give and the meaning of mutuality were expressed by one senior this way:

> I feel a tremendously strong desire to have one particular person to whom I can personally give who will need and want me when she thinks of needing or wanting someone and from whom I can really, almost selfishly, take and know that she will be happy that I'm doing it because she can do the same with me. And it's been with these people that I've been probably totally unguarded and whatever is really me comes out without my trying to inhibit it.

Accompanying these profoundly moving, enriching—"humanizing" in the words of one senior—relationships comes a much more sympathetic understanding of women. The men are wise enough not to claim they understand a woman but they do become more sensitive to how a woman thinks,

> I'm learning a little about how a female mind works, call it that, if you might. I'm learning different patterns of thought. . . . It's an ability to think out loud with someone, to share things with someone in a very total and complete way, and be able to work things out together. . . .

These are major personal changes; some of the most important ones a maturing young man experiences. To be able to be so moved by another person is to be in a highly educable state. The perceptive educator should not be surprised therefore that such friendships also have manifold effects upon the maturing of the men's values and intellectual skills. In particular, the men's growing interpersonal allocentrism seems to also increase their value and intellectual allocentricism. They become more aware of their values, valuing others and loving relationships more highly; they report a widening of their intellectual interests and a growing sensitivity to how others, particularly women, approach issues and problems.

INTELLECTUAL AND ACADEMIC DETERMINANTS

The two most powerful determinants producing change in the undergraduates and alumni samples were their roommates and the intellectual atmosphere and traditions of the college. It is no accident that these two are so powerful, for not only are their effects similar but each reciprocally reinforces the power of the other at Haverford College—though not necessarily at other colleges. Each increases the educability or openness of the student to a wider range of ideas and to his own impulse life. As a committee of the Amherst faculty has recognized (1965), the quality of the students' interpersonal relationships is a primary determinant of the effectiveness of the faculty. The assertion should be pushed further. The quality of the intellectual life of a college also affects the type of personal relationships that students establish.

The intellectual impact of a college is shaped by many factors not exclusively academic. Roommates and friends with whom one discusses intellectual topics and the type of student receptive to such intellectual conversations inevitably create an aura that defines for the entering freshmen what is and is not important. If the students discuss Dostoyevsky's view of religion rather than the pennant standings, or listen to Beethoven's sonatas rather than the Monkees, the freshmen get the message.

Intellectual atmosphere and expectations. Since the effects of the intellectual atmosphere and the faculty academic expectations were so similar, students found them difficult to disentangle. They will be discussed together. The principal maturing effects for both the freshmen and seniors were to increase their awareness of themselves (Sym–SC), the stabilization of their achievement needs (S–V), the expansion of their intellectual interests and relationships (I–IS), and the formation of a more stable and consistent image of themselves (S, I–SC). The undergraduates were quite conflicted about the effects of the intellectual atmosphere. The freshmen suffered a major loss in their self-confidence (Unstable SC). The seniors, apparently, felt the immaturing effects of the academic pressures more widely. The intellectual atmosphere evoked the highest ratio of immaturing to maturing statements (42 per cent) of any determinant for them. For the freshmen, only the determinant of roommates produced a higher percentage of immaturing effects (51 per cent). For the seniors, the principal immaturing effects of the intellectual demands of the college were, paradoxically, the reduction in the quality of their intellectual work (Lack autonomy IS), decreased value of the intellectual life (Lack autonomy V), and inability to integrate their intellectual processes with their emotional and social needs (Nonintegration V, SC).

The conflict of the freshmen about the academic demands of the college had a different implication for the maturing of the men than did the conflict of the seniors, which we discuss later. Since the maturing effects of the intellectual life of the college grow up like the phoenix out of the ashes of the destroyed self-confidence of the budding freshman intellectual, we examine the nature of his first major trauma before describing the maturing effects of the intellectual life of the college.

Of the high faculty expectations, one freshman said, "comparing myself with what I should be doing, I feel very inadequate . . . sent me into despair other times."

The feelings of inadequacy and despair of many freshmen result, of course, from suddenly competing with a more select group of peers. A high school valedictorian must, as a freshman, adapt himself to the possibility of being mediocre or even of failing a course for the first time in his life. The despair of contemporary students may become even more accentuated when, as Chapter Three described, their *raison d'etre* had become increasingly focused on their intellectual prowess, frequently to the meaningful exclusion of other sources of self-regard. The threat to their identities as "intellectuals," not absorbed by secondary defensive positions of self-esteem, thereby becomes magnified. Rather than blame and resist the faculty, who emerge from the interviews like white knights, the undergraduates respond by maturing dramatically, though not without considerable conflict for some or attempts to change the "grading system" by others.

The men soon become aware that their intellectual motivation is more shallow than they thought, their reading and study skills abysmally inadequate, and their other needs more central to their development. They become more aware of themselves and their relation to other persons. A freshman said, "Well, it's made me more aware of what I am. I certainly have gotten broken down." A senior said,

". . . made me aware there are a lot of people that have a lot more ability than I as well as a lot more drive and more achievement."

Another effect is to force the men to question, in the words of a freshman, "Why you're learning." The answer for many is a marked deepening and stabilizing of their intellectual values. They identify with the college's intellectual tradition and begin to enjoy "learning for the sake of learning rather than learning for the sake of getting grades." In the words of one freshman,

> I think it's increased very much my appreciation of an education. . . . I was struck from the first . . . with the interest for education's sake.

Their interest in intellectual activity for its own sake increasingly stabilized and, as the alumni reported, was one of the more enduring effects of becoming liberally educated. Interestingly, the principal effect of the college's intellectual atmosphere for the alumni was not the development of their intellectual skills (which the previous chapters have described) but the maturing of their identity as a person motivated to excel intellectually.

But paradoxically, as the men developed a more solidified and genuine commitment to intellectual work, such work became less singularly valued by becoming integrated with other motives and interests. As Chapter Five described, their interests became more differentiated and complex; their aesthetic interests integrated some of their emotional needs; their social lives became more important.

> You don't have a lot of free time for yourself . . . and oh, because of this, I guess, this partly explains my frustration in relationships. . . . These external forces make one suppress any internal wishes or desires or impulses. . . . They perhaps made me take my course work a little less seriously; in other words, sort of pushed things into perspective and I realize that perhaps it's not as important as I used to make it out to be.

A principal adaptive way to meet the demands of the college is to identify with the intellectual values of the faculty. When such an identification is congenial to one's talents and temperament, a more certain and integrated identity emerges, as it did for many seniors.

The intellectual atmosphere . . . has [made] me satisfied
with the way I am, insofar as I am an intellectual person,
and self-confident.

I felt more at home right from the beginning in an intellectual sort of atmosphere. . . . It's just a more comfortable
situation; it allowed me to integrate myself to it.

But when the academic demands are excessive or not congenial, conflict and immature reactions may develop. It is a cardinal
assumption of the theory of maturing that excessive development in
one sector of the personality eventually creates internal resistance, frequently unconsciously, to further development in that sector until other
sectors have matured similarly. About 20 per cent of a class find they
are not mature enough to meet the intellectual demands of the college
and leave for a period of time before returning. Of the remaining, if
the samples are representative, 25 per cent are in conflict about the
intellectual life of the college. Three seniors illustrate in their terms
the theoretical assumption that maturing proceeds organismically.

Well, I've survived. I think the emphasis on intellectual attainment is a very good one, but I think the college, to keep
you from having the feeling of breaking apart, which I often
had, that my head's going to explode, I think you need
some kind of safety valve. And that hasn't been found at all,
so it leads to periods of depression.

I think my own intellectual facilities have become greater
with restriction upon emotional outlets. . . . As I fit into
this sort of environment and become more intellectually
motivated myself, I think our relationships are much less
spontaneous. . . . I feel less taken up in the cares of other
people, their particular opinions.

Well, as a result of being so deeply involved, in purely
intellectual abstract concerns, the nonintellectual personal
emotional needs that I have have been accentuated, I suppose, and when I feel a need for that kind of personal emotional involvement, it's a good deal stronger than it would
have been if I simply had been floating along, not being
terribly wrapped up in impersonal mental problems.

Omnipresent and even unobtainable intellectual expectations
stretch the men further out of shape than they were as entering fresh-

men. They feel that academic demands intrude on their increasingly more important intimate personal lives. Increasingly, some unconsciously, others consciously, withdraw energy and commitment from their formal academic courses, but *not* from the value of their intellectual work or from those particular courses that most resonate with them at the time. They begin to grow in their personal relations with men and women, which come to be their major preoccupation, as we have seen, in college. Little time and energy are left for spontaneous and creative activities like hobbies, writing, or musical composition, unless they be indulged in at the expense of achieving at the intellectual level they value.

To resolve the guilt induced by the discrepancy between the level of achievement they value and the level they can realistically obtain, given their other needs, a number of seniors, including some of the college's more prestigious students, devalue the intellectual life (temporarily, according to the alumni data), or decrease their academic involvement, manifested by dramatic and seemingly inexplicable changes in academic performance, for example, major drop in grade average, failure to complete projects or term papers, or reluctance to participate in honors programs.

Although the devaluation of the intellectual life of the college reduces one's guilt for not fulfilling its expectations, it may be unadaptive if the asserted autonomy of the college's values is excessive and violates the person's own talents and temperament.

> I rejected the values which I considered Haverford College to hold, mainly intellectual values, because they're not satisfying in themselves. I want other things which seem to conflict. In other words, throughout my career here, I was not able to spend day and night in the library.

The devaluation of the importance of the intellectual may lead to the blocking of intellectual development. While the redirection of energy into less developed areas of one's personality may have greater eventual maturing effects, too frequently the blocking is too extreme and uncompromising to be integrative. One senior in academic difficulty said,

> I resolved not to close the library every night. If you're going to be consistent, you can do it two ways: learn every-

thing or learn nothing and pray. I'm sure there are just as
many people doing it my way (learn nothing, but he didn't
pray) than the other way. I think people caught halfway in
between are the ones that suffer.

Counseling experience suggests that satiation and withdrawal
experiences occur most frequently with the scientists, many of whom
entered college already too stretched out of shape. The prospect of
more intense graduate work, so they believed, perhaps falsely, would
further alienate them from their undeveloped emotional and interpersonal needs.

The upperclassmen struggle to find a workable synthesis between feeling like an intellectual "hothouse tomato" and their unsatis-
fied allocentric and sexual needs. Some learn to live with nonintegrative
solutions.

Well, yeah, I realize I'm capable of becoming a grind. I
haven't been motivated to become a grind because I'm motivated in several directions to do several things. But I realize that I'm capable of doing high quality work over a long
period of time, I guess, if I don't have conflicting motivations.

Courses and faculty. It is primarily the faculty that keeps alive
the intellectual tradition and atmosphere of the college. Through their
courses they provide inspiration and discipline, example and style. The
freshmen talked of specific courses quite independently of the faculty
who taught them. The seniors and alumni talked of faculty quite independently of the specific courses they taught. We examine briefly the
types of effects of certain courses and then those of the faculty.

The freshmen agreed surprisingly well about the different effects
of a few courses, like their required English or nonrequired courses like
psychology and philosophy.[3] These courses may be so determining because they impinge most directly on the freshmen as human beings and
it is with themselves they are most preoccupied. Other courses may
have their principal maturing effects later in the maturing process.

[3] The English, psychology, and philosophy courses were selected
by 76, 44, and 22 per cent of the sample respectively. No other course
was selected by more than 15 per cent to have had influential effects
upon them.

These courses greatly expand the capacity to reflect (Sym–IS), particularly about themselves and their values (Sym–SC, V), encourage more stable ideas about themselves (S–SC) as well as more allocentric and stable intellective skills (Al, S–IS). In different ways and with different materials, these human-centered courses stimulated and challenged the freshmen to think about their own behavior. Psychology and philosophy provided means by which to objectify the process of self-exploration, challenged the students' assumptions about themselves, demonstrated the similarity of one person to the next, and provided an intellectual framework by which to order and understand their and others' feelings and needs. "It opened up a whole new understanding of human beings that I had never had or hardly thought of before I took the course."

But it was the English course that stimulated the largest range of maturing effects. Its tutorial emphasis on the men's values and closely criticized weekly papers not only made the men more reflective about themselves and their values, but taught them to reflect and think more clearly and logically, to express themselves concisely, to write efficiently and quickly. By the end of the year, these fundamental allocentric intellective skills had become stabilized.

> Before I wrote to myself and not for other people . . . but now I have a constant awareness when I write that I'm writing to give more clarity to my papers so that other people can understand them. Again, Haverford has helped me in this movement from the subjective to the objective in my way of looking at . . . different things.

Other courses have other effects. No course has a hegemony over any particular type of maturing effect. For example, their history course taught some freshmen how to assimilate and integrate a great deal of information; a French course affirmed another's belief in his own intellectual and creative powers; and a political science course markedly liberalized the ultraconservative views of another.

The seniors and alumni are very clear that the more enduring effects of the intellective life of the college are worked not through its curriculum, outside speakers, special programs, or other impersonal academic rules and procedures. As has long been known, it is the lives of the faculty that educate.

The data give the impression that there has been a dilution

in the effect of the faculty upon the maturing of the students during the past several decades. The replies of the alumni of the thirties and forties suggest they had been more strongly and enduringly influenced by a few members of the faculty than the alumni of the fifties, perhaps because in a smaller college in days when faculty were not as specialized, the communal experiences with faculty members may have been more compelling and pervasive. As a measure of the mobility of the faculty that heralds the probable decrease of faculty influence and communal identification, only five of the eighteen different faculty identified by the alumni of the fifties to have influenced their development were at the college a decade later. For the men of the sixties, no faculty member stood out as *the* exemplar of *the* Haverford professor, for no person was singled out by more than three seniors to have been influential in his development. Given the centrality of the development of their values, it perhaps is no accident that it was primarily men of the humanities faculty who were identified to have had detectable effects on the men.

The principal effects of the nominated faculty were to stimulate the men to become more aware of and consistent in their images of themselves (Sym, I–SC), to develop more logical, orderly, and integrative intellectual skills (Al, I–IS), as well as more socially centered values (Al–V). The alumni agreed with the undergraduates about the characteristics of the effective faculty that encouraged such effects.

The effective faculty are those who, out of genuine personal concern, seek out a young man to help him know himself and find his direction.

> He pointed out to me, what I hadn't realized before, that I had a great deal of potential in interpersonal relationships which I hadn't been using up to that time and which he noticed and made me aware of.

The men also value those faculty for what the men have not yet become, namely, those who are professionally competent but who do not let their intellectual competence shield them from "being very human persons." Those faculty whose own lives were highly integrative, who revealed a humanness, including their frailties, who put into action what they believed, and who had developed a perspective within which to locate their own intellectual interests, strongly and emotionally moved many of the men who were looking for models by which to make a similar integration in their own lives. Narrow commitment to one's specialty did not offer the men a satisfying solution to the conflicts induced by the intellectual demands of the college. Nor did a personal, permissive warmth or indiscriminate friendliness command the respect of men who so valued intellectual control and discipline. The seniors said:

> They strike me as being extremely successful people in organizing their lives and as members of the academic community. And to that degree they could act as a pattern for what I view as my own probable future. I regard them as men who are well trained in their fields, have a considerable amount of personal integrity and a unified way of life.

> He's one of the few faculty members that I've ever met who is not only extremely competent in his field but is also a human being. . . . He is an inspiring individual in that he combined my ideal of warmth and intellectual capacities. He certainly helped me organize my own thoughts. I'd generally classify his influence as bearing on almost every aspect of my intellectual life here at Haverford.

Faculty were also appreciated for their ability to reveal new patterns and meanings within and between intellectual fields as well as for their demands that the students learn to analyze problems from diverse or more allocentric viewpoints.

> He was able to relate practical experiences to the theoretical work and that had a very great effect on me.

> He was primarily interested in awakening the imagination of the students and trying to get them to see things in a fresh way, to approach things in a different way, so perhaps things can be seen differently than they've been seen before.

Finally, a strong social commitment of an engaging and liberal faculty member also impressed young men who saw their teachers living in action their social beliefs. The lives of such faculty contributed to the development of more allocentric values in their students.

We can summarize the effect of a faculty member very simply: a liberally educated and mature teacher has liberally educating and maturing effects.

THE QUAKER TRADITION

There is less agreement among the samples about the importance of the religious-ethical tradition of the college as a determinant
of their growth. The freshmen and alumni agreed that the academic
and social honor systems had important maturing effects. But the undergraduates disagreed with the alumni that the Quaker tradition of
the college exercised significant effects; the alumni rated it to have
been one of the five most important influences on their development.
How should we understand such inconsistencies? Several reasons combine to account for the differences. The rejection of the ethical tradition and its institutionalized form by the seniors may reflect, in part,
what Chapter Five hypothesized to be a negative identity reaction that
developed in their last semester, that is, unconscious rejection of the
college to facilitate breaking their dependency ties to it.[4] Or the disagreement may reflect the diminution of the Quaker presence on the
campus as a result of the changes in the character of the student
body and faculty described in Chapters Two and Three. Or, as some
alumni have claimed, perspective about the reasons for one's development changes when one is no longer a querulous undergraduate,
rebelling against compulsory religious forms or other symbols of virtue. To check this observation, the ratings made by the Alumni Senior sample about the importance of the college's religious-ethical tradition when they were seniors were compared with those they made
as alumni. The claim is valid. As seniors, the sample rated the Quaker
tradition to have had a *moderate* influence; but as alumni, just two to
three years later, they rated it to have had *considerable* influence; a
difference that was statistically significant ($p < .01$). Two thirds of
the Alumni Seniors changed their judgments toward the "more" influential end of the scale. This was the only determinant for which the
sample changed its judgment so markedly.

Just as it was difficult for the men to separate the effects of the
various academic determinants from those that contributed to the intellectual atmosphere of the college, so was it difficult to separate the
effects of the honor systems from the Quaker tradition of the college.

[4] This is not to suggest that the religious tradition had no effects
on the seniors. If the ranks of its indices were combined with those of its
most clearly institutionalized form, Quaker Meeting, then it ranked 13.5
for the seniors.

The community's high and explicit value on honesty, integrity, independence, and dissent were viewed as the necessary and reinforcing conditions for a psychologically meaningful honor system to survive. Interestingly, some undergraduates and alumni even assimilated the intellectual atmosphere to the college's religious-ethical tradition, as one undergraduate tried to do when he said,

> There is something specifically Haverfordian about (the intellectual atmosphere), probably a trust in the student, the whole idea of giving him a lot of freedom and independence. It's probably because of the whole Quaker idea of giving him as much freedom to work out his own values as possible.

Recognizing, then, the limitations of our arbitrary analytic scheme, which violates the subtle meaning and patterning of situational and psychological factors, let us examine briefly the effects of the Quaker tradition.

Religious-ethical tradition. Why did the alumni increasingly identify the religious tradition of the college to have had the more persisting effects upon their maturing? As the previous chapter suggested, the world tests different aspects of one's growth than a college tests. When their growth was subsequently tested by their post-college experiences, the alumni developed a different perspective about their college years. They said the most enduring and significant effects of the college had been the stabilization and integration of their identities as valuing persons who prized excellence, the self-discipline of sustained work, integrity, honesty, and a compassionate concern and respect for others. Apparently it became clearer to the alumni that this type of development was their most meaningful growth in college and they changed their assessment of the importance of different determinants. The college's religious and ethical tradition was identified to be *the* principal determinant of this development by the alumni. Other than their roommates, whose effects were felt primarily in the maturing of their personal relationships, no other determinant produced so many maturing statements by the alumni.

When describing in Chapter Six the development of the alumni's values, we were, in fact, describing primarily the principal effects of the college's Quaker tradition: the stabilization and integration of their identities and values (S, I–SC, V) around an allocentric way of life (Al–V). Rather than describe these effects further, we cite the general meaning of the college's religious tradition to several non-Quaker alumni before turning to the honor systems which institutionalized the spirit of the tradition. A Presbyterian wrote,

> Haverford instilled an enormous sense of ethical responsibility. . . . We were made to feel responsible for the welfare of our community and for individuals in it. Even the suicide of a classmate was impressed upon us as our failure to speak to his condition. . . . The enormity of Haverford's moralism forced the issue. It was either apathy or responsibility. I chose responsibility and experienced grace—a surprising bonus which nobody had talked about much.

And a Methodist wrote, in part,

> As the ethical-religious tradition reflected itself in courses, college rules, and social intercourse, it has a great effect on students' religious and ethical values. My values changed from those of a typical Protestant in the Calvinist tradition to those of an atheistic humanist. My strong beliefs are now that humans, with their impossibly weak, irrational, and paradoxical qualities, nevertheless hold the seeds of their own redemption. . . . This belief generalizes to a strong belief in civil rights, the right of people to reject parts of their cultural tradition, and a feeling that humans (that's us) must look to ourselves, not to a Christian (anthropomorphic) God for a source of strength and help.

Finally, for 23 per cent of the alumni, but for no Jews or Quakers, Fifth Day Meeting—the institutionalized form by which the Quaker philosophy was communicated to the students—was spontaneously identified to have been instrumental in developing a more religiously based orientation to life:

> Believe it or not, in one Fifth Day Meeting in one of those years I had my personal conversion experience. Haverford gave me the moment when I passed from a religious upbringing to knowing it for myself. The exposure to many ideas and personal philosophies and interpersonal relationships collided one day and I came out of it a believer. This might not have happened in a religiously protected college or in an agnostic environment.

The honor system. The Quaker insistence that a person's values must be individually and honestly forged, but shaped within the boundaries of his responsibilities to his community, was inescapably impressed upon each freshman not only in Fifth Day Meeting but also through his commitment to the honor system. The honor system provided the impetus as well as the psychological support to a seventeen-year-old to assert his individuality, even to oppose, if necessary, his parents, social group, or religion in his search for a more autonomously formed personal morality. The honor system required personal self-confrontation with and decision about three of the men's most important conflicting problems: sexual, work, and personal responsibilities to others. As a result, the freshman was immediately drawn into a communal search that dominated his personal relationships, that was reinforced academically by his English course, that was reworked at different levels of understanding and intellectualization in other courses like psychology and philosophy. Without being doctrinaire or authoritarian, the honor system provided the common experience of belonging to a community self-consciously united by similar goals and faced by common problems.

The maturing effects of the academic and the social honor systems differed but neither was perceived to have had any appreciable immaturing effects. The academic honor system stabilized the men's conception of themselves and their values (S–SC, V) and developed more allocentric values and personal relationships with other men (Al–V, MR). The social honor system provoked different effects for the freshmen than for the seniors who were more ambivalent about it. It encouraged the freshmen to become more aware of their values (Sym–V) and develop a more independent and integrated value system (Au, I–V). It stimulated the seniors to become more aware of themselves and others (Sym–SC, MR, FR) and to develop more allocentric values (Al–V).

Many freshmen were incredulous and even shocked their first week of college to discover that the upperclassmen meant what they said when they asserted that no one cheated at Haverford. Over 30 per cent of the sample spontaneously reported that cheating was rampant in their high schools, that their own cheating sapped their interest in intellectual work, and that they had become cynical and distrustful about other people. Seven months later, the freshmen reported they didn't cheat and, because the honor system was so much a part of themselves, didn't even think about cheating.

> Throughout high school I cheated like hell. . . . The fascinating thing I find here is I didn't even think about cheating on a take-home exam.

> In high school just about everybody I knew cheated and it always bothered me a lot and it often made me feel as though maybe it wasn't worth trying to learn the stuff. . . . And here there's no cheating and everybody's in here to learn and not even have any thought of cheating as far as I know. It's just something you never even think about and it takes off a whole lot of pressure and it makes it now fun to study, almost interesting; takes the grind out of work. I think it's a really wonderful thing.

They felt themselves to be part of a community that values honesty and integrity, which gave them a feeling of greater freedom.

> It forced me to realize what I do, well only ultimately, what I do, I do not only for and against myself, which is half of it; the other half is for or against the community.

Some developed a "much greater faith" and trust in others because they felt themselves to be trusted.

> I feel less pessimism, more faith in humanity. . . . Here it's become part of our lives and practice, even by those who aren't quite sure of it, and once you start practicing something it becomes part of your belief.

In contrast to the academic honor system, the behavior that trespasses the social honor system is left unspecified, so each freshman is forced to define for himself the boundaries of his acceptable social behavior with women and then worry if his definition will agree with that of his peers seated on the Council. So it is no surprise the primary effect of the social honor code is to make the freshmen more aware of their values.

> Well, again the social honor system makes the assumption that I'm mature. I like that. Plus it makes me think a little bit more about my ideas regarding women. It has also led

> to discussions among my friends . . . discussing them has
> helped me to crystallize my ideas a good bit.

The humanization, but not the dissolution, of conscience, already described in Chapter Five, may result in a break with the conventional
sexual mores of their parents and society as the men fashion a more autonomous and integrative value system.

> I see coming out the influence of my parents . . . but com-
> ing out into my own form and this has meant a great deal
> to me. Where before this was an alien influence, now I feel
> this is mine and I feel better about it. I'm much more stable
> . . . and I've been able to resolve my moral questions.

The seniors, on the other hand, pressured by more urgent sexual
desires and closer relations with women, argued more with themselves
about the social honor system, which tested them more than the academic honor system. In American society, it is good to be honest and
have integrity in one's academic and professional work; but it is not
necessarily good to refrain from sexual relationships when a woman is
in your bedroom. So the social honor system forced some young men
to deny their impulses when much of society would not deny them.
The seniors thought the social honor system was good for them as
freshmen but they found it necessary to liberalize their interpretation
of it with their growing maturity. The men were forced to become
more aware of what they and their girls wanted and what their responsibilities were to their girls and the community. For many seniors,
sexuality became incorporated into more allocentric values that emphasized responsibility to the social community.

> I think there's a great deal of emphasis on responsibility and
> respect for the women guests and also for your roommates
> and the college community. . . . I think this emphasis
> makes you think of what you're doing and how it fits. You
> say to yourself, "Well, why am I doing this?" It makes you
> look at your own motives.

The social honor system served a liberating purpose. Eventually, the men worked out for themselves a more liberal humanistic
ethical code they felt to be part of themselves and for which they themselves were responsible.

[My moral standards] are based on what I feel is a very high moral plane. But it is not the same moral plane I would have defined as a "high moral plane" when I was a freshman, [which was] more one that I could have cited by rote from my parents and my relatives and my church. Over the four-year period, [I have] changed more toward letting myself emotionally decide what is right and what is wrong. If I feel right about it, then it is right. And this is what I have come to believe and discover.

NONCOLLEGIATE EXPERIENCES

The determinants of personality change are many and the collegiate ones we have discussed are only some of those that have significant effects during young adulthood. Two noncollegiate determinants, the men's summer vacations and their relationships with their parents, were also judged by the undergraduates to have had important effects upon their development. We briefly illustrate their effects to remind ourselves again of the complexity and multiplicity of determinants of personality change.

Summer vacation.   The principal maturing effect of the freshman's prior summer vacation was the development of more self-confidence that he could exist independently of his parents (S, Au–SC) and that he could adapt to and appreciate a wider range of other types of people than he had known before (Al–MR). It was the upperclassmen for whom their summer vacations were both a psychological necessity and a test of their own development in college. Their summers expanded their understanding of themselves and their relations with a greater diversity of persons (Sym–SC, MR) with whom they were progressively more able to feel comfortable and at ease (I–MR).

An intense and absorbing intellectual life invokes needs for complementary experiences. Accumulated strains and frustrated needs require resolution and gratification. The summer permits the dissipation of emotional and intellectual fatigue as well as of the inevitable psychological resistances induced by the highly intense utilization of only part of their personalities. One man said he got a "chance to bounce back"; another said the summer's hard physical labor was his "natural therapy" during which "things sorted themselves out," enabling him to return to college "feeling as though [he had] worked a lot of cobwebs off."

Their vacations not only tested how the men had matured during the year but also provided the opportunity to grow in ways perhaps not possible for some during the academic year. Many men used their summers to discover whether they measured up to their intended vocational plans; others to explore new strengths that renewed their self-confidence.

> As a counselor of boys, I found this was very definitely a major strength of mine. . . . I felt very much more at ease, much more effective. I could do things and see good results. It made me feel I was worth something. I was meaningful. I had something to do.

The men also learned how diverse others are as well as how seemingly different people are very much like themselves.

> I think I have a greater feeling of the universality of people, that all people seem to be sensitive to the same kinds of things. There was a broad band of underlying human-ity. . . .

To feel increasingly secure and comfortable with many different people, to recover and fulfill one's needs to belong to others, was prized very highly by the men, perhaps because the contrasting academic life was of necessity so self-involving and solitary, demanding long and lonely hours of independent work. One student commented, "I was for six weeks part of a group that was traveling and working . . . I felt a sense of oneness with the group."

Parental relations. Another noncollegiate determinant of maturing is the men's relationships with their parents. Although not all of the samples agreed about its importance, it was of sufficient importance to the seniors to be mentioned. Almost all of the seniors reported their parents had many more maturing than immaturing effects upon them and, unexpectedly, described their parents as highly supportive and tolerant persons against whom they tested their ideas and values rather than as persons against whom they rebelled or whom they resented. Apparently strain occurs more in secondary school, persists into the early college years and culminates in a crisis, if one is to occur, at the time of the men's occupational decision. The effect of their parents is to develop in their sons more stable and autonomous images (S, Au–SC) of themselves as well as more autonomous values (Au–V).

To illustrate how one very mature father assisted his son to develop more autonomous values, we quote his son's résumé of his advice:

> When you have gained some maturity and thought out a value system, you stick by this and you stand up for it, whether it's inconvenient or even dangerous to do this. The only way you can really live with yourself is to believe in something and stand up for it.

As a result of their growing emotional distance and independence of their parents, the men come to appreciate and respect their parents as human beings for whom they have some responsibility.

> Now, I'm able to just enjoy being with them and to accept them for what they are and to have some respect for the people they are.

"Why did the students change in the ways they did?" The chapter suggests but does not confirm that some aspects of the college environment did have decisive effects upon the men's development. It suggests that change is mediated primarily by the quality of one's personal relationships with others and the expectations that others have of the type of person one should become—results not incongruent with those of other studies on development in college (Sutherland *et al.*, 1962). Although the results of the varied samples are consistent and, to one who knows Haverford College well, compelling, the chapter does not *confirm* either that the students matured as much as they believed or that the "causes" of the specific changes we have described were what our procedures identified. Even if our analytic model of maturing and procedures do provide a more systematic way to relate personality development to institutional determinants, the relation between maturing and environmental "causes" is far from simple. For the data are very clear. There is no univocal relation between a particular determinant and a particular maturing effect. A determinant may produce a variety of effects, and an effect, as the following chapter summarizes, can be produced by a variety of different determinants. Similar maturing effects as those reported may therefore occur in seemingly very different environments. Whether they do so occur and to what extent awaits, of course, empirical test. If similar effects can be so demonstrated, then closer analyses of the apparently dissimilar environmental determinants producing similar specific personality effects may—or may not—reveal underlying structural or genotypic similarities. To begin the task of identifying such genotypic characteristics, the next chapter collates the different determinants found to produce similar specific personality effects.

CHAPTER VIII

The Determinants
of Maturing

Little more than speculation exists about the social and environmental conditions that encourage the development of mental health, ego strength, or maturing. The failure to identify specific behaviors indexing healthy development and then to develop procedures to relate them to specific aspects of the environment has limited research. No hard data are available, for example, on the factors that promote autonomous values or integration of the self-concept. In summarizing and synthesizing the results of the preceding chapters, we now illustrate how the model of maturing and the analytic scheme it provided for coding the type of interview data we secured *could*, in principle, supply such data. Unfortunately, to illustrate the determinants of the dimensional development of a particular self-structure would be to make too fine and unreliable analysis of the data of our too small samples. Instead, we summarize only the determinants of the principal self-structures and developmental dimensions.

DEVELOPMENT OF SELF-STRUCTURES

Table 8.1 lists the most important determinants that affect the development of different self-structures. The ranked importance of each determinant for each self-structure was determined by combining the ranks of two objective indices: (1) the number of maturing effects attributed in the interviews to that determinant, and (2) the student's ratings of the importance of each determinant, made prior to their interviews. Similar alumni rankings are also listed, though they are less reliable because they are based solely on the number of scored effects each determinant had upon each self-structure.

INTELLECTUAL DEVELOPMENT

No student complained that the faculty "let him down." All felt they had been stretched intellectually and expressed, in many different ways, their awareness of the new intellectual powers they had acquired. Their growing confidence in their own hard-won intellectual achievements was not unrealistic. Most do exceedingly well in graduate and professional schools. We have discussed the determinants of such intellectual maturing and have examined the specific effects that their English and some social science and humanities courses had upon them. The data contain many suggestions that different types of courses have similar but also different effects upon personality development. In effect, the students recognized the reasons why the faculty required them to distribute their course selections among the academic departments. We have deliberately refrained from investigating curricular effects in detail, for that thorny problem is too complex to examine in a small college and really requires a different and more focused type of study.

It is not surprising that both undergraduates and alumni agreed that their peer relationships influenced their intellectual development. That the conversations and arguments were frequently centered around

TABLE 8.1
Importance of Determinants of Personality Maturing

Freshmen Rank	Freshmen Determinant	Seniors Rank	Seniors Determinant	Alumni[a] Rank	Alumni[a] Determinant
			INTELLECTUAL SKILLS		
1.5	Freshman English course; Intellectual atmosphere	1	Intellectual atmosphere	1	Intellectual atmosphere
3	Faculty academic expectations	2	Faculty academic expectations	2	Freshman English course
4	Social science courses	3	Freshman English course	3	Humanities course
5	Humanities courses	4	Specific faculty	5	Social science courses; Specific faculty; Faculty academic expectations
6.5	Roommates; Specific courses	5.5	Independent project course; Specific course		
8	Male friends	7	Natural science courses	7	Roommates
		8	Male friends		
			VALUES		
1	Intellectual atmosphere of college	1	Female friends	1	Religious-ethical tradition
3	Social honor system; Type of student; Male friends	2	Roommates	2	Academic honor system
		3	Intellectual atmosphere	3	Intellectual atmosphere
5	Academic honor system	4	Male friends	4	Specific faculty member; Social honor system
6	Roommates	5	Social honor system		
7	Freshman English course	6	Parental relations	6	Faculty academic expectations
8	Faculty academic expectations	7	Summer vacation	7	Roommates
		8	Type of student		

TABLE 8.1 (*Cont'd*)
Importance of Determinants of Personality Maturing

SELF

1	Male friends	1	Female friends	1	Specific faculty
2	Roommates	2	Male friends	2	Roommates
3	Type of student	3	Roommates	3	Academic honor system
4	Female friends	4	Summer vacation	4	Intellectual atmosphere
5	Faculty academic expectations	5	Intellectual atmosphere	5	Male friends
6	Specific course	6	Type of student	6	Religious-ethical tradition
7	Intellectual atmosphere	7	Parental relations	7	Faculty academic expectations
8	Living arrangements	8	Faculty academic expectations		

INTERPERSONAL RELATIONSHIPS

1.5	Roommates; Male friends	1	Female friends	1	Roommates
3	Female friends	2.5	Roommates; Male friends	2	Male friends
4	Type of student	4	Living arrangements	3	Female friends
5	Living arrangements	5.5	Summer vacations; Type of student	4	Type of student
6	Parental relations	7	Bryn Mawr College	5	Bryn Mawr College
7	Summer vacation	8	Social honor system	6.5	Social honor system; Athletic activities
8	Bryn Mawr College				

a The reliability of the more limited alumni data does not permit the inclusion of more than the seven, and occasionally fewer, most important determinants.

TABLE 8.1 (*Cont'd*)

Importance of Determinants of Personality Immaturing

	Freshmen		*Seniors*
Rank[b]	Determinant	Rank	Determinant
INTELLECTUAL SKILLS			
1	Type of student	1	Intellectual atmosphere of college
VALUES			
		1	Intellectual atmosphere of college
SELF			
1	Roommates	1	Female friends
2.5	Faculty academic expectations; Intellectual atmosphere of college	2	Roommates
		3	Intellectual atmosphere of college
INTERPERSONAL RELATIONS			
1	Roommates	1	Female friends
2	Female friends	2	Roommates
3	Male friends	3	Type of student
4	Type of student		

[b] Determinant included in table if 3 per cent or more of the total immaturing statements for the sample were attributed to that determinant. Too few immaturing statements were given by the alumni to the determinants to merit their inclusion.

intellectual topics reinforced the development of intellectual skills, just as such skills and intellectual interests reciprocally facilitated the initiation and stabilization of their interpersonal relationships.

As the upperclassmen got drawn into their academic majors, found their specialized studies more directly relevant to their own emerging directions, they discovered that independently testing their own creative intellectual powers was highly rewarding. Most men reported that their independent project courses helped them to confirm and stabilize their emerging vocational identities and to become more autonomous of the faculty and of the dominating academic atmosphere. Their independent work fulfilled their needs for a sharper contrast to their usual intellectual diet. Efforts to encourage a graduated series of increasingly more independent intellectual projects from the freshman year onwards could well be one effective antidote to the resistances and conflicts the academic routine induces.

VALUE DEVELOPMENT

Our results show that Jacob (1957) was right when he claimed the college powerfully effected a reformation of the consciences of its students. They became more liberal, less tied to conventional ritual and rite. The more formal religious beliefs and values of the men became transformed into a more immediate personal morality and ethical humanism under the combined impact of the college's intellectual and ethical traditions. The men were encouraged to go behind and beyond the shibboleths and emotional slogans of their parents, religions, and country to form value systems they could genuinely defend as their own. That most students did just this was the result of the ethos of the college, consistently manifested in those determinants that touched their immediate lives most personally.

The honor systems touched the students in those areas about which they were most sensitive, particularly those defining a responsible intellectual and a socially and sexually adult male. They provided the "laboratory experiences" that made the freshman English and other similar courses much more potent than they otherwise would have been. Their values were more personally worked through in the close physical associations with the type of reflective person admitted to the college.

Interestingly, the men did not report drastic changes in the content of their political and economic values. They did not become socialist miniatures of some of the faculty; certainly, they do not even approach the left-wingism of a few of the faculty. They did not break with the value tradition of their parents. They broadened and humanized it, made it their own, but did not repudiate it.

The effect of the intellectual atmosphere of the college upon the students' values was paradoxical. Its pervasiveness was inescapable except by physical withdrawal from the college, or by such a severe denial of its importance that a man risked closing himself to any subsequent educative effects of the college. The majority of the men developed a more genuine appreciation of the intellectual life. Yet, its salience in their value hierarchy receded because the men found its too great impingement on their lives led to immaturity in other increasingly more important personal areas. In the process of reconciling the intellectual demands of the college with their more allocentric needs, many students discovered William James was right: you can't be a philosopher and a ladies' man, not to speak of a saint, simultaneously. You have to define for yourself who your Number One self is to be. Many resisted identifying themselves as philosophers, perhaps because they were still not sure about how much of a ladies' man they could be. They knew they could not be saints.

If a college wishes to educate liberally the consciences and values of its students, it must have a genuine tradition and atmosphere that prizes the unfettered development of a personally wrought mature value system.

SELF-CONCEPT DEVELOPMENT

No student reported that he had not changed his conception of himself as a consequence of his college experience. The college very effectively challenged its young men to confront themselves and to begin the more arduous task of reforming sounder identities. Plunged into intimate relationships with other men to whom they were forced to adapt, goaded to a level of academic attainment they never imagined possible, and encouraged to refashion their central values in a way they had not anticipated, the men discovered much about themselves and their ability to adapt.

The process of discovering more and more about their traits, talents, and values involved reaching successively more complex equilibrium levels. One such level was approached when the college's demand that a person select an academic department in which to concentrate precipitated the vocational identity problem. For college males, the spring semester of their sophomore year is a time for decision and commitment. Some, prepared by their diverse summer experiences and greater maturity, need make no decision—the direction of their lives is already clear to them. But much of the ennui and restlessness of other sophomores is symptomatic of their inner resistance, in Erikson's words, to foreclosing prematurely their options for the future.

Another equilibrium level was reached when the upperclassman, catalyzed by his increasingly more intimate relations with young women, resolved his doubts about his masculinity and its related complex of imponderables like his attractiveness, his potency, and his capacity to love and to be loved.

Another consolidation point in the men's development occurred when they began to think of themselves as adults, when their youth and college days became their irrevocable pasts. The confirmation that such an equilibrium level had been reached is frequently witnessed by the changed quality of their relations with their parents. Other nodal points around which the men's identity becomes integrated will surely develop after they leave college and must confront themselves as responsible communal members, as creative workers, as fathers, and so on. It is not until their basic values are tested outside the shelter of the college's permissive freedom in these new roles and relationships do they appreciate how much of themselves had become organized around a few central values while in college, values reflected in the lives of one or two faculty members and in the college's ethical institutions.

Just because the college was so effective in upsetting its students' ideas about themselves, it risked provoking considerable disorganization and regressive behavior. Frustrated intimate emotional experiences with roommates and girl friends as well as conflict about or inability to meet the intellectual expectations of the college were the primary blocks to the formation of a student's concept of himself as a mature person.

INTERPERSONAL DEVELOPMENT

The data very clearly demonstrate that a small residential community powerfully influences the students' personal relationships by making accessible within a small area a large number of persons of similar interests and temperaments who are potentially open to the educable influences of their peers. The most persuasive determinant of personality change is another human being whom one respects or toward whom one must adapt. We doubt that any impersonal "teaching machine" will ever induce the range and depth of maturing effects that a fellow human being can induce in another, particularly in persons who need to grow in their emotional lives before they can fulfill their intellectual potentials.

Our data also suggest that the aggravated narcissistic potential observed in the entering freshmen was more likely a secondary effect or defensive screen protecting them from an unsympathetic and frequently alien high school peer culture. The college was quite successful in transforming the culturally induced autocentricism of the freshman into a more mature social allocentricism. How this development occurred we've already described. In one sense, the college threw up a protective wall around its young men. They worked out in a sympathetic setting an identity that they would be able to maintain autonomously and that would not defensively inhibit their fuller development as human beings upon leaving college for a world similar to the one they had left behind.

It was somewhat surprising to discover, given the importance that such personal relationships had for the maturing of the men, how infrequently the faculty and nonacademic relationships with them were rated to be important determinants of maturing in any area other than the intellectual. The emotional distance of even the younger faculty from the personal lives of their students was greater than we anticipated or than what is implied by the college's advertisements about the advantages of attending a small college. The real advantage of a small college is that it optimizes student-student and not necessarily student-faculty personal relationships. Perhaps this is as it should be in a college where the student ambivalences about the intellectual demands and the potential conflict involved in personal relationships are so great.

We have already observed that interpersonal determinants so crucial for the maturing of young men can also be decisive in producing disorganizing effects that seriously interfere with their adaptation to the demands of the college. Reduced or inhibited academic motivation or sudden academic difficulty may be symptomatic, not of "laziness" or low ability, but of unhappy personal relations. Some young men may make too precipitate decisions affecting their futures, especially if they don't understand how closely academic efficiency depends upon emotional stability, which in turn depends partly on a student's personal relationships.

DIMENSIONAL DEVELOPMENT

What factors encouraged and discouraged development on the dimensions that define maturing? Table 8.2 lists the determinants that produced the largest number of reported stabilizing, integrative, and other maturing as well as immaturing effects. The tabulated ranks may be less reliable than those reported in Table 8.1 since the students did not also rate the effect of each determinant on each dimension.

AWARENESS

The principal psychological condition that promoted reflectiveness and expanded the capacity of the men to symbolize their experience seems to have been their encounter with opposition and contrast. The college was most effective in challenging its students by ideas and values that directly confronted and contradicted what many students had known, believed, and assumed for most of their lives. Such challenges were picked up by a freshman's roommate or friend who frequently deliberately provoked by asserting seemingly scandalous ideas or by manifesting disconcerting personal traits and habits. Students and faculty who took nationally publicized stands—advocating medical aid to the Viet Cong, refusing to pay income taxes for war purposes, conscientiously objecting to war—forced other members of the community to define their own positions, not only about such issues themselves but also about the right to use the college as a platform for such ideas. The men's girl friends offered a contrast in another way, for by just being women—who, according to the men, think differently—they provoked the men to consider and reconsider what they wanted and what they wanted to do and what kind of men they were to become.

Another condition that produced reflectiveness was the college's expectation that its students would become more aware of themselves, others, and their relationships. The college's atmosphere was a truly reflective one, not limited just to the faculty's expectations that students were to go far beyond and behind just the factual mastery of

TABLE 8.2

Importance of Determinants of Developmental Dimensions of the Theory of Maturity

AWARENESS

	Freshmen		*Seniors*		*Alumni*
Rank	Determinant	Rank	Determinant	Rank	Determinant
1	Roommates	1	Female friends	1	Roommates
2	Specific course	2	Roommates	2	Freshman English course
3	Freshman English course	3	Male friends	3	Specific faculty
4	Male friends	4	Summer vacation	4	Fifth Day Meeting
5	Intellectual atmosphere of college	5	Type of student	5	Male friends
6.5	Faculty academic expectations; Female friends	6	Intellectual atmosphere	6	Intellectual atmosphere
9	Specific faculty; Living arrangements; Social honor system; Parental relations	7	Social honor system		
		8	Specific faculty		

ALLOCENTRICISM

	Freshmen		*Seniors*		*Alumni*
Rank	Determinant	Rank	Determinant	Rank	Determinant
1	Roommates	1	Female friends	1	Roommates
2	Male friends	2	Roommates	2	Type of student
3	Type of student	3	Male friends	4	Intellectual atmosphere; Religious-ethical tradition; Freshman English course
4.5	Living arrangements; Freshman English course	4	Type of student		
		5.5	Living arrangements; Summer vacation		

6 Academic honor system
7 Female friends
8.5 Parental relations; Intellectual atmosphere of college

2.5 Roommates; Male friends; Female friends; Type of student
5 Intellectual atmosphere of college
6 Specific course
7.5 Social science courses; Specific faculty member

STABILITY

1 Intellectual atmosphere of college
2 Male friends
3 Female friends
4.5 Academic honor system; Faculty academic expectations
6 Type of student

7.5 Specific faculty member; Intellectual atmosphere of college

INTEGRATION

1 Female friends
2 Male friends
3 Roommates
4 Specific faculty member
5 Intellectual atmosphere of college
6 Type of student
7 Specific course
8 Summer vacation

STABILITY

1 Female friends
2 Intellectual atmosphere of college
3 Male friends
4 Roommates
5 Faculty academic expectations
6.5 Summer vacation; Type of student

6.5 Specific faculty; Social honor system

1 Roommates
2 Intellectual atmosphere
3 Religious-ethical tradition
4 Specific faculty member
5 Academic honor system
6 Social honor system
7 Faculty academic expectations

1.5 Roommate; Intellectual atmosphere
3 Specific faculty
4 Faculty academic expectations
5 Religious-ethical tradition
6.5 Academic honor system

TABLE 8.2 (*Cont'd*)

Importance of Determinants of Developmental Dimensions of the Theory of Maturity

	Freshmen		*Seniors*		*Alumni*
Rank	Determinant	Rank	Determinant	Rank	Determinant
8.5	Freshman English course; Specific course; Summer vacation; Roommates	8	Independent project		

AUTONOMY

	Freshmen		*Seniors*		*Alumni*
Rank	Determinant	Rank	Determinant	Rank	Determinant
1	Intellectual atmosphere of college	1.5	Female friends; Parental relations	1.5	Independent project; Academic honor system
2.5	Type of student; Social honor system	5	Independent project; Summer vacation; Intellectual atmosphere of college; Roommates; Male friends	3	Social honor system
4.5	Academic honor system; Summer vacation			4	Religious-ethical tradition
6	Parental relations	8	Social honor system	5	Intellectual atmosphere
7.5	Roommates; Religious-ethical tradition of college				

Importance of Determinants Producing Immaturing Effects on Developmental Dimensions

	Freshmen		*Seniors*
Rank[a]	Determinant	Rank	Determinant

REDUCED AWARENESS

AUTOCENTRICISM

Freshmen Rank	Freshmen Determinant	Seniors Rank	Seniors Determinant
1	Roommates	1	Roommates
		2	Type of student

REDUCED INTEGRATION

Freshmen Rank	Freshmen Determinant	Seniors Rank	Seniors Determinant
1	Roommates	1	Female friends
2	Type of student	2.5	Type of student; Intellectual atmosphere of college
		4	Roommates

INSTABILITY

Freshmen Rank	Freshmen Determinant	Seniors Rank	Seniors Determinant
1	Roommates	1	Female friends
2	Intellectual atmosphere of college	2	Roommates
3	Faculty academic expectations		

REDUCED AUTONOMY

Freshmen Rank	Freshmen Determinant	Seniors Rank	Seniors Determinant
1	Roommates	1	Intellectual atmosphere of college
2	Intellectual atmosphere of college	2	Roommates
		3	Female friends
		4	Parental relations

[a] Determinant included in Table if three percent or more of total immaturing statements made by sample attributed to that determinant.

their courses or just to the English or other specific courses whose content was peculiarly reflective. The wider atmosphere of the college was reflective as well. The social honor system, for example, was designed to compel a student to think about the quality of his social relationships. Other institutions like Fifth Day Meeting also stimulated such reflectiveness, as Chapter Two described.

Given the nonauthoritarian character of the college, its high value on honesty and plain speaking, and its receptivity to any ideas, it is understandable why no determinant was judged to have had repressive or inhibiting effects on the development of awareness.

ALLOCENTRICISM

For the undergraduates and alumni, their relations with their roommates and friends were their principal experiences that transformed their egocentricism into a greater acceptance and affection for others. Many of the freshmen and seniors spontaneously confirmed the test results reported in Chapter Three, describing themselves to have been, as entering freshmen, isolated, egocentric, overly intellectualized and defensively superior. But at college, forced to live with another whom they could not ignore without great effort, the young men began to accommodate themselves to other men, gradually becoming more acceptant and tolerant and eventually forming some close friendships, often for the first time in their lives. Also, with increased physical distance from their parents came a greater positive concern for them. The freshmen, under considerably more academic pressure than the upperclassmen, with limited access to transportation for "dates," tended to become more dependent upon each other for satisfying their needs for relaxation and play. Under such conditions of enforced intimacy, many of the young men matured rapidly in their allocentric relations with other men, reclaiming in the process a portion of what should have been for many a developmentally earlier experience. But from their close friendships at college the young men gained social experience, confidence, and security, which gradually freed them to expand their relationships to young women. By the time a student became a senior, his capacity for intimate emotional relations with his girl was both the sign of his more mature allocentric development and the spur to even greater emotional involvement and devotion.

For some, however, to live with roommates or students whose

own lives were not well integrated or were too narrowly and selfishly directed was to inhibit allocentric development. Some students retreated into an even deeper autocentricism in response to what they saw in others.

The maturing interpersonal relationships of the men also affected their intellectual development. Through the continuous intellectual discussions and arguments that characterized much of the content of such relationships in a college with the intellectual atmosphere of Haverford, the men learned how to take the perspective of other persons, to anticipate arguments, to defend their views logically, to think more realistically. Our results strongly confirm Cardinal Newman's assessment of the liberally educating strengths of the Protestant residence institutions he was holding up as an ideal for his fellow Catholic educators:

> When a multitude of young men, keen, open-hearted, sympathetic, and observant, as young men are, come together and freely mix with each other, they are sure to learn one from another, even if there be no one to teach them: the conversation of all is a series of lectures to each other, and they gain for themselves new ideas and views, fresh matter of thought, and distinct principles for judging and acting, day by day. . . . Here then is a real teaching, whatever be its standards and principles, true or false; and it at least tends towards cultivation of the intellect; it at least recognizes that knowledge is something more than a sort of passive reception of scraps and details; it is a something, and it does a something, which never will issue from the most strenuous efforts of a set of teachers, with no mutual sympathies and no intercommunion . . . and with no common principles, who are teaching or questioning a set of youths who do not know them, and do not know each other, on a large number of subjects, different in kind, and connected by no wide philosophy (1852, pp. 146–148).

Fortunately, the college provided the intellectual atmosphere for its inquiring students and an atmosphere of trust in the intellectual achievements of others that gave value to such accomplishments. The college gave to the freshmen a closely supervised and guided intellectual experience in their English course and to the seniors experiences with certain faculty that combined and mutually reinforced each other to produce more socialized intellectual growth and interests.

The increasing integration of the men's selves, values, intellectual skills, and personal relationships resulted primarily from their personal relationships, with male and female peers and their family. It is through their direct confrontation with the ideas, interests, and lives of other persons that the young men began to open and expand themselves as persons. We have noted the personality constriction, the emotional inhibition, social immaturity, and heavy intellectualization of many freshmen, particularly of those entering in the post-Sputnik years. Intense and close living with other persons in an environment valuing honest self-examination inevitably leads to the release of other, more humanizing needs and feelings. The young men found their interests widening as well as deepening, they became aware of their loneliness and need for other persons, they opened themselves to more creative aesthetic impulses, they strove to form a philosophy of life that placed the intellectual within a more personally meaningful context of values. The stereotype of the typical student as an inconsiderate and egocentric intellectual spurred this reevaluation and reintegration of the value of intellectualism within a larger Weltanschauung. For some, the stereotype had immaturing integrative effects leading them to reject the intellectual life altogether.

From the perspective of the alumni, and in noticeable contrast to that of the undergraduates, it was the college's religious-ethical tradition and its manifestation in the honor systems that compelled them to place their lives within a larger, more consistent and integrative system of meanings. The progressive integration of the students' values, temperament, and traits was also encouraged by their relation with those faculty who had formed such an integration in their own lives. Most of the students did not find specialists emotionally satisfying models of the person they would like to be; in fact, some students vigorously rejected such persons as models, even though such rejection occurred at the sacrifice of their own best talents. The effective faculty were those who lived more than just a narrowly circumscribed professional life. The students reacted similarly to the academic courses of the faculty. Narrow, technical, or highly specialized courses that didn't anchor their content or method within a larger set of relationships and implications, particularly for the humanistic and philosophical concerns of the students, tended not to have integrative effects upon the students. Specialized courses and faculty may have value for students only after the students have broadened themselves and have settled upon a direction that is integrating.

Paradoxically, perhaps, the college may have had such strong integrative effects upon its students just because of some of its excesses. Too intense saturation, as the theory of maturing predicts, invokes resistances to even further saturation and leads to attempts to develop the more neglected parts of oneself. Certainly, the prevailing intellectual atmosphere, reinforced by the intellectual type of student, induced temporary anti-intellectual reactions in many students and led to an increased valuation of more social and emotional forms of expression. One might conjecture that the increased academic pressures and the devaluation of other than intellectual types of growth reported throughout the country's colleges and universities may be, in part, the cause of the student psychological "flight" out of the colleges into the world of hippies and drugs, civil rights and protests, in order to find a way of life that speaks more honestly and directly to their emotional and social needs.

STABILITY

We have discussed at length the extent to which a student's roommates and the intellectual atmosphere of the college, manifested particularly in the expectations of the faculty, induced severe and occasionally traumatic crises in self-confidence and disorganized behavior in the freshmen. Most of the freshmen survived such a painful baptism. Why?

The college's ethos and central values, more clearly recognized by the alumni than by the undergraduates to have been important stabilizing influences, provided clear expectations and ideals of what the young men were to become. But by not prescribing the specific economic, political, religious, or social values they were to develop, the college avoided for the most part inducing resistance and rebellion to its basic ethical values. Such an ethos, highly unified and integrated, served as a very supporting external directing control, which became the model of the type of internal stabilizing control the students eventually developed. The atmosphere of the college, the academic (and social) honor system, and the close personal support of the freshman English faculty reinforced each other in a communal value pattern that provided direction and stability to the men. The freshmen were drawn into a communal, though individualized, quest for self-knowledge and integrity.

The young men lived with or found as close friends, perhaps for the first time, other men similar to them and their interests, with whom they began to work out their own meaning of the college's demands. The utopian ideals of the college's religious-ethical tradition did induce strains and disorganization. But they also provided the shared directing values that enabled the students to converge in their development toward a more communal identification. The commonly shared and accepted vision of what they were to become was, for the undergraduates, a principal stabilizing influence that, perhaps, they came to value once they were no longer under its more silent influence.

Another important stabilizing influence was the men's discovery that they were competent persons who had something of genuine value to contribute to others and that they could adapt to the intellectual demands of the college. Frequently, the discovery of their own worth emerged from a summer experience in which they found they could adapt effectively to the world "outside," from their independent project work when they found they could produce an acceptable piece of original work, or from their relations with their women friends when they confirmed they were men capable of loving another person. The resolution of inner doubt and gnawing uncertainty about their intellectual capability, in particular, frequently occurred as a result of seemingly trivial or unrelated events. One student's discovery that he could play the guitar released him from inhibitions that had paralyzed him academically; another found his ability to reach children at a summer camp gave him the confidence to return to his academic work, for which he had lost interest and hope; another's love for his girl encouraged him to settle down more full-heartedly to prepare himself for his own professional future.

Finally, being recognized and accepted by their friends and roommates for what they were reinforced and stabilized the men's emerging identities as valued human beings. To find that one can be appreciated, liked, or loved just because of what one is and not just because of what one has achieved contributed to that self-esteem necessary for subsequent maturing and productivity.

AUTONOMY

For the freshmen and alumni, the college's atmosphere, both

intellectual and religious, institutionalized in its honor systems, and supported by a skeptical and questioning student body, encouraged the development of autonomy. The college's basic values and expectations were very clear. A young man was expected to take charge of his own life and do something constructive with it. Interestingly, for both the freshmen and seniors it was the social more than the academic honor system that encouraged their independent reworking of their values and personal relationships. The college said to its freshmen: "You are to reexamine your own self, values, and personal relationships to make them more true to your experience. We trust your judgment because we believe that you will, in the process, come to terms with what your relation to the community and others should and is to be." The social honor system gave permission to the students to oppose temporarily many of the traditional values of their society, parents, and even of the Friends themselves. The consequence for many was the emergence of values, more frequently than not, very similar in content to those with which they entered college, but which were their own. Studies that show students do not change their values may not be measuring the real change that occurs. They felt themselves to be independent, more firmly anchored on their own ground, and more able to talk as an adult, even with their parents. The lives of the alumni unqualifiedly demonstrated that the college did not produce social psychopaths; instead, the college liberalized but sensitized the conscience, moral idealism, and humanism of its students.

Frequently, the test for, as well as an additional determinant of, the students' growing independence was their activity during the summer vacations. Students felt proud of themselves if they had been able to survive on their own outside the shelter of the college, whether in a job or in a strange land. They began to trust their own resources and skills and no longer feared the economic and emotional independence that was shortly to be theirs.

By the time a student became a senior, his intellectual motivation had become more intrinsically based and found its test and reinforcement in his independent research work and in his independently formed intellectual views. He was critical, evaluative, questioning and no longer as deferential to the faculty. He was beginning to look outward to the world and to sever his emotional ties to the college—very frequently by devaluing the college, as so predictably happened in Fifth Day Meeting each spring, or by rejecting even more strongly the intellectual life of the college with which some felt satiated. Table 8.2 indicates that the seniors reported that their roommates, female friends, and parents had immaturing effects upon their developing autonomy. We interpret these immaturing effects to be qualitatively different from those occurring for the freshmen. The seniors had consolidated a more maturely developed autonomy, were at a new equilibrium level so to speak, where it was now necessary to become more dependent and open to influence to be able to become even more maturely autonomous. Many of the seniors had become mature enough to allow themselves to be dependent on their girls and roommates, even their parents; they no longer flaunted their individualism and independence. Our coding scheme did not take into account the higher level of maturity at which such apparent immaturing effects occurred.

WHAT MAKES A COLLEGE LIBERALLY EDUCATING?

To create an institution that will have maturing or liberally educating effects upon its students is not simply a matter of introducing into that institution the potently maturing determinants. We are acutely conscious of the limitations of both our analyses of the students' personality development and the situational determinants influencing that development. The complexity and reciprocal interrelationships of both types of data have eluded our methods of analysis. The data might better have been presented in the form of a novel or in a very detailed elaboration of a single student's development. To rectify the deficiency of our more objective methods, we now try to induce the basic organizational structure, the binding seams, that made the men's experience as powerfully maturing as they felt it to have been but which our limited data only feebly revealed it to have been.

Our more subjective hunch is that the power of a college to mature, to educate its students liberally, depends upon three primary characteristics: (1) The educability of its students; that is, the congruence of their personality organization with the psychological demands of the college. (2) Its communal character; that is, the extent to which it elicits a pervasive identification of its students with the college and its purposes. (3) The internal coherence of its purposes; that is, the degree of clarity and consistency of its goals and expectations and of their implementation in the lives of the faculty and all the activities of the community.

EDUCABILITY OF STUDENTS

It is obvious that the material with which one works limits the types of effects one can produce. It is not so obvious, however, what educable potentials a person should have to adapt to specific colleges. The question, "Who is educable?" cannot be answered independently of the demands of the situation in which that educability is to be tested.

Different colleges make different demands upon their students. By "demands" we do not mean the social rules, the number of required courses, or the number of spelling mistakes allowable in a term paper. Nor are the ostensible demands of a college the necessarily *effective* ones to students. The measure of the true demands of an institution are the real effects it produces. Probably few educators are aware of the full range of effects their colleges produce in their students. Even fewer educators can probably identify those traits that make one person more educable than another for a particular college. The dilemma of the admissions office, in particular, is that no college clearly specifies the types of effects it wishes to produce in its students. No college has more than a vague, diffuse, and frequently ignored statement in its catalogue of its liberally educating goals, and none explicitly, systematically, and regularly assesses whether it is in effect achieving such goals. Because no college really seriously examines its entering freshmen and reexamines them when they graduate in terms of its educational goals, no college knows whether it is accomplishing its larger purposes. In reality, "educability" is defined negatively as the student's ability not to fail so many courses that he must be asked to leave college. Educability is seldom defined positively as the potential for becoming liberally educated in certain specific ways.

To illustrate the meaning of an institution's "demands" and of "educability" we must be specific. Like most other colleges, Haverford has no explicit statement of the precise types of effects it wishes to produce in its students. Yet, as Chapter Two described, contained within its traditions are clear and consistent expectations about the kind of person a Haverford student should become. The effects we have described in the previous chapters indicate that many of the students and alumni did change in the ways expected of them. The educable potentials of many were congruent with the basic psychological demands of the college.

In effect, we have sought to identify the *de facto* liberally educating goals of the college by identifying its principal effects upon its students. If we have been successful, we can now ask, "What are the characteristics of the person most educable for a college that produces such effects—that has such *de facto* goals?" Although we have not studied this question specifically, the analysis of the entering students and of how they matured permits us to make some tentative inductions about the principal demands of the college and the types of adaptive potentials its entering students should have.

The college demands that the student:

1. be emotionally stable enough to permit himself to become disorganized.

The college expects its students not to be so rigid and preformed that they resist the pain of disorganization that is a potential consequence of any challenge it makes to the students' conception of themselves, their values, and modes of thinking. Students must be mature enough to live with uncertainty. Premature commitment to or specialization of interests that is primarily defensively motivated will limit their educability in the Haverford setting.

2. be receptive to the emotional and social influences of his peers.

The student who does not have the potential for and willingness to establish and sustain close personal relations with others, who prefers to live alone or off campus, risks closing himself to the allocentric—both social and intellectual—effects of the college.

3. achieve academically with some degree of excellence.

Students must have more than high intellectual aptitude to profit from the academic program of the college. They should have, in addition, a reflective type of mind that enjoys abstract philosophical discussions as well as the ability to inhibit their emotions from persistently disrupting their intellectual processes.

4. develop his own values and the independence to defend such values.

Students who are not sensitive to ethical issues, who are asocial or who have psychopathic tendencies, who are unable to identify with communal ethical expectations, or who are rigidly tied to familial or religious patterns may feel constantly in opposition to the predominant ethos of the community. Such opposition risks creating overt conflict with the honor systems as well as resistance to faculty demands, particularly those faculty in the humanities.

5. have a basically liberal and caring attitude about others.

The authoritarian or prejudiced student who is emotionally committed to strong ideological views, particularly conservative ones, about authority, social organization and its change will find little emotional support from his fellow students and the faculty. He may react to constant questioning by over-defending his views and so risk shutting himself to any educable influences.

One might extend the meaning of "educable for Haverford" further. Our point is not to prescribe for a specific college but to suggest that the power of a college to educate its students depends upon the educability of its students for its *particular psychological demands*. The pattern of effective demands will surely vary from one college to another. There must be any number of colleges and universities for whom the above educational potentials, while perhaps nice to have, are not really necessary or crucial for a successful adaptation to their demands. Current research examining the typical presses or demands of different college environments may generate more generalizable hypotheses about the types of personality structures most educable for different types of environmental presses.

COMMUNAL CHARACTER

We asked the alumni to assess the relevance of a former president's statement about the college to the education of a contemporary student, thereby hoping they would reveal the conditions they felt were important to their own development in college. The statement is:

> Some persons have claimed the college has been effective in liberally educating its students because of its small size, its intellectual tradition, and its Quaker history and atmosphere.

Table 8.3 lists the responses of the alumni of the different generations. Because of the question about Quakerism, the responses of the Quaker alumni were eliminated in a retabulation of the data.

As Table 8.3 shows, it is imperative to the alumni for every decade since the thirties that the college remain small. Limiting our discussion just to those alumni of the fifties and sixties, numerous grad-

TABLE 8.3

Percentages of Alumni Identifying as Important
for a Liberal Education

	Alumni Seniors (1960s) %	Alumni Sample (1950s) %	Alumni Council (1930–40s) %
Small size	81ª	89	77
Intellectual tradition	88	76	73
Quaker history and atmosphere	80	65	77

	Omitting Quaker Alumni		
	Alumni Seniors (1960s) %	Alumni Sample (1950s) %	Alumni Council (1930–40s) %
Small size	83	88	79
Intellectual tradition	87	74	64
Quaker history and atmosphere	81	62	64

ª These per cents are based on too small numbers of alumni to be interpreted as anything but indicators of a general sentiment.

uates who had experienced the impersonality of the university and occupational world insisted the college should remain small.

What does "small" mean? It does not mean just the opportunity for informal contacts with the faculty (a determinant not ranked to be very influential by any sample), nor just small classes, nor just the opportunity to participate in a large number of activities. One alumnus captured the meaning other alumni sought to communicate this way:

> The intimacy of the campus . . . provides an attitude of community interest which is quite apart from "school spirit" or similar concepts and which provided me with a sense of identity then and now which some never find. This sense of community provides an important social context for many activities of later life and helps to foster a sense of purpose which might otherwise not develop.

"Small size" means to the alumni to experience being a member of a community. Preoccupation with the numerical size of a college obscures the real significance of the issue of "size," which is the experience of belongingness. To experience being a member of a community is (to paraphrase Newmann & Oliver's analysis, 1967),

1. To value being a member of a corporate group of persons.

The contemporary student needs to identify more with a total group of individuals.

Haverford's size allows one to identify with the whole institution, the people and the physical layout in a beneficial way. The atmosphere is one of independence, respect for the individual, and appreciation of the spiritual and the good in man and life. There seem to be few institutions which provide these qualities; I hope Haverford continues to do so for they are a vital part of a liberal education.

2. To know that one's college is concerned with *significant* parts of oneself, that is, not with unimportant or isolated aspects of one's life.

Not just small size *per se,* but a small, organically integrated unit of faculty, students, administration and campus. The individual must be made aware of himself and given the opportunity to flourish in a close and personal society . . . it is not the intellect itself but the "whole man" which is and should be developed and motivated.

3. To feel that one's college is concerned about and values individual differences.

It was important to have small classes and to be recognized by name and not number.

Its size enables a fair degree of latitude for the student to develop as he wishes.

4. To feel responsible for the continued vitality of the college and its activities.

The size did not allow anyone to hide. One was almost forced to accept an active role in the community.

Many [from large universities] lack a sense of involvement with each other and with the profession of medicine. Many feel no debt . . . to give to others.

5. To experience "enduring and extensive" personal relationships with other members of the college.

I have a warm feeling for each of my Haverford classmates as a result of sharing the intimate and deep Haverford experience. . . . [My graduate school] contained little of the sharing situation that Haverford had.

The personal relationship of students to one another—each student can reasonably know well all of his classmates and professors. This [provided] an atmosphere of caring about one another.

6. To agree about the important values and goals for the college and the means to reach these goals.

I think that this type of education is man's only hope of humanizing himself. The college was the first step in my finding myself . . . I can't help wishing that everyone were able to experience life such as that at Haverford.

I am bound to say that a small college, with an intense intellectual and community life, exposing young people to the concerns of the Friends, is likely to be a rewarding—perhaps most rewarding—undergraduate experience for many though clearly not all, outstanding contemporary students.

These are the communal values that define for the alumni the meaning of "smallness." Perhaps another adaptive potential should be added to those that define "educable for Haverford," namely, the capacity to identify with a communal but scholarly group. Certainly, not to be able to experience being an integral member of a corporate group is to close oneself to its influence.

INTERNAL COHERENCE OF PURPOSES

Another, and more ineffable, reason for the power of a college to educate is the clarity and coherence of its vision about the liberally educating effects it hopes to produce. A community that has an ideal or vision has, in effect, expectations of what its members are to become. Such ideals or expectations, so out of fashion nowadays, may be more silent than vocal; they may work their effects outside of awareness; they may constitute the invisible college of which we spoke in Chapter Two. And when such expectations are consistently expressed in all structures and activities of the institution, then different communal experiences may mutually reinforce one another. It is rare that a specific type of educational experience is very significant in a person's life, as our data so clearly show. Rather, it is the coherence, the consistency, the "atmosphere" of one's environment that makes its impact upon development.

One Alumni Senior, who as a senior felt strongly opposed to the Haverford community, expressed this coherence this way:

> I have been in a position to compare two small schools—Haverford and my Graduate School. The former educated me; the latter only instructed me (a comment made by many more than just this alumnus). Thus, the effectiveness does not arise only from *size*. Rather, it arises from the centralization of the school, both traditionally and physically. There is a body of shared experience between and within student generations that builds up a certain spirit. I couldn't recognize it there, any more than the fish recognizes water, but it exists. And it is this which changes one-sided instruction into participant education.

As an example of this coherence, this centralization, both students and alumni reported that a principal effect of their college experience was the development of a more integrative value system. This effect was most succinctly stated by the alumnus who described his education to have been a "process of intellectual and spiritual integration." The college's intellective effects were primarily analytic and critical and its personal and moral (spiritual) effects primarily synthetic and reconstructive. The power of the college was that it insisted its students integrate both the intellectual *and* the moral. To have emphasized only intellectual analysis and criticism risked perpetuating the narcissism of the entering freshmen. To have emphasized only moral synthesis and reconstruction risked encouraging an emotional dilettantism and moral authoritarianism. The integration of the intellectual and moral in the men's experience resulted in a meaningful identity centered in a core of values that synthesized, on the one hand, the values of excellence, integrity, and self-realization with, on the other hand, the development of a genuine concern, respect, and felt responsibility for others and their welfare. These values defined the substance of the enduring effects of their college experience and made clear its fundamentally moral character.

The intellective-moral integration was the product of the coherence of the institutional pattern of demands. It is most doubtful that such a major change would have occurred as a result, say, of just the freshman English course or just of adherence to the honor system. The English course had powerful effects on the values of the students *because* it was an integral and consistent expression of a larger coherent philosophy that was expressed in many other communal activities and customs as well as in the relationships between the older and younger members of the community. It would have been a much less powerful course if the college did not attract a type of student who enjoyed reflecting about his values and discussing them with his roommates and friends, if the college did not have an honor system that demanded students form their own social and intellectual values, if the college did not have a religious tradition and Meeting for worship that expected and encouraged such value integrations to occur. But even this combination of determinants would have been relatively powerless to induce the intellectual and spiritual integration of the men if it had not had a basic core of respected faculty whose own lives testified to and supported the implicit demands of the college. A college is indeed a procession of people. When there is an intercommunion, as Newman says, of purpose and spirit among the members of that procession, then specific education programs and forms are unconsciously and intuitively developed and implemented in ways that are integrative and consistent with the college's historic vision. When there is no such intercommunion among a significant element of the faculty and administration, then educational changes do not emerge out of consensus or produce an immediate intuitive understanding and appreciation of their effects on the invisible college. In other words, the power of any single institutional determinant to produce change is profoundly affected by the coherence of the context of other reciprocally supportive determinants demanding similar development. Communion of values among the faculty guarantees the continued coherence of the community. It is too frequently forgotten that a genuine community—not just a collectivity—is a *system* of mutually reinforcing and respecting persons, the activities of any one of whom subtly affect the power of others to affect and liberally educate their students.

What has given coherence to Haverford's community in the past? Our hunch, and one that will be rejected by many contemporary students, faculty, and some alumni, is that the college's religious-ethical tradition provided the unifying framework of expectations of what type of person a student should become. The Quaker view of man as a perfectible person led historically to demands not only for moral but also for intellectual excellence, demands that were never viewed as contradictory and inconsistent in the larger history of the college. Both moral and intellectual excellence were related expressions of the larger Quaker vision of human excellence. Because students encountered demands for integrity, honesty, simplicity, and respect by other students and faculty and from the college's institutions in *all* areas of their lives, they were forced to develop an integrative core to their lives.

Let us examine what the alumni, from their perspective, identify to have been the important traditions of the college that gave it its power. That the college should continue to maintain its traditionally high standards of academic excellence has never been an issue to anyone. No one has seriously argued the college should retreat from its high academic expectations. Given the singularly personal meaning that excellence does have to the identity of the alumni, that several alumni insisted the college should cease to exist if it abandoned its pursuit after intellectual excellence is quite understandable.

But few alumni said the college should pursue only intellectual excellence, without incorporating it into a larger view of the purposes of human beings. How to define this larger perspective was a livelier issue for the alumni. About three quarters of the alumni identified the Quaker tradition to be relevant or central to this larger conception of man's development. But in analyzing the alumni responses, we encountered some paradoxes. Although the older alumni consistently rated the college's religious and ethical traditions to have been the fourth to fifth most important determinant of their growth in college, they were less certain about its relevance to the educational experience of contemporary students. On the other hand, those alumni most similar to contemporary students (Alumni Seniors) rated the tradition not to have had as important effects on their own development as the older alumni did. Yet, these younger alumni, more explicitly and consistently than the older alumni, claimed the college's religious tradition to be central to its identity as a liberally educating institution. Several non-Quaker Alumni Seniors who, either as seniors or as alumni, had never identified the tradition to have had a *major* influence on their own development said this:

> But I think that Haverford's Quaker atmosphere is the most vital factor of those named above (size, intellectual tradition). The emphasis on the worth and responsibility of the individual—in academics, in social life, in normal dealings with fellow students—at Haverford is important to the development of an individual sense of value and ethics, and that, I think, is the heart of a liberal education.
>
> I think that for me the Quaker traditions (as reflected in the confidence the faculty and administration have in student honor) is an essential element of a liberal education. From what I understood of a liberal education, its goal is to make well-rounded responsible men.

The alumni may be saying that they value very highly the college's principles and testimonies that are historically associated with the Quaker tradition, that they find such values to be as relevant today as to their own day, but that the college is no longer as effective in implementing its tradition. If the college is to continue to be as powerfully educative in the future, it must find more meaningful ways to translate its historic vision into real maturing effects on the undergraduates. If our interpretation that it was the Quaker philosophy of man and his relationships that gave the community its coherence and "centralization" is correct, then, unless that philosophy be miraculously revitalized or replaced by as consistent a philosophy, we would be forced to predict that the college may not be as effective in the future in producing the particular pattern of liberally educative effects that apparently marked its efforts for a number of decades. The college may indeed no longer wish to produce such effects, but it has yet to define just what pattern of effects it would like to produce in the future. It can no longer rely on its historical tradition to provide the coherence necessary to educate in the same ways it has in the past.

Our attempt in Chapter Two to capture the coherence, the "special character" of the college now must be modified. We underestimated the power of the communal aspect of the college and the importance of the men's interpersonal relationships to their development. While the intellectual tradition is obviously important, we failed to illuminate its integral relation to both the communal and the religious-ethical tradition of the college. And, finally, we did not anticipate that the men's value reorganization and consolidation would emerge as prominently as it did, particularly for the alumni. The integrative effect of the college's religious-ethical tradition was underestimated.

Cardinal Newman's (1852) insight is our best summary of a liberally educating college. He said a *collegium* does not rise just out of buildings, students, faculty, and a curriculum of whatever scope or depth. For him, a collegium came into being when certain types of men, keen, open-hearted, and sympathetic, came together to mix freely with each other, to learn actively about ideas, principles, and values. Teachers were most helpful in this educative process not only when they knew both their students and each other intimately but also when they shared an "intercommunion" (not just "intercommunication") with each other. Such an intercommunion about basic values helped form a wider philosophy of life within which the faculty's educational efforts were made meaningful and reciprocally supportive and which served as an integrative model to their students.

Our data compellingly confirm Cardinal Newman's insights of over a hundred years ago. The college's historic power was, according to the undergraduates and alumni, that it attracted a type of student who was open to the basic purposes of a resident community of teachers and other students who mutually shared high expectations and values of the kind of person he should become. The college's religious-ethical and intellectual traditions defined a way of life that was very consistently, though frequently imperfectly, translated into a variety of communal structures and activities whose maturing effects were mutually reinforcing and supporting. The college community had an internal coherence which, when internalized, helped stabilize and integrate the developing identity of its members.

CHAPTER IX

A Reevaluation

The studies have drawn us very far into the interior lives of the students of one small college. Our purpose is not to understand the maturing only of the students of one particular college, but to discover how maturing occurs in any person in any environment. Though the particular has been used to illustrate the general, we have tried not to trespass across the border that separates the two when inducing generalizations about the maturing process. Just as the seniors had to grow inwardly to be ready to test their growth outwardly, so are we now ready to turn away from Haverford College to examine the implications of the results for more general and significant issues. Three questions frame this chapter. How adequate is the theory of maturing? What should be the priority goals of a liberal educator who seeks to further the maturing of his students? What implications do such goals and the conditions that lead to their attainment have for educational practice and policy, for the future of liberally educating institutions, and for the relation of a liberal education to contemporary American society?

ADEQUACY OF THE THEORY

The model of maturing should probably not have been dignified by calling it a "theory." The theory has been used more to plan, order, and systematize the maturing process and its relation to the environment and to educational goals than to test carefully delimited relationships whose basic terms have been precisely defined and unambiguously coordinated with operational procedures. We considered the latter approach to be too premature when the studies were initiated.

It is now time to assess the adequacy of the theory. The criteria that define the adequacy of a theory are its comprehensiveness, validity, generality, generativity, and utility.

COMPREHENSIVENESS

The theory of maturing is comprehensive when tested by the criterion of becoming liberally educated; but it may not be when tested by the maturing of young adults. The model does include, as Chapter One suggested, the principal goals of a liberal education cited by educators and philosophers. Although the empirical studies of the maturing person reported in Chapter Five did not uncover growth trends not includable in the model, we distrust this finding. What is and is not discovered is a function of one's methods. For example, the interviews revealed emotional qualities not codable by the categories we used to define maturing. Playfulness, emotional expressiveness, enthusiasm, excitement, liveliness, gaiety, and humor are signs of freed energy that should also, perhaps, define maturing. Our hunch is the model may not adequately comprehend energic and motivational changes. Whether to add an energic dimension to the model or to consider the freeing of energy to be a consequence of maturing waits upon more precise specification of the basic model itself.[1] To

[1] A factor analytic study of the data supporting the theory of

make the theory more comprehensive and its hypotheses more precise, it may also be necessary to expand the types of interpersonal relationships whose dimensional maturity is being assessed. For example, the rate of maturing varied for the men's male and female relationships. Similarly, the men became more autonomous in their relationships with their parents than with their peers.

VALIDITY

The validity of the theory was generally not refuted by the results. This conclusion is phrased obliquely for several reasons. The validity of a theory depends upon the precision with which its hypotheses are specified and the reliability of the measures designed to test them. Vague hypotheses tested, in part, by diffuse methods, like interviews, may be more readily verified just because of their imprecision. The validity of our developmental hypotheses was also affected by the educability of the samples, as Chapter Three argued, by the power of the college to evoke a wide range of predicted maturing effects, as described in Chapters Two and Five, and by the stage of the adaptive sequence being investigated, if there is an orderly sequence, as Chapter Six hypothesized. Although the formal tests of the theory reported in Chapter Five generally confirmed its expectations, informal indices about the theory's validity were more persuasive. The theory adequately encompassed and ordered most of the data. Although the students did not know the theory, they frequently used the "words" of the theory to describe their own change. They said they became more aware of themselves and others, autonomous of their parents and of the opinions of others, efficient, rational and logical intellectually, consistent and integrated in their values, and so on. The theory did not violate the way the students described their own development. Furthermore, some hypotheses have been confirmed by studies of students in other colleges. Vassar women became more stable and autonomous in their ego identities and "freed" in their personal relationships; they developed deeper and more complex interests and humanized values (N. Sanford, 1966). Sarah Lawrence women be-

---

maturing tentatively identified one dimension to be the readiness with which impulses and emotions were assimilated into the self (Heath, 1965). The factor accounted for too little variance in those data to warrant including it as a dimension defining maturing in this book.

came more aware of themselves and others, more stable and confident; they developed new interests and more articulate ways of communicating to others (Murphy & Raushenbush, 1960). Other studies of student growth identify greater autonomy, increased integration and stability (Chickering, undated, 1965; Lehman & Dressel, 1962), increased responsibility and cooperativeness (Carter, 1949), and so on.

GENERALITY

The theory of maturing is based on the very powerful assumption that there are universal genotypic developmental dimensions that define the maturing of any person regardless of his age, sex, social class, and cultural or religious values. It is this assumption that justified our intensive analysis of a highly selected group of young men. But such a belief about the generality of the results must be tested. Evidence is accumulating that the theory holds for a variety of different samples. The theory has been translated into questionnaire items to assess the maturity of five- to eight-year-olds. Teachers have found the measures useful and appropriate. The theory also predicted reactions of mature and immature five-year-old boys to frustration (Lowry, 1967). Studies of the development of other college students, primarily women, also confirm that they mature similarly, at least in those areas of the theory tested by the studies (Murphy & Raushenbush, 1960; N. Sanford, 1956, 1966). The applicability of the theory for describing personality development between the ages of twenty-two and thirty-two is being investigated by replicating the initial studies that validated the theory on the same men a decade later. The generality of the theory is also being tested in the principal cultural-religious areas of the world. Exact replications of the original studies of American Protestant and Jewish young men have been completed with comparable Italian Catholic and Turkish Moslem men. The results so confirm the basic hypotheses that tests of the theory's generality in Confucian, Buddhist, and Hindu cultures are now theoretically more defensible.

GENERATIVITY

Another criterion of a theory's adequacy is its power to generate new methods and questions. As a model of maturing, it has facilitated the development of a variety of new measures. For example, the Perceived Self Questionnaire was developed to measure the dimensional maturing of each self-structure. The pattern of its correlates with many other measures of maturing has been more consistently replicated in a variety of samples than that of any other psychological test used in the studies, including the MMPI and Rorschach.

The studies challenged the theory with several new questions. Since no independent data are available by which to answer them, we but briefly mention them. Is there an orderly sequence to the adaptive process during which growth is differential for each dimension? Is maturing on a dimension contingent upon the prior development of other dimensions? For example, a problem to which one must adapt requires symbolization of its components in order to identify the sources of difficulty. Such heightened awareness facilitates the search for alternative reality-oriented or allocentric means that when integrated appropriately lead to their stabilization. Progressive stabilization in turn leads to the eventual automatization of such adaptive means from disruption. Chapter Six illustrated how such a sequential model of the problem-solving process ordered the growth trends of the freshmen, seniors, and alumni. Development cannot, of course, be so simply ordered. Growth occurs organismically but the emphasis varies at different points in the sequence. Also, problems differ in their complexity and in the temporal duration required for their solution. A person may struggle for forty years to adapt to a mother-in-law. The person is at any one time solving a variety of different problems. But if such an adaptive sequence does describe the general pattern of growth of a student, then it has some important implications. Testing the theory of maturing requires that studies be made at different points in the adaptive sequence. Another implication is that different educational practices and goals are relevant at different stages in the process of becoming liberally educated. For example, a college must create an adaptive problem; it must "shock" its students. Then it must have means to help its students learn how to reflect about their new problem. It should then educate them how to discover and construct more appropriate solutions. The unknown strength of Haverford College was that it induced marked instability and then—by means of its honor system, English and other reflectively value-oriented courses, religious tradition, and form of communal worship—educated its freshmen to use reflection in a socialized way to understand themselves and to integrate their values.

The studies also suggest that maturing is a much more complicated process than Chapter One implied. Is not the process of maturing one of reaching successively more complex and stable equilibrium levels at which a person's growth may "pause" temporarily—or forever? Development is not a progressively increasing and linear process. There are periods in one's life in which one grows more rapidly and deeply than in others. The assessment of the "maturity" of development on a dimension depends upon the stage in the adaptive sequence or the level of equilibrium at which it is observed. For example, the entering freshmen seem to have been more "autonomous" and emotionally self-sufficient in their personal relationships than they were seven months later. But within the context of their maturing generally, the apparent "regression" in autonomy was necessary to become more autonomous. Similarly, the apparent "integration" of the entering freshmen's talents, values, and interests may have been a less mature form of integration than the "disintegration" the same men experienced later in the year. To continue their development the men had to form an even more mature integration that assimilated their emotional and social needs into their images of themselves as cool professionals. Their "disintegration" was more "mature" than their earlier integration. Sanford has noted that the entering Vassar woman was stable but immature and the Vassar senior more mature but also more unstable (1956). Such observations suggest that comparing isolated differences in test scores between freshmen and seniors is not an adequate test of a theory of maturing. The meaning of the differences is a function of the freshmen's and seniors' maturity. For this reason, we do not know how to interpret those findings that indicate seniors are more disorganized and "neurotic" than freshmen. We would want to examine the entire context of the results before accepting such an interpretation.

Clearly, another question the studies provoke is the meaning of disorganization. Disorganization is indispensable to maturing. Not infrequently, the analysis of the men's Rorschachs included comments like these:

May have to allow himself to become more disorganized and upset in order to sense how strongly he needs other people and thereby learn how to love.

Looks as if the stability in the self-report tests is defensive and that he has not opened himself to the maturing forces

within him . . . he has yet to confront the real strength of
his impulses and emotions and allow himself to become unstable and disorganized from which state to develop more
fully.

A person who fears and resists disorganization is no longer educable
or "maturable." He remains stuck at the stable level of development
he has achieved or, to avoid the pain of anticipated inner tumult and
disintegration, regresses to simpler adaptive solutions.

The question is, "When is becoming disorganized maturing and
when is it immaturing?" How does a psychologist distinguish between
the seemingly chaotic and disorganized person who is maturing and
one who is regressing? How does an educator distinguish between the
apparent personal chaos and academic disorganization of the student
who is becoming educated and of the one who is not? "Disorganization" has different meanings. It can mean becoming more unstable,
disintegrated, autocentric, unable to symbolize, or less autonomous in
one or more of the different structures of the self. But our organismic
assumption implies that as disorganization becomes more severe and
persistent it involves increasingly more dimensions and self-structures.
Such an assumption provides some guidelines by which to define *maturing* disorganization.

1. The more mature the person, the greater is the likelihood that the
   disorganization he experiences will have maturing effects.
2. The disorganization is selective. It involves only a limited sector
   of a person's personality. To become disorganized in academic work
   and personal relationships may be less maturing than to become
   disorganized only in one's academic work.
3. Growth continues to occur in other sectors of the personality.
   Growth in interpersonal relations, for example, may require the
   abandonment of inhibitions that formerly maintained academic
   motivation. Although a person's academic work may be disrupted,
   he may be growing in his personal relations.
4. The disorganization does not persist and the temporary adjustment
   made to it does not become stabilized. Probably one of the more
   practicable tests of how maturing is a person's disorganization is
   its duration and the type of adjustment that has been made to it.
5. The disorganization is reversible. Disorganization may be under the
   control of the person or the immediate demands of the environment. That is, a person can adaptively regress and control its extent

and reversibility. Such control is a function of his maturity (Heath, 1965). It is also a characteristic of the creative process (Kris, 1952; Pine & Holt, 1960). Or if the disorganization had been primarily induced by the adjustmental demands of the environment, it should be reversed if the demands are altered or the person enters another environment that requires a different adjustment.

6. The affect and energy of the person remain freed. He continues to be interested and enthusiastic about other activities. A person does not exhaust his energy while searching for new ways to resolve the disorganization. He may even seek out experiences like "turning on" with LSD that are temporarily disorganizing to test himself and to be spurred to form other types of adaptation.[2]

UTILITY

The theory of maturing has been useful in organizing a variety of research programs, developing new methods of personality assessment, and collating varied information about the developmental process. This book is a measure of its utility.

In conclusion, the theory of maturing has been a useful model that has comprehended the goals of liberal educators. It may validly describe the maturing process of any human being. The new methods and ideas it has generated, as well as its generality, must be explored further.

GOALS OF A LIBERAL EDUCATION

A liberal education—any education as Dewey would also say— is the process of promoting growth and health, maturity and adaptability. Such a noble but hopelessly unrealistic and vague ideal does not get us very far. The YMCA also promotes growth and health; so do the Boy Scouts and some families. We must be more precise. People mature in specific ways. We could say a liberal education should stabilize, integrate, symbolize, and make more allocentric and autonomous

[2] Erikson also identifies similar characteristics when he distinguishes between "neurotic" and "normative crises." Normative crises "are relatively more reversible . . . and are characterized by an abundance of available energy which . . . supports new and expanded ego functions in the searching and playful engagement of new opportunities and associations" (1959, p. 116).

a person's concept of himself, his cognitive-intellectual skills, his values, and his interpersonal relationships. But even this more detailed statement of goals is unrealistic. No institution can be expected to develop any person—let alone hundreds—twenty or so different ways. Now, we don't want to abandon the ideal of promoting maturity for it is the context of the model of maturing that is the criterion by which the specific effects of a liberal education can be judged to be maturing or not. But we must establish some realistic priorities that distinguish the efforts of a college from those of the Experiment in International Living and Episcopal Church.

We do not believe there is *a* definition of the goals of a liberal education to which all educators would agree. Some educator would want to add just one more goal to any list of priorities. But there may be agreement about the more important maturing effects a liberal education should produce.

How shall such priorities be established? Several considerations are relevant. First, the priorities should reflect the core goal of a liberal education which is to further the growth of an individual. A person should be educated to be educable, that is, more adaptable. The rapidity of change in contemporary society just demands that man be taught how to adapt as maturely as possible. This shifts the emphasis in the adaptive sequence we have outlined from stability and autonomy to symbolization, allocentricism, and integration. Second, the priorities should be congruent with the growth potentials most characteristic of the young adult period. Young adulthood traditionally has been considered the critical period when a person was most receptive to the maturing effects of a liberal education. How can the specific potentials for growth that define this period be identified? We would argue that the principal maturing changes the studies discovered define substantively the types of growth for which young adults are psychologically most ready. Not all the identified effects, however, necessarily define the goals of a liberal education. Third, the priorities must, of course, accord with the means or resources available for their attainment. A college does not have the resources of a finishing school to shape debutantes or of a mental hospital to cure patients. A college has the resources to educate students. Its basic concern is intellectual development; its basic value is truth; its basic mode is cognition. And finally, the priorities should approximate the principal maturing effects that were empirically discovered to occur in a powerfully liberally educating environment.

What priorities should define all liberally educating institutions? We propose they should develop more symbolized, allocentric, and integrative intellectual skills and values. Why? Why do we not accept as a goal the stabilization of a student's self-concept and values, which were the two most important maturing effects for the alumni? Why do we not accept Socrates' advice, "Know thyself," which was the second most important maturing effect for the undergraduates?

We reject that a college's *primary* emphasis should be to stabilize and make more autonomous its students' self-structures. Why? For one thing, educational philosophers have not emphasized these dimensions. For another, the evidence presented in Chapter Five suggested that the process of maturing in college involved primarily symbolization, allocentricism, and integration. Furthermore, the analysis of the process of adaptation in Chapter Six suggested that autonomy was the consequence of increased stability, which itself results when a person has found an adaptive integrative solution to a problem. The process of stabilizing one's self-structures, particularly one's self-concept, values, and personal relationships, is given a strong push in college, but the process becomes more important after college, as the alumni clearly told us. The test of the integrations one has formed must be made in those situations in which they are to be applied. The college can assist its students to anticipate imaginally the tests they may encounter but it cannot usurp them. Young persons require the opportunity to live "as if" in order to learn how to adapt. They need to learn how to formulate many different possible integrations, to make realistic judgments and selections. But they also need to learn without being bound too rigidly by the consequences that inevitably come when judgments must be implemented in action. One knows who one is and what one values only when one acts "for keeps." Of course, we do not mean a college should not provide searching tests and demand responsible action. But its tests should be less binding and not close off the opportunity to test other alternatives.

We also reject that a college's *primary* emphasis should be the development of a person's self-concept and interpersonal relations. It should be clear we do not consider such goals to be less important for maturing than the development of a person's cognitive skills and values. Given all of the evidence we have presented about their centrality to the maturing process, how do we defend their exclusion as high priority goals for a liberal education? We view the development of a more accurate, allocentric, integrated, stable and autonomous self-concept not to be a practicable goal but a *test* of the power of a college to educate. Maturation of the self-concept is, we hypothesize, a consequence of having developed more symbolized, allocentric, and integrative intellectual skills and values. Another reason is that the analysis of the adaptive sequence suggested that the integration and stabilization of the self occurred in connection with and as a consequence of the development of one's values. The alumni reported their basic identity had become organized around the values they had internalized during their college experiences. The development of one's values then is a prior task. A third decisive reason for us is that a college's concern, ethic, and mode are basically intellectual. Faculty are scholars whose primary mode of understanding and communicating is cognitive. To believe that most faculty are psychologically oriented, sensitive to the inner lives of their students, motivationally, personally equipped, and effective in helping a young adult explore himself is a magnanimous but unrealistic view of many faculty. Even in a college like Haverford that sought such faculty, less than a third were identified to have had significant maturing effects on the students. Given the centrality that a person's values has to his developing concept of himself, a liberally educating institution that really has maturing effects on the values of students will also have similar effects on their self-concepts. Chapter Eight did suggest that specific faculty members, their expectations, and the intellectual atmosphere of a college do encourage the development of a student's values. Since intellectual skills can be used to help a student examine, reformulate, and synthesize his values, is it not realistic to expect such a goal to be appropriate to the competence of most faculty?

We also reject that a high priority goal of a liberally educating institution should be the development of the personal relationships of its students. Although three of the five most important maturing effects of the college experience involved the maturing of the undergraduates' personal relationships, we view such maturation not as a goal but as a singularly important condition that affects the attainment of the college's proper and most important goals. Lest we be misunderstood, we must stress again what the evidence has so clearly and consistently said. The quality of the personal relationships the students have with one another is probably the most important determinant of the largest number of enduring maturing effects that a college has. If our data are correct, a large impersonal non-residential university is probably such an educationally deprived and poverty-stricken place it should not be called liberally educating—a judgment many students are apparently making also. But the primary goal of an educational institution whose basic mode is cognition, whose ethic is truth, and whose concern is intellectual is not the development of stable love relationships. Of course, some students might disagree.

We now return to defend the high priorities we have given to the development of more symbolized, allocentric, and integrative intellectual skills and values. Surely, there is little doubt that a foremost goal of a college is the development of intellectual skills. But many educators doubt that a principal purpose of a college should be the development of values or specific ways of acting when confronted by choices. We consider such a goal to be primary for several reasons. First, we just cannot ignore the judgments of the alumni that the central enduring maturing effect of college was the development of their values. Also, the undergraduates matured more generally in their values than in their intellectual skills. Second, to become more educable is to develop those values associated with continued educability. For what purpose is it to teach a person how to learn, organize information, make judgments and think allocentrically if he is not receptive to new information nor motivated to seek wider integrations, if he forms dishonest judgments and resists further growth? Third, we believe that the most critical growth potential for young adults to realize is the formation of more mature values. Intellectual development is clearly secondary for most students, as can be seen by their disinterest in academic work when they believe it has no purpose or meaning. Interpersonal development is also crucial to young adults and, as Chapter Three described, is becoming even more so as entering freshmen are increasingly more autocentric interpersonally. But the focal issue in much of their relationships concerns their values. And as we have seen, the stabilization of one's self-concept depends upon the maturation of one's values. Finally, and more compelling, maturing of certain values is so intrinsically a part of intellectual development that the failure to develop one limits the growth of the other. Intellectual activity requires honesty, objectivity, openness to alternatives, flexibility, humility, respect for dissenting views and so on. Associated with intellectual activity is an ethic about what is appropriate intellectual activity. A person who fabricates or distorts information, consciously ignores contradictory data, plagiarizes the work of others, and interprets information to fit some purpose other than truth loses the trust and respect of others. A liberal education must educate for the ethic of truth if it is not to produce intellectual psychopaths.

Our last problem is how to order the priorities we suggest. We do not believe one list of priorities can be formed, because the primary goal of a liberally educating institution changes as its students develop. The educative emphases of the college should be different for the underclassmen than upperclassmen, if the hypothesized process of adaptation to college is valid. The highest priority goal for the freshmen should be the development of their ability to symbolize, primarily by helping them to analyze and understand their values. They should become more reflective and learn how to go beyond appearances. The freshman is peculiarly receptive to the exploration of his inner life and that of others in his first year at college. Analysis of his values is the doorway into an understanding of himself and others. Concurrent with the development of the ability to analyze reflectively, to search for hidden structure and meaning, to identify less obvious alternatives, the freshman should learn the discipline of socializing his symbolizations. Unless he learns how to order and organize his reflections to relate them logically, to communicate clearly to others, he risks not having his symbolizations available for future adaptation. He has learned only how to think with himself, not for and with others. When he does learn how to think more allocentrically, he learns to value taking the view of others, becoming more objective and critical, as well as communicating with others. The socialization of thought and of value should be and, we suggest, are mutually reinforcing.

Although the underclassman has also been spinning his own subjective theories, forming new but usually vague syntheses and relationships, creating diffuse patterns and meanings, it is not until he has learned how to symbolize accurately and think more precisely and logically that he is ready to respond to the integrative demands of the college. The primary goal now becomes the integration and more differentiated organization of the student's intellectual processes and values. His generalizations should become more disciplined, his thinking more relational and constructive, his knowledge less encapsulated.

Similarly, his values should become more consistent and ordered. He should begin to develop a philosophy of life with its own priorities. He should begin to act with greater integrity.

To summarize, a liberal education should help a person become more mature by educing those potentials that enhance his educability and adaptability. The most important adaptive potentials for a liberally educating institution to educe are, in temporal order of priority, the symbolized, the allocentric and the integrative development of a person's cognitive-intellective skills and values. The extent to which such goals can be realized is contingent on the maturing of other self-structures. The test of becoming liberally educated is the maturing of the individual, not *just* the attainment of more reflective, allocentric, or integrative intellective skills and values.

IMPLICATIONS

The work of the book is now completed. The theory of maturing has been tested. It may adequately order the developmental process. How the specific maturing effects of different environmental determinants might be studied has been illustrated. We have tried to fulfill Dewey's charge to discover "what actually takes place when education really occurs." And we have suggested the types of maturing effects that should be the principal priorities of a liberal education.

Educators believe, and our work supports their belief, that a liberal education can be a potent means of maturing. What implications can now be drawn about how to realize such potential power to further the maturing of young persons?

EDUCATIONAL PRACTICE AND POLICY

Of the many implications the findings provoke about specific educational practices, only a few will be noted. That a particular maturing effect is produced by a variety of different determinants suggests that the goals of a liberal education may be attained by different educational arrangements and practices. Furthermore, the effectiveness of an educational practice to have maturing effects depends upon how its effects are reinforced by those of other determinants. Consequently, it is unlikely there is any one pattern of educational practices that defines *the* most favorable liberally educating environment. The transposition of a specific practice, like the great books curriculum of St.

Johns or the honor system of Haverford, from one college to another does not guarantee it will produce similar effects in a different context. So rather than examine the implications of idiosyncratic educational practices, we note instead more general implications.

Given the importance that disorganization has in the educational process, a faculty should analyze most closely how it can best disorganize its entering freshmen so that the disorganization will be maturing rather than immaturing. If to become liberally educated is to develop more mature values and intellectual skills, then a college must challenge both to educe either effectively. Failure to produce such disorganization in the first weeks of college probably means the college has lost the optimal opportunity to educate its students.

To disorganize successfully is dangerous and morally irresponsible unless powerful educative supports are provided that convert that disorganization into a maturing rather than immaturing experience for most students. Our hunch is few colleges have self-consciously and judiciously examined the kinds of psychological supports they provide to help students to remain educable. Most faculties abandon the freshmen to work more closely with seniors, and so lose the opportunity to affect profoundly the development of either. By psychological support we do not mean clinical psychologists and deans, as necessary as they are to help students whose disorganization is not maturing. The most powerful support is an institutionalized vision of a way of life that is consistently manifested in the lives of both faculty and upperclassmen. The absence of valued guiding expectations as well as of direct intimate faculty support in the freshman year enhances the early internalization and stabilization of the values of the freshman's peers that may well impede the liberally educating process. If a college really wishes to educate liberally it will concentrate much of its best effort and resources in the first semester of the freshman year.

What about the acquisition of knowledge and its curricular organization? Other exploratory studies indicate the appalling complexity a more general systematic analysis of such development would entail (Raushenbush, 1964). We can only offer some illustrative suggestions. All freshmen should become personally involved in a highly reflective, rigorous, but sympathetic analysis of their own values during their first year at least. Such involvement could be reinforced by other coordinated but more substantively oriented studies that take up similar concerns from different points of view. The freshman should become personally involved in practicing different systematic and disciplined modes by which to analyze similar problems. Hopefully, students would be encouraged to integrate their self-exploration about an issue with their studies of the related factual content and analytic modes. The senior should return to similar issues to rework more integratively his basic value orientation. How he has matured in his intellectual skills and values since his first freshman paper would be the measure of his having become more liberally educated. Another implication might be that no course that is not liberally educating should be included in a curriculum; that is, the college should concern itself with developing explicitly more reflective, allocentric, and integrative thought *and* values. We would ask every educator to describe how he planned, for example, to encourage integrative thinking and the maturation of values in his courses. We would ask him to assess how well he liberally educated his students at the end of the course and then examine his students to confirm his judgment. Other implications will come readily to practicing educators.

Another implication is that if a college is to educate liberally, the character of its faculty must be congruent with the goals of a liberal education. We would select faculty who are competent scholars *and* mature persons, who have developed highly reflective, allocentric, and integrated values as well. To select for either intellectual competence or value maturity but not for both may subvert the maturing effects either may have upon students.

The power of a college to educate liberally also resides in the contextual pattern of its principal educative determinants. All pending policy decisions about a particular determinant should be explored for their potential effects on the power of other determinants to educate liberally. Ideally, administrators, deans, faculty, and students should make basic policy together. The potential maturing and immaturing consequences of every student, faculty, and administrative policy should be spoken to by the other. The president should be perceptive about the context of real strengths that defines the effective liberally educating power of the institution. His primary responsibility is to defend and promote the educative coherence of the entire community.

Finally, a liberally educating institution seriously concerned about its power to educate will develop means to assess just how liberally educated its students are becoming. The inability of faculties to agree about the goals that define their efforts results in reliance on

numerical grades, whose relevance to the goals of a liberal education
is remote at best. Students receive little relevant feedback about how
they are becoming liberally educated. They seldom know how to become more liberally educated. But a clearer conception of the primary
goals to be achieved means that methods of evaluation can be made
more relevant. If after two years, a student has not demonstrably matured on some of the dimensions in either his intellectual skills or values, though not necessarily in both, he should seek some other maturing
environment. We would not be adverse to ask a traditionally catego-
rized "A" student to leave after two years if his high quality work did
not represent noticeable improvement from when he entered or if he
showed no maturing in his values. An upperclassman should have
matured noticeably in how reflectively, allocentrically, and integratively he has learned to think *and* value. He should graduate when he
has reached the level of maturity that he and the faculty define his
potential growth to be in that setting.

THE FUTURE

One of the most influential researchers of the effects of colleges on student development has titled a recent book *Where Colleges
Fail* (N. Sanford, 1967). Other educators talk of the dying liberal
education tradition (Barzun, 1963; McGrath, 1959). The perceptive
reader may already have developed a similar concern from the studies
and changes we have reported. How may the changing character of
contemporary students and their colleges affect the power of liberally
educating institutions to have maturing effects in the future?

Chapter Eight identified three conditions that defined a particularly powerful liberally educating environment: the educability of
its students, its communal educative conditions, and the coherence of
its purposes and means. Just how educable are young adults generally?
Just how educable are contemporary young adults specifically? With
respect to the first question, a number of educators reject the assumption that a young adult is highly modifiable. One distinguished educator, who reviewed our efforts, well expressed one point of view:

> You would probably agree that alterations in character *de-
> crease* in something like a geometric ratio with age. If Freud
> is right, almost no significant changes will ordinarily occur
> after the onset of the latency period which are not causally
> determined by potentialities acquired before that time. Isn't

it important *not* to give the impression, which I think the students themselves have, that these rather sudden changes were almost exclusively produced by the present situation? Whereas, in fact, the present is a stimulus setting off the reaction. "Cause" here is like a weak electric current exploding a stick of dynamite (Kennedy, 1967).

Evidence that might be cited to support the assumption that "almost no significant changes will ordinarily occur" in college might include the increasing number of studies that seem to show that a liberal education does not have powerful effects on students. Our own results of the standard psychological tests may be similarly interpreted. The pattern of interests of the seniors as a group remained qualitatively though not quantitatively similar; the men still valued intellectual and aesthetic and devalued economic activities. Their personality profile as measured by the MMPI did not change significantly, though the profiles of individual students did change. Psychoanalysts have long claimed that a person's basic personality structure and conscience are shaped and "fixed" by late childhood. Studies of intellectual development have demonstrated that intellectual growth reaches its optimum about seventeen. A synthesis of longitudinal studies of development supported the hypothesis that the basic personality and talents of a person are stabilized very early in his life (Bloom, 1964). Despite the weight of this and other evidence that a young adult is not very modifiable, the issue is far from settled. None of the evidence is free of criticism. We have spoken of the limitations of the studies on student development that question their conclusions. The psychoanalysts have not studied in depth the growth of healthy persons; their conclusions are based on unhealthy persons who are not free to grow. Other data suggest that the age at which intellectual growth ceases has been underestimated, particularly for persons of high intelligence who continue their education (Bayley, 1955). And Bloom's conclusions are not well supported for a person's values and personality traits. But more importantly, no longitudinal study has been guided by any comprehensive model of development (Neugarten, 1966). More specifically, most of the types of liberally educating effects about which philosophers have talked have never been systematically investigated. There are few data available about the development of most of the types of maturing effects we have proposed. Researchers may not have been studying the types of changes that do occur or may not have been interpreting them within a more comprehensive context of development. The issue as we have stated it is overdrawn and too vague anyway to be meaningfully discussed psychologically. A more testable statement of the issue would be, "What are the characteristics of those persons who are modifiable and open to continued growth?"

Sanford, who has studied the development of healthy young adults, has concluded that psychologists underestimate the modifiability of a young adult (1967). Our studies support the conclusion that significant growth can continue through college and, more specifically, that there are important types of growth that occur more readily than others in young adults. We would strongly reject so extending Kennedy's assumption to suggest, as he certainly would not, that

> . . . the rate and quality of psychological and characterological development between the ages of seventeen . . . and twenty-one . . . are not so marked as to make those years particularly valuable for exploring the forms of human thought and feeling and for establishing the habit of searching for relations, conflicting and compatible, among them; in consequence, the liberal arts college has no distinctive educational function to perform (Truman, 1966, pp. xi–xii).

Our data give no support to those educators, whom Truman is paraphrasing, who wish to convert the liberal education process into a more specialized academic training on the grounds of such an argument.

Our real concern is not that a liberally educating institution cannot have powerful maturing effects. Our concern is that the types of changes now occurring in contemporary students, as well as in their colleges and society, dilute the power of a college to educate liberally just at the time young adults and their society need to grow more in the ways a liberal education has the power to educe.

Chapter Three described the increasing personality constriction, overintellectualism, narcissism, and interpersonal autocentricism of many entering freshmen. Just how educable are such students? Our hunch is they are simultaneously highly uneducable and educable. The principle that excessive development in one self-structure induces resistance to its further development until some developmental equilibrium among other self-structures occurs applies at this point. Contemporary students may be less educable, despite their high scholastic aptitudes, for the intellectual requirements of the better colleges (Heath, 1968a). Increasingly, the students are resisting the encroachment of continued academic demands upon their time and energies. But simultaneously they are in a state of heightened educability for growth in their values and interpersonal relations, as the data have illustrated only too clearly. Can not the uninhibited excesses, the anti-intellectualism, and corporate "love-ins" of the hippies also be understood as excessive reactions against their earlier "cool," intellectual vanity, and interpersonal isolation? The hippie solution, unfortunately, does not seem to make the hippie any more educable, for he remains closed to the discipline required for the development of his intellectual talents. A more integrative adaptation may be made by the student who involves himself in civil rights or other socially constructive actions. But much of his motivation is to discover and affirm convictions and values. Too frequently, his motivation is a flight from academic sterility and too exclusive attention only to intellectual development.

The contemporary freshman increasingly needs just the opposite of early academic specialization, which may stabilize too prematurely an identity that is not basically integrative. He needs a powerfully liberally educating experience that does not feed into his intellectual and interpersonal self-centeredness but does severely shock his conception of himself as a cool intellectual and as a full person. He needs a maturing experience that frees him from his "cool" so he can develop more allocentric and integrative social relationships.

The tragic paradox is that just at the time the freshman needs to become more reflective, allocentric, and integrative in his values and personal relationships, the older generation that controls liberally educating institutions is abandoning its historical commitment to liberal education as a means to promote the maturing of a student and, more specifically, to help him clarify, socialize, and integrate his purposes and values. The intensity of the reaction of the students of the New Left to their colleges, for example, suggests how strongly they feel betrayed by the erosion of the ideals of liberal education. The needs of the students are becoming less congruent with the demands of their colleges (Katz & Associates, 1968).

The second condition that characterizes a powerfully liberally educating environment is its communal or corporate character as it was described in Chapter Eight. Ironically, the better colleges are modeling themselves after the university while the better universities are reinstituting some of the educative conditions of the communal college. Because of many pressures—the need to compete for faculty, the federal government's policies about the distribution of funds, societal expectations—the college is "universitizing" its character. To illustrate how the colleges are assuming the values and expectations of the university, we cite only one type of change occurring in the better colleges. Colleges are increasingly using their limited educational resources to provide extensive research facilities and space for faculty, increasing their size in part to provide colleagues for specialized faculty, providing for auxiliary nonteaching research personnel, adding more specialized courses to a heterogeneously organized curriculum, rewarding increasingly on the basis of research publication, establishing satellite research units, and so on. A faculty member may as well go to the university, which can more persuasively act like a university. Do such changes really affect the maturing of students? Would not a college dedicated more firmly to some meaningful vision be better able to attract and hold faculty and also be more liberally educating?

A college becomes less of a community when it adds different types of members whose interests and identifications are with ways of life not resonant with the principal ideals of the community. To universitize a college is to risk tranforming it from the *collegium* of Newman into a "collversity" in which there is no longer a society of persons of common interests and values. A collversity becomes a loose federation of departments competing for better students and over-training them in their specialties. Allegiance is to, and the educational focus is on, the departmental specialty, not to the college or on the integrative goals of a liberal education. The integrative effect of a liberal education recedes as insulated specialties emerge. The development of intellectual skills supplants rather than complements the development of values. A community, to survive, must perhaps pay the price of some measure of simplicity in organization and program, of guardedness from the conforming pressures of the outside world, and of the restrictions that come from a commonly shared vision that captures the devotion of its members. Universities are not noted for any of these characteristics.

The third condition that described a powerfully liberally edu-cating institution was the coherence of its purposes and means, as Chapter Eight also illustrated. To claim a liberally educating institution develops a person's intellectual skills *and* values is dishonest unless these goals are institutionalized in very specific and harmonious ways. Some colleges are committed to values that contradict the ethic of truth, thus creating conflicting claims that reduce their power to have maturing effects on either the students' intellect or values. The goals of the college must be consistently integrated. Similarly, the means used to attain such goals must be consistent with the basic values of the institution. Students do not become more reflective about their values if they are not allowed to be confronted, for example, by dissident groups espousing challenging and obnoxious ideas.

Colleges are becoming increasingly secularized, "freed" of particularistic but organizing traditions of values. Such secularization has been abetted by many forces—the changing religious climate, the challenge of science to myths, and the cultural homogenization that accompanies a mass communication society. It was the religious tradition that supported the goal of character reformation or maturation of values, though sometimes at the expense of intellectual integrity. But in severing their historic ties to a distinctive source of values, colleges have not created any more viable and persuasive myth or vision of a way of life that integrates a person's values and serves as the organizing center of his identity. The consequence is that colleges have lost not only a sense of distinctive identity but also coherence of purpose. The college increasingly risks producing disembodied intellectuals of weak conviction, tamed passion, and insipid courage— except the students won't let this happen. When pushed too far, they will revolt.

What may be the consequences of the changes we have described? Prediction can be treacherous, as our results tell us. The types of effects a liberal education educes may be produced by different types of conditions. Our studies of one powerfully liberally educating environment identified the educability of its students, its community and coherence to be singularly important liberally educating conditions. But other, equally powerful colleges might be characterized by other conditions. We don't know. Our results, however, are in accord with psychological principles and insight. For example, Sanford has also identified an institution's coherence to be a central liberally educating condition (1967). Our analysis, in fact, our use of the same word, "coherence," was made independently of his own conclusion. Given, then, the qualification about the generality and applicability of our own findings, what do we predict? We predict that a college that passively succumbs to the changes we have described —that is, one that does not adapt to the changed educability of its students, abandons its communal attributes, and loses its coherence—will lose much of its power to educate liberally in the future. The range of its maturing effects will constrict and be less enduring; fewer students will be as liberally educated. The college that actively sets its poets and philosophers to the task of rediscovering and retranslating into modern language and educational forms its own more valid traditions and myths may become even more powerful, given the potentially heightened but selective educability of contemporary students and society's need for a communally based but more coherent way of life. To speak to today's students, a liberally educating college must create a way of life that includes what the multiversity cannot: a communal identity and vision that integrates both the intellectual and value development of its students.

FOR CONTEMPORARY SOCIETY

Neither the educability of contemporary students nor the power of a college to educate is independent of the influence of society's expectations. We have suggested the changed educability of students might be a reaction to changing societal expectations of them. The liberal arts colleges have probably become more open to the influence of our highly seductive culture, as Trilling calls it (1965), than at any time in their history. No longer tied inwardly to some historic but stabilizing tradition that gave them autonomy of the immediate pressures of the outside world, eager to extend their educational processes into the problems of society, flattered by and responsive to societal demands for their knowledge and talents, colleges have turned almost passionately outwardly. There will be a Stanford University extension on the moon by 1975. The universalizing of the college has many consequences, many of them very maturing. But for colleges to be unguardedly and unselectively open to the expectations and blandishments of the world beyond their campuses is to court forced adjustments that may undermine their power to educate liberally. It takes a faculty and administration most perceptive about the educative strengths of its college and the potential consequences each new opening to the world may have upon those strengths to make a mature adaptation to change. A college must adapt; it must not merely adjust.

Better to be a poor relation but independent in purpose and spirit than to be affluent but without integrity and a soul.

The relation between liberally educating institutions and society is becoming increasingly more interdependent. Society is becoming more open to the influence of educators as it becomes more dependent upon their knowledge and talents. In many subtle ways, the universities and colleges are assuming more direct responsibility for promoting the maturing of society. What potential strengths do liberally educating colleges have that may contribute to the healthy growth of their society?

Their greatest potential contribution is to serve as models of a way of life that integrates the power that comes from a freed intellect with the passion that comes from matured values. Their greatest potential strength is they can witness visibly the vision of a democratic society—the development of human excellence.

The ability and willingness of a democratic society to realize its vision of human excellence for all its members is sapped by many forces which a liberally educating institution has the potentiality of challenging. Among the more destructive of such forces are the homogenization of the society's values and the nihilization of its common purposes. A democratic society that values human excellence encourages the development of differences that distinguish individuals. A vital democratic society must promote pluralistic values, as Gardner has insisted, if it is to promote the fulfillment of all of its members (1961). The dominant Zeitgeist of the twentieth century is, however, the homogenization of values. It should be a matter of deep concern lest the "ecumenization" of religious differences impoverishes rather than enriches myth; lest the rationalization of the universities and colleges diminishes rather than multiplies models of living; lest the "technicalization" of industry dehumanizes rather than humanizes modes of living; lest the "mass-communicationization" of information conforms rather than individualizes attitudes and beliefs; lest the internationalization of the world reduces rather than encourages cultural variety. All of these manifestations of the homogenization of value can impede the development of a vital individuality and the maturing of human excellence.

It is the liberally educating institution that has the potential autonomy of such forces, the potential wisdom of its liberal education tradition, the potential coherence of its communal forms, and the potential socialized and reflective means to create the pluralistic models of living indispensable to a maturing democratic society.

Perhaps the inevitable accompaniment of the homogenization of values is also their nihilization. When a society is not clear about its priorities, several consequences occur. A society loses the power to attract the devoted efforts of its members. Corporate purposes are replaced by private purposes. The community becomes a collectivity whose energies are diffused into self-serving activities. Bell has described the growing nihilistic temper of society this way:

> . . . nihilism has begun to attack the very core of culture and to proclaim a way of life that is really a withdrawal from society, a retreat into the "interior distance," a new gnostic mode which beats against all the historic, psychological taboos of civilization. . . . The post-modern sensibility seeks to abolish constraint by substituting experience for art, sensation for judgment. And it wants to impose that sensibility of undifferentiated experience upon all realms of culture (1966, pp. 308, 309).

Perhaps such a trend is one way to adjust to the homogenization of values!

Another consequence is that decisions are made not within the context of some grander vision but in response to the most immediately persuasive demand. For example, the reaction to Sputnik was the overthrow of the ideal of human excellence to embrace a narrower and less appropriate goal for a democracy—the development only of intellectual excellence. For a decade, intellectual but not human excellence has been the criterion of educational progress and only now are the consequences of such a partial goal becoming manifest. The accentuation of the characterological changes of contemporary students, their paradoxically improved academic preparation and scholastic aptitude but reduced educability and motivation for continued intellectual involvement and their growing dissatisfaction with their narrowing college training may be related consequences of the failure to locate educational innovation within the broader and more appropriate goal of human excellence. One tragic example to us is the plans to bring together eight to ten thousand students—even one or two thousand may be too many—into educational parks, presumably to offer increased intellectual advantages and to further racial integration. We predict that such travesties may well make more students even more uneducable and rob them of the intimate and corporate educational experiences they need for their fuller development as human beings. The only stable primary group of the student in this Orwellian world will be his bus group—a highly appropriate symbol of the nihilization of values.

It is the liberal education tradition that preserves the record of man's adaptations and provides the means to assess their significance and relevance to the problems of contemporary society. A liberally educating college is committed not to a prescribed parochial set of values but to those associated with the pursuit of human excellence, that is, the ethic of truth. Individual colleges have different visions about how such an ethic can be best institutionalized and realized in the lives of their students. Such visions provide society the models it needs to assist all its members to become fuller more mature persons.

Goals of a Liberal Education

∿∿∿∿∿∿∿∿∿∿∿∿∿∿∿∿∿∿

Using the categories of the theory of maturing, I systematically analyzed the writings of a number of influential educational philosophers and identified and organized specific developmental goals. Of the goals consistently cited by at least several philosophers, all could be assimilated to the model that forms the basis of this study. To illustrate how the developmental dimensions that characterize the maturing person apply to the process of becoming liberally educated, I shall redescribe each developmental dimension in the educational language used by representative educators.

A maturing person becomes more able to represent experiences symbolically. A liberally educated person should have a richly developed, vivid imagination (Eliot in Thomas, 1962; Hook, 1946; Spaulding in Curti, 1959) that enables him to entertain the possible (Van Doren, 1943) and foresee consequences (Dewey, 1933b; Thorndike, 1912). A liberal education is a reflective education that expands a person's awareness of the world, his ability to inquire and test his inquiries, to state the reasons for his thought (Dewey, 1933a), and to place any immediate end-in-view within the total pattern of likely consequences that enmesh that end-in-view (Dewey, 1939). A condition for such reflective thought to develop, for educators like Dewey, is the inhibition of impulse and desire, since the immediate translation of a wish into action forestalls the development of any internalized or symbolic modes of adaptation.

A few educators like Bode (1927), Hook (1946), and Dewey (1896, 1903, 1928) have addressed themselves specifically to the symbolization of values, claiming that a liberally educated person should be aware of his own and others' values as well as how his own character and desires influence his values.

No one contradicts Socrates' dictum, "Know thyself." To be aware of one's desires and motives, to have an accurate concept of self, to have self-insight is a widely accepted goal of liberal educators.

Finally, both Hook (1946) and Dewey (1937) insist that liberal education should develop insight about other people as well as an understanding of social problems. By the highly conscious use of the scientific method to criticize and to reconstruct social life, these social problems can be solved (Dewey, 1897).

A maturing person becomes more allocentric. Agreement among educators that a liberal education should socialize a person is universal. We can capture the flavor of their agreement by citing only a few examples. A liberally educated person can project himself into the thought of others and will "endeavor to rear within himself that third man who is present when two men speak, and who is happy when they understand each other" (Van Doren, 1943, p. 68). To understand a multiplicity of viewpoints (Dewey, 1933a; Newman, 1852; Whitehead, 1916), as Piaget has shown (1928), is a condition for the development of logical, ordered, consistent, or, more generally, allocentric thought.

There is also near unanimous explicit agreement that a liberal education should promote allocentric values and personal relations. Good citizenship (Newman, 1852), abstract (Russell, 1931) and imaginative sympathy for others (Bode, 1927; Hook, 1946), tolerance (F. H. Sanford, 1966; Syrkin, 1944), social interest, cooperation, and good will (Bode, 1927; Russell, 1931), democratic ideals and devotion to human values (Hook, 1946), "social consciousness and a social conscience" (Hutchins, 1943), "respect for the rights and views of others" (McGrath, 1959) define the content of the values educators hope a liberal education produces. A liberally educated person, because he fully accepts and shares his humanity with others, develops respect and love for others, learns how to accommodate himself to the needs of others (Newman, 1852; Syrkin, 1944), shares imaginatively and physically with others (Bode, 1927). From such reciprocally developed mutuality feelings, there emerges a stable and "sound community life" (Parker in Curti, 1959), as well as an unlimited extension and application of man's intelligence, worked through organized cooperative endeavor, to the solution of the common problems that beset mankind (Dewey, 1899).

A very persistent theme is that liberal education should help an individual experience his basic humanness and social identity with all other men. Liberal education humanizes. It draws out of man potentialities that create in him a deeper identification with other humans (Bode, 1927; Dewey, 1897; Hutchins, 1936; MacLeish, 1920; Thomas, 1962; Van Doren, 1943). A truly liberally educated person will not think of himself as just unique, but will understand himself as an integral part of mankind.

A maturing person becomes progressively more integrated. Educators have much to say about the integrative effects of education. Almost every educator, among those I reviewed, agreed that a liberal education should enlarge a person's skill to think more integratively. No two educators used the same words but the message was the same. They spoke of connecting each individual mind with some general mind (Thomas, 1962), welding "together imagination and experience" (Whitehead, 1927), making reflective syntheses (Wriston in Thomas, 1962), "understanding human endeavors . . . in their relations to one another" (Meiklejohn, 1920, p. 38), breaking down artificial barriers (Hook, 1946), training for generalizations (Hutchins, 1936), and "discovering combinations of ideas before their worth is known" (Bruner, 1963, p. 6). General education has been defended because it supposedly provides the opportunity for coordinating and generalizing skills to flourish (Thomas, 1962). Some educational philosophers, like Newman (1852), define the task of liberal education to be primarily the nurturing of such generalizing skills.

Many educators feel more comfortable discussing liberal education solely as the development of intellectual skills. Others do dare to consider that a liberal education should also assist a person to systematize, order, and integrate his values. Most shy from suggesting that the educator should proselytize for a particular value. Instead, they emphasize that a person's intellectual training not be isolated from ethical concerns (Dewey, 1933b; Conant, 1945). Hook says students should know how their values are interrelated (1946). Dewey emphasizes the importance of the integrative effect that an ideal has for a person and the necessity for "consistency and harmony in belief" (1933c, p. 226).

Stemming from the Greek emphasis on wholeness comes a persistent interest in uniting, connecting, integrating the different components of the self. "Man is in the same breath metaphysician, philosopher, scientist, and poet," says Van Doren (1943, p. 57); man needs to develop a more "coherent and integrated self" according to Dewey (1928, p. 177); Brinton says, "Every man in his own heart is at once priest, scholar, and worker" (1958, p. 100). Liberal education should assist a person coordinate and integrate those aspects of himself into a more consistent self.

Finally, liberal education should give man a sense of his connectedness with other men (Hutchins, 1936; Van Doren, 1943) and an understanding that his own development is fully contingent upon the fuller development of other men with whom he is organically related because of his essentially social nature (Dewey, 1934).

A maturing person becomes more stable. Only a few educators speak about the desirability of stabilizing intellectual skills and values. Newman claimed a liberal education should develop a "steadiness of intellect," equitableness, and repose (1852). For Dewey, a genuine intellectual organization had "its own principles of order and continuity" (1928). With respect to the development of more stable values, both Hook and Dewey emphasize the necessity for internalizing the scientific attitude itself as the criterion of value. Only an "unswerving moral rectitude" or intellectual integrity, that constitutes the very core of the scientific attitude, would be the permanent value of a maturing person (Dewey, 1895). For McGrath, a liberally educated person will have a "provisionally firm set of convictions, an examined philosophy . . . which . . . structures the purposes and directs the activities of his existence. . . . They give stability to his being" (1959, p. 6). Other educators fear a student's values may become too stable, rigid, and closed to future modification (Bode, 1927; Hook, 1946).

Those who identify the development of individual talents (Thomas, 1962), the acquisition of self-knowledge (Whitehead, 1916), or the fulfillment of one's humanity (Van Doren, 1943) as goals of a liberal education imply a stable identity will result. All educators we reviewed remained quiet about the stabilization of a person's personal relationships with others.

A maturing person becomes more autonomous. Educators also emphasize the development of independence or autonomy. A person becomes "free to use the intellect" (Van Doren, 1943) which is no longer distorted by passion, desire, appetite, and prejudice (Dewey, 1933a; Newman, 1852; Van Doren, 1943). Phrases such as "freedom of thought," "freed intelligence," "intellectual courage," "capacity to weigh evidence dispassionately" (Gardner, 1956, p. 6) recurringly appear in the writings of these and other educators.

A similar tone marks the attitudes of educational philosophers about a more liberally educated person's values and, presumably, personal relationships, though no educator specifically addressed himself to the manifestation of autonomy in such relationships. A person should be prepared to "meet resistance" to his values (Van Doren, 1943) with courage (Russell, 1931), if not by rebelliousness (F. H. Sanford, 1966).

A liberally educated person has a sense of inner freedom and control over his own destiny. Again, this increased autonomy is phrased in words that differ but have a similar meaning. A maturing person secures "command over [his] own powers" (Newman, 1852; Van Doren, 1943), control over himself (Hyde in Thomas, 1962), can stand alone (Hook, 1946), and becomes self-reliant and independent of "external tutelages" (Dewey, 1933a, 1934).

The Perceived Self
Questionnaire (PSQ)

The Perceived Self Questionnaire consists of fifty bipolar scales designed to assess the developmental maturity of the dimensions and self-structures that define the theory of maturing described in Chapter One. Listed below are the test scales and a code for identifying those items that define the hypotheses of the theory. Appropriate steps have been taken to minimize known sources of error. For example, to control for response sets, item position and right-left hand location of the mature and immature ends of each scale have been systematically randomized.

Each item is an eight point scale that defines a continuum from immature to mature or mature to immature. The test is *subsequently* scored by assigning point values of one (for the least mature scale position) to eight (for the most mature scale position). For example,

I can maintain a high level of intellectual efficiency for many days and weeks.	I cannot maintain a high level of intellectual efficiency for more than a few hours or days at a time.

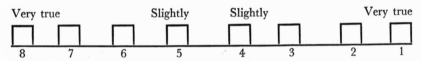

Very true			Slightly	Slightly			Very true
8	7	6	5	4	3	2	1

Scores for each pair of items that define one of the hypotheses, for the ten items that define each developmental dimension or self-structure, and for all fifty items that define overall maturity are obtained by summing the appropriately assigned scores.

The PSQ is self-administered and takes about twenty minutes to complete. Students find the test interesting for it requires them to think about themselves in ways they usually have not explicitly considered before. The test has been administered under a variety of conditions and to different samples. Translated copies of the test have been administered to two Italian and two Turkish college male groups who represented different regions of their countries. The tests were administered as part of a study testing the generality of the theory of maturing in different cultures by replicating the early research that demonstrated the validity of the theory with selected American samples (Heath, 1965). The principal American samples were described in Chapter Four. The men of the Freshman sample took the PSQ within the first several days of their first weeks at college and six to seven months later. The Senior samples I and II were first given the test in their senior year. Half of the men of each sample first rated themselves as they recalled what they were like when they entered college as freshmen. Several days later they rated themselves as seniors. The remaining seniors rated themselves as seniors first and several days later what they were like as entering freshmen. Although the ratings by the seniors of themselves as freshmen are subject to several sources of error and are, therefore, of dubious reliability, they do permit us to infer how the students judged themselves to have changed. The seniors did not find it difficult to rate themselves as freshmen, perhaps because the break between secondary school and college is a sharp one for many young persons and may be represented more saliently and clearly in their memories than most other times in their lives.

PERCEIVED SELF QUESTIONNAIRE

1. I can maintain a high level of intellectual efficiency for many days and weeks.

   I cannot maintain a high level of intellectual efficiency for more than a few hours or days at a time.

   Very true   Slightly   Slightly   Very true

   ☐   ☐   ☐   ☐   ☐   ☐   ☐   ☐

2. I could not describe in detail my feelings and thoughts about the male friends I had four or five years ago.

   I could describe in detail my feelings and thoughts about the male friends I had four or five years ago.

3. I have not found a way of life that integrates most of my values and desires and that gives me some direction.

   I have found a way of life that integrates most of my values and desires and that gives me some direction.

4. My closest male friends could not persuade me to do something that I might consider mistaken.

   My closest male friends could persuade me to do something that I consider to be mistaken.

5. Fundamentally, I am very different from most other persons.

   Fundamentally, I am like most other persons.

6. My values and beliefs are centered more on the lives and needs of others than myself and my desires.

   My values and beliefs are centered more on myself and my desires than on the lives and needs of others.

7. I frequently am not able to understand why I have misunderstandings with a girl I feel close to.

   I usually can understand why I have misunderstandings with a girl I feel close to.

8. My ideas about myself are quite changeable; sometimes

   My ideas about myself are quite stable; I think I am the same

I think I am a different person now than I was several months ago.

person now that I was several months ago.

9. I seldom feel I impulsively act as if I were much younger when I am with a male friend.

I frequently feel I impulsively act as if I were much younger when I am with a male friend.

10. My thinking is frequently inconsistent, vague, and tends to simplify too much the complexities of a problem.

My thinking is usually consistent, precise, and takes into account the full complexity of a problem.

11. I usually remain reasonably certain about what I believe and value when someone directly challenges my convictions.

I frequently become very uncertain about what I believe and value when someone directly challenges my convictions.

12. I have felt so fond of a girl that I have done things for her even at the expense of my own interests.

I have not yet felt so fond of a girl that I did things for her at the expense of my own interests.

13. I readily remember the facts necessary to analyze and solve an intellectual problem.

I frequently cannot remember the facts necessary to analyze and solve an intellectual problem.

14. I develop new interests and become more sensitive to new feelings and thoughts as a result of a close male friendship.

I seldom develop new interests or become more sensitive to new feelings and thoughts as a result of a close male friendship.

15. What I think of myself is not easily influenced by what my friends and family tell me.

What I think of myself is easily influenced by what my friends and family tell me.

16. A quarrel with a close male friend usually changes my friendship with him.

A quarrel with a close male friend usually does not change my friendship with him.

17. I rarely feel I can just be myself with a close girl friend; there are parts of me she doesn't know.

I am very much myself with a close girl friend; there is little I hide from her.

18. My thoughts and judgments about intellectual problems are usually realistic and practical.

My thoughts and judgments about intellectual problems are often unrealistic and impractical.

19. I don't know myself very well and could not describe myself very accurately if asked to do so.

I know myself reasonably well and could describe myself quite accurately if asked to do so.

20. My beliefs and values are still very much influenced by experiences I had when younger.

My beliefs and values are now no longer influenced by experiences I had when younger.

21. I seldom feel I am a divided, inconsistent, and contradictory person; I am sure of what I am and what my direction is.

I frequently feel I am a divided, inconsistent, and contradictory person; I am unsure of what I am or what my direction is.

22. Because I frequently reflect about why I believe and act as I do, I find these questions easy to answer.

Because I seldom reflect about why I believe and act as I do, I find these questions difficult to answer.

23. When I really like a girl very much, my feelings persist for many months.

I have never liked a girl very much, or if I have, my feelings have not lasted more than a month or two.

24. The interests of a close male friend seldom become my interests.

The interests of a close male friend frequently become my interests.

25. My evaluation of contemporary issues is often influenced more by the opinions of other persons than by my own judgment.

    My evaluation of contemporary issues is usually influenced more by my own judgment than by the opinions of others.

26. I find it difficult to reflect on my motives and values and to understand the reasons for much of my behavior.

    I find it easy to reflect on my motives and values and to understand the reasons for most of my behavior.

27. I have so liked a male friend that I did things for him even at the expense of my own interests.

    I have not yet so liked a male friend that I did things for him at the expense of my own interests.

28. A quarrel with a girl I like usually changes my relationship with her.

    A quarrel with a girl I like doesn't usually change my relationship with her.

29. My desires and values seldom influence my judgments about the adequacy of an intellectual issue or theory.

    My desires and values often influence my judgments about the adequacy of an intellectual issue or theory.

30. I am not what I believe other people think me to be.

    I really am what I believe other people think me to be.

31. My values are really my own and are not easily influenced by what my friends and family believe.

    My values are not really mine and are easily influenced by what my friends and family believe.

32. I am able to remember in detail how I was and what I felt when I was much younger.

    I am not able to remember in detail how I was and what I felt when I was much younger.

33. In analyzing a problem, I seldom anticipate how other people look at the problem.

    In analyzing a problem, I frequently anticipate how other people look at the problem.

34. I have developed new inter-

    I have not developed new interests and become more sensitive to new feelings and thoughts as a result of a close relation with a girl.

ests or become more sensitive to new feelings and thoughts as a result of a close relation with a girl.

35. My close friendships with other men tend to last many months or years.

My close friendships with other men tend not to last for more than a month or two.

36. My ideas about myself are still influenced by experiences and feelings I had when I was much younger.

My ideas about myself are now no longer influenced by experiences and feelings I had when I was much younger.

37. I rarely feel I can be just myself with a close male friend; there are parts of me he doesn't know.

I am almost completely myself with a close male friend; there is little I hide from him.

38. It is difficult for me to remember exactly what I thought some years ago about various intellectual issues.

I can remember exactly what I thought some years ago about various intellectual issues.

39. The interests of a girl I like seldom become my interests.

The interests of a girl I like frequently become my interests.

40. My beliefs and values are rather changeable and now differ considerably from what they were several months ago.

My beliefs and values are rather stable and don't differ too much from what they were many months ago.

41. I constantly try to relate and integrate intellectual ideas and facts into more comprehensive patterns.

I have no great drive to relate and integrate intellectual ideas and facts into more comprehensive patterns.

42. A girl I love could convince me to do something which I believe to be wrong.

A girl I love could not easily persuade me to do something which I believe to be wrong.

43. When a new experience

When a new experience chal-

challenges my opinion of myself, I remain reasonably certain of what I am basically like.

lenges my opinion of myself, I become very uncertain of what I am really like.

44. I can describe in detail the feelings and thoughts I had four or five years ago about my relations with girls.

I find it difficult to remember in detail the feelings and thoughts I had four or five years ago about my relations with girls.

45. Most people who know me consider my convictions and values to be unrealistic and impractical.

Most people who know me consider my convictions and values to be realistic and practical.

46. I usually know what other people think of me.

I usually don't know what other people think of me.

47. I frequently impulsively act as if I were much younger when with a girl friend.

I seldom impulsively act as if I were much younger when with a girl friend.

48. I don't often feel torn and divided between several inconsistent and conflicting values, beliefs, and desires.

I frequently feel torn and divided between several inconsistent and conflicting values, beliefs, and desires.

49. I frequently can understand why I have misunderstandings with my close men friends.

I frequently cannot understand why I have misunderstandings with my close men friends.

50. My thinking frequently becomes impaired and confused when I encounter intellectual ideas that are personally disturbing.

My thinking usually remains efficient and clear when I encounter intellectual ideas that are personally disturbing.

How reliable is the PSQ? Without presenting the detailed results of the seven samples, we can make the following general statements: The pattern of the internal relationships between the scores indexing the maturity of different self-structures and dimensions was remarkably similar for all of the samples, despite test item, instruc-

KEY TO PSQ ITEMS
Dimensions of Maturing

Self-Structures	Stability	Integration	Allocentricism	Autonomy	Symbolization
Intellectual Skills	1(M)[a],50(I)	10(I),41(M)	18(M),33(I)	25(I),29(M)	13(M),38(I)
Values	11(M),40(I)	3(I),48(M)	6(M),45(I)	20(I),31(M)	22(M),26(I)
Self	8(I),43(M)	21(M),30(I)	5(I),46(M)	15(M),36(I)	19(I),32(M)
Relations with males	16(I),35(M)	14(M),37(I)	24(I),27(M)	9(M),42(I)	2(I),49(M)
Relations with females	23(M),28(I)	17(I),34(M)	12(M),39(I)	4(M),47(I)	7(I),44(M)

[a] (M) and (I) indicate whether left-hand side of bipolar scale is the mature (M) or immature (I) end of scale.

tional, geographical, and cultural differences among the samples. Generally, the dimensional and structural scores correlated very highly with the total maturity score and less highly with each other, as the theory of maturing would predict. For example, persons who reported themselves to be more integrated also reported themselves to be more stable or more maturely developed in their values. These results do not violate, therefore, the holistic assumption about maturing; neither do they confirm it, since the same self-report data were used to measure both dimensional and structural maturity. The PSQ may measure least reliably the autonomy dimension. Although highly correlated with the total maturity score, it tended not to be consistently related with the integration, symbolization, and particularly, allocentric dimensions. The autonomy and allocentric dimensions seem to be the most contradictory theoretically and our data suggest that these dimensions are more independent in young adults than we assumed them to be. Conflict over autonomy at young adulthood may obscure its meaning. In fact, Chapter Five presents data that suggest that the autonomy dimension may need to be theoretically clarified. The scores indexing the maturity of the students' male and female relationships are also not highly predictive of their other PSQ scores. But the consistency with which this pattern was found among widely different samples combined with other information about the samples suggests the scores may not be, in fact, unreliable. Other data suggest that the men of all of the samples were quite defensive and conflicted about how mature their relationships were with other persons, particularly women. That the pattern of the validity correlates of the interpersonal scores was as predicted indicates that in spite of their questionable reliability, they still may be useful indices of interpersonal maturity.

Table B.1 lists the stability coefficients for the different samples.

Although the samples differed in their test instructions, procedures, and retest time intervals, their PSQ scores are moderately stable. We did not expect high stability since we were predicting that students would become more mature during the interval of time. That the stability coefficients of the senior samples were generally similar to, and occasionally lower, than those of the Freshman sample was not anticipated. If the ratings by the seniors of their freshman selves, made within several days of their ratings of their senior selves, had been primarily reflections of their judgments of themselves as seniors, the stability coefficients would have been much higher than those ac-

TABLE B.1

Stability Coefficients of the PSQ Scores

PSQ Scores

Samples	Total	Intell.	Values	Self	Male	Female	Stabil.	Integ.	Alloc.	Auton.	Symbol.
Freshman[a]	.78	.65	.74	.59	.62	.69	.47	.56	.55	.64	.51
Senior I	.57	.42	.27	.43	.45	.66	.62	.40	.50	.76	.64
Senior II	.73	.73	.54	.55	.80	.40	.64	.61	.78	.65	.45

[a] Time interval between the first and second PSQ administrations was six to seven months for the Freshman sample and three to five days for the Senior samples, whose instructions differed for each of their two ratings.

tually obtained. The senior ratings of themselves as freshmen may be more reliable than we had anticipated.

How valid are the PSQ total, dimensional, and structural scores? Just what do they measure? It is impossible to report in detail the very extensive data available on seven different samples, some of whom had taken the PSQ as well as other validating tests more than once. We must be both highly general and selective. Only statistically significant findings found in at least several samples will be reported. One-tailed significance tests were used for the MMPI, SIQ, Holt Rorschach scores, and judge evaluations of maturity; two-tailed tests were used for the AVL, SVIB, academic achievement, intelligence, and other measures for which no directional hypotheses were made in advance. To facilitate the interpretation of the results, they were ordered by their degree of confirmation which is defined in Table B.2. Table B.3 defines the different scores used in the validity studies; Table B.4 cites the specific correlates for the PSQ Total score; Table B.5 summarizes the types of measures found to correlate with each PSQ structural and dimensional score.

Recall the total PSQ score summarizes the extent to which a person agreed with fifty items, each measuring the components of the theory of maturing. A high PSQ total score was expected to covary directly with other measures of maturity. As Table B.4 indicates, such was the case. The PSQ Total score is most consistently and significantly correlated with other questionnaire-type indices of maturity, though in neither the MMPI nor the SIQ, nor the SVIB for that matter, does a person directly rate this own maturity *qua* maturity. Nor, when he completes the PSQ, does he know that he is making judgments about his own maturity. PSQ-defined maturity is not related with Rorschach, academic achievement, and most intelligence measures.

More specifically, a mature person thinks of himself as healthy (MMPI Sr) and mature (SIQ SE), correctly believes others think similarly of him (SIQ SSE; Judge), has more mature interests (SVIB IM), and is relatively free of crippling neurotic complaints and symptoms (MMPI Tot). He is intellectually efficient (MMPI Ie), reflectively controlled (MMPI K), and able to bounce back from stress (MMPI Es). His energies move strongly outwardly (MMPI Do), particularly toward other persons. He is highly tolerant (MMPI To), socially responsible (MMPI Re-r), and deeply interested in others and their welfare (SVIB).

The less mature person, as defined by a low PSQ Total score, does not have stable control of himself. His behavior is both very rigid (MMPI Rgm) and chaotic, inconsistent, and impulsive (MMPI F, Im, Nu). He is also anxious (MMPI At), dependent (MMPI Dy), self-doubting, obsessional (MMPI Pt), and depressed (MMPI D). His energies tend to be turned inwards. He is a more socially intro-versive (MMPI Si) person, who may be quite aloof and emotionally isolated from other persons (MMPI Sc). His self-image is inconsistent and nonintegrative, unstable, autocentric, and inaccurate (SIQ, NI, Un, Auto, Inac).

Table B.5 illustrates that the same basic personality pattern is associated with most of the PSQ dimensional and structural scores. That the scores of any one test are not independent of each other inflates, of course, the number of significant relationships. But what is of interest is that some of the PSQ dimensional scores are associated, though weakly at times, with the appropriate scores of other different measures. For example, an allocentric person is more socially poised (MMPI Sr) and not socially withdrawn and isolated (MMPI Sc, Si). He consciously values loving relationships with others (AVL So-cial) and is more motivationally similar to those persons who are suc-cessful in service or other-centered types of occupations. And his self-image is more allocentrically organized. Generally, the PSQ stability, integration, intellectual, value, and self-concept scores seem to be the most valid dimensional and structural scores.

Although we have questioned the reliability of the retrospective PSQ ratings made by the seniors of themselves as freshmen, we do plan to use them and so we must briefly assess their validity. Compar-ing these retrospective ratings with the personality material secured from the men *when they were freshmen* revealed little change in the pattern of the results just reported (data not reported), even though, as Chapter Five reports, the senior samples' PSQ scores of their senior selves differed significantly from their PSQ judged freshman selves. One intriguing difference between the pattern of validity correlates was obvious, however. The seniors' ratings of the maturity of their interpersonal relations when freshmen, particularly with other men, were the ratings most predictive of the largest range of MMPI scores and were even more powerful predictors than their ratings of the ma-turity of their personal relations as seniors. Could it be that the seniors, anxious and uncomfortable about their contemporary personal rela-tionships, did not need to protect their images of themselves as freshmen as much and could therefore rate their freshman selves more honestly? A similar trend occurred for the ratings of intellectual skill maturity. Could it be that both interpersonal relationships and intellectual development are foci of strain and unresolved conflict? As Chapters Five and Seven show, such was indeed the case. Apart from these differences, the data do suggest, however, that the PSQ pattern of validity correlates is unusually stable.

Given the great differences among the samples, administration conditions, experimenters, and other factors that attenuate the magnitude of the relationships the results are most reassuring. They indicate not only that the PSQ may validly measure the theory of maturing and that it can be used to assess maturing, but also that the senior retrospective ratings of their freshman selves may have been quite accurate. Finally, the very remarkable similarity of the results of seven samples from three different cultures supports the generality of the theory of maturing whose validity the book seeks to test with students who are becoming liberally educated.

TABLE B.2

Definition of Degrees of Confirmation[a]

Degree	Criteria
Very strong confirmation	The correlates of at least five of the seven samples are significant at the .05 p level; three of the correlates are significant beyond the .01 level; no correlate is markedly discrepant in the opposite direction.
Strong confirmation	The correlates of at least four samples are significant at the .05 p level; two of the correlates are significant beyond the .025 level; no correlate is markedly discrepant in the opposite direction.
Confirmation	The correlates of at least three samples are significant at the .05 p level; at least one correlate is significant beyond the .025 level; other correlates are generally supporting; no correlate is significant in the opposite direction.
Weak confirmation	The correlates of at least two samples are significant beyond the .05 p level; no correlate is significant in the opposite direction.

[a] These definitions have been modeled on those found useful in earlier studies (Heath, 1965) and modified to take account of the number of samples, intersample differences in test forms, test administration conditions, sociocultural factors, and experimenter errors.

Definitions of Abbreviations of Test Scores Used in Tables

AVL — Allport, Vernon, and Lindzey *Study of Values*[a]
Aes: Aesthetic; *Ec:* Economic; *Pol:* Political; *Rel:* Religious; *Soc:* Social; *The:* Theoretical.

CEEB — College Entrance Examination Board scores[a]
Eng: English Achievement; *Quant:* Quantitative score; *Verb:* Verbal score.

DC — Departmental Chairman ratings[b]
Det: Determination (+); *EmoS:* Emotional stability (+).

Gd.Av — Grade average[a]
Fr: Freshman; *J:* Junior; *S:* Senior; *So:* Sophomore; *Tot:* Average for the four years.

Judge — Judge rating of maturity
Rtg: Independent faculty and student ratings of maturity (+).

MMPI — Minnesota Multiphasic Personality Inventory[e]
At: Anxiety (−); *D:* Depression (−); *Do:* Dominance (+); *Dy:* Dependency (−); *Eo:* Over-control (−); *Es:* Ego strength (+); *F:* Inconsistency (−) *Hs:* Hypochondriasis (−); *Hy:* Hysteria (−); *Ie:* Intellectual efficiency (+); *Im:* Impulsivity (−); *K:* Defensive or reflective control (+); *Ma:* Manic (−); *Mf:* Femininity; *Nu:* Under-control (−); *Pa.* Paranoia (−); *Pd:* Psychopathic deviate (−); *Pt:* Psychasthenia (−); *R:* Repression (−); *Re-r:* Social responsibility (+); *Rgm:* Rigidity (−); *Sc:* Schizophrenia (−); *Si:* Social introversion (−); *Sr:* Social presence (+); *To:* Tolerance (+); *Tot:* General maladjustment (−), average of basic pathological scales.

PSQ — Perceived Self-Questionnaire
Allo: Allocentricism (+); *Aut:* Autonomy (+); *Fem.* Female relationships (+); *Integ:* Integration (+); *Intell:* Intellectual skills (+); *Male:* Male relationships (+); *Self:* Self-concept (+); *Stab:* Stability (+); *Symb:* Symbolization (+); *Tot.* General maturity (+); *Value:* Values (+).

ROR — Holt's Rorschach scoring system.
%DD: Degree to which response requires some defense against it (−); *%FAcc:* Degree of accuracy of image (+); *%L1:* Degree to which images are dominated by markedly unsocialized primary process drives (−); *%L2:* Degree to which images less markedly unsocialized (−); *%Form:* Degree to which thinking is organized by primary process (−); *MDE:* Degree to which the primary process manifestation has been successfully defended against (+).

Definitions of Abbreviations of Test Scores Used in Tables

SIQ   —   Self-image Questionnaire

Auto: Autocentric self-image (−). Discrepancy between social self and ratings by other persons; *Inac:* Inaccurate self-image (−). Discrepancy between private self and ratings by other persons. *NA:* Nonautonomous self-image (−). Effect of experimental challenge to self-image; *NI:* Nonintegrated or incongruent self-image (−). Discrepancy between private and social selves; *Judge:* Student judged maturity (+). Sum of ratings made on scales describing mature persons by peers; *SE:* Self-esteem (+). Sum of self-ratings made on scales describing mature persons; *SSE:* Social self-esteem (+). Belief others rate self highly on traits describing mature persons; *Un:* Unstable self-image (−). Discrepancy between private selves at time one and time two.

SVIB   —   Strong Vocational Interest Blank[a]

Chem: Chemist; *CSS:* City School Superintendent; *Dent:* Dentist; *IM:* Interest maturity (+); *LifI:* Life Insurance Salesman; *Pers:* Personnel Manager; *PubA:* Public Administrator; *SalM:* Sales Manager; *SocW:* Social Worker; *Y-PD:* YMCA Physical Director; *Y-Sc:* YMCA Secretary.

W-B   —   Wechsler Bellevue Intelligence Scale[a]

DS: Digit symbol test.

[a] No directional hypothesis predicted for these scores except SVIB *IM*.

[b] (−) or (+) indicates the predicted direction of the relation between the test score and the PSQ scores of maturity.

[c] The labels attached to the MMPI scales, particularly *D, Hs, Hy, Ma, Pa, Pd, Pt,* and *Sc,* should be interpreted in accordance with the cautions suggested elsewhere (Dahlstrom & Welsh, 1960).

Personality Correlates[a] of PSQ Total Score of Maturity
Sample

Degree of Confirmation	Fresh.	Sr. I	Sr. II	Istanbul	Ankara	Pisa	Palermo
Very strong							
MMPI Dy	−25	−38*	−53****	−41**	−59*****	−34*	−54****
Ie	09	42**	76****	18	64****	49****	59****
Sc	06	−39*	−48***	−34*	−63****	−37*	−69****
To	02	34	65****	50****	43**	39**	50****
SIQ SE	69****	57****	71****	71****	76****	70****	64****
SSE	77****	65****	47***	63****	63****	58****	63****
Strong							
MMPI At	−15	−33	−45**	−38**	−70****	−35*	−56****
D	−18	−48***	−61***	−29	−54*****	−27	−41**
F	−20	−22	−47**	−22	−46**	−44****	−69****
Im	01	−28	−40*	−42**	−48***	−34*	−56****
Re-r	07	05	49***	17	39*	63****	46***
Rgm	01	−51***	−41**	05	−25	−33*	−52****
Si	−46***	−49***	−57***	−48*****	−31	−29	−32
Sr	49****	42**	47***	17	23	13	45***
Tot	15	−18	−51***	−19	−66*****	−33*	−71****
SIQ Ni	−07	−15	−42**	−34*	−24	−35*	−50****
Un	−01	−29	−40*	−41**	−50***	−09	−39**

Confirmed							
MMPI Do	09	31	26	42**	52****	21	37*
Es	06	12	37*	10	67****	31	68*****
K	26	17	37*	52*****	34	22	38**
Pt	16	−33	−40**	−21	−63****	−26	−72*****
Weak							
MMPI Nu[b]	13	03		−57***	−40*	−33	−26
SIQ Auto	24	−09	−51***	03	−22	−25	−45***
Inac		08	−46**	15	07	13	−46***
Judge[b]				10	33	32*	43**
SVIB[b] CSS	−10	61***	43*				
IM	08	60****	50***				
Pers	03	53***	63***				
SocW	06	49**	45*				
Y-PD	10	49**	53***				
Y-Sc	03	64***	45*				

* $p < .05$
** $p < .025$
*** $p < .01$
**** $p < .005$

[a] See Appendix C for other validity correlates of PSQ scores.

[b] Score not available for samples for whom no correlates are reported.

TABLE B.5

Summary of PSQ Score Correlates for Three American,[a]
Two Italian, and Two Turkish Male College Samples

Degree of Confirmation	PSQ Score	

MATURITY OF SELF STRUCTURES

Intellectual Skills

Very strong	SIQ:	SE (7)[b]; SSE (6).
Strong	MMPI:	At (4); D (4); Dy (5); Pt (4); Rgm (4); Sc (5); Si (4); To (4).
	SIQ:	Un (4).
Confirmed	MMPI:	Do (3); Es (3); Ie (3); K (3); Sr (3); Tot (3).
Weak	AVL:	Ec − (2)[c].
	MMPI:	Im (2); Nu (2)[d]; Re-r (2).
	SIQ:	Auto (2); NI (2).
	SVIB:	Y-Sc + (2).[e]

Values

Very strong	MMPI:	D (5); Sc (5).
	SIQ:	SE (7); SSE (7).
Strong	MMPI:	At (5); Do (6); F (4); Ie (4); Si (4); To (5); Tot (4).
Confirmed	MMPI:	Es (3); Im (3); Pd (3); Pt (3); Re-r (3); Sr (3).
	SIQ:	NI (3); Un (3).
Weak	MMPI:	Do (2); Hs (2); Hy (2); K (2); Rgm (2).
	SIQ:	Auto (2).
	SVIB:	IM + (2); Pers + (2).

Self-Concept

Very strong	MMPI:	At (6); Dy (6).
	SIQ:	SE (7); SSE (7).
Strong	MMPI:	Im (4); Sc (4); Sr (4); To (4).
	SIQ:	NI (4).
Confirmed	MMPI:	Es (3); F (3); Ie (3); K (3); Nu (3); Re-r (3); Rgm (3); Si (3); Tot (3).
	SIQ:	Auto (3).

297

TABLE B.5 (Cont'd)

Summary of PSQ Score Correlates for Three American,[*] Two Italian, and Two Turkish Male College Samples

Degree of Confirmation	PSQ Score

MATURITY OF SELF STRUCTURES

Self-Concept

Weak	MMPI:	D (2); Ma (2); Pt (2).
	SIQ:	Inac (2); Un (2).
	SVIB:	Chem — (2).

Relations with Men

Very strong	SIQ:	SE (5).
Strong	MMPI:	Ie (4); To (4).
	SIQ:	SSE (4).
Confirmed	MMPI:	At (3); K (3); Sc (3); Tot (4).
	SIQ:	Auto (3).
Weak	MMPI:	Dy (2); F (2); Im (2); Si (2).
	SIQ:	Inac (2).
	SVIB:	Dent — (2); LifI + (2); Pers + (2).

Relations with Women

Strong	MMPI:	Sc (4).
	SIQ:	SE (4); SSE (4).
Confirmed	MMPI:	Ie (3); Re-r (3).
Weak	AVL:	Ec — (2).
	MMPI:	D (2); Do (2); K (2); Nu (2); Pt (2); Rgm (2); Sr (3); To (2); Tot (2).
	SIQ:	Un (2).

DIMENSIONS OF MATURING

Symbolization

Very strong	SIQ:	SE (6); SSE (5).
Strong	MMPI:	Pt (4).
Confirmed	MMPI:	Ie (3); Si + (3).

298

TABLE B.5 (*Cont'd*)

Summary of PSQ Score Correlates for Three American,[a] Two Italian, and Two Turkish Male College Samples

Degree of Confirmation		PSQ Score

MATURITY OF SELF STRUCTURES

Symbolization

Weak　　　　AVL:　Pol + (2).

MMPI:　At (2); D (2); Do (2); Dy (2); Eo (2); Es (2); F (2); Im (2); K (2); Nu (2); R (3; one other sample significant opposite direction);[f] Sc (2); Sr (2); To (2); Tot (2).

ROR:　%Form (2).

SVIB:　CSS + (2); Pers + (2); Y − PD + (2); Y − Sc + (2).

W-B:　DS + (2).

Allocentricism

Very strong

Strong　　　MMPI:　At (4); F (5); Ie (4); Pt (4); Sc (5); Si (4); Sr (5); Tot (4).

SIQ:　SE (6).

Confirmed　MMPI:　D (3); K (3); To (3).

Weak　　　　AVL:　Aes − (2); Soc + (2).

MMPI:　Dy (2); Es (2); Rgm (3).

SIQ:　Auto (2); Inac (2); NI (2); SSE (2); Un (2).

SVIB:　CSS + (2); Pers + (2); SocW + (2); Y − PD + (2).

Integration

Very strong　MMPI:　F (5); Sc (6); Si (5).

SIQ:　SE (7); SSE (7).

Strong　　　MMPI:　At (4); Dy (4); Im (4); K (4); Rgm (4); Sr (4); To (4).

SIQ:　Auto (4); Un (4).

Confirmed　MMPI:　D (3); Es (3); Ie (3); Pt (3); Tot (3).

SIQ:　Inac (3); NI (3).

299

TABLE B.5 (*Con'td*)

Summary of PSQ Score Correlates for Three American,[a] Two Italian, and Two Turkish Male College Samples

Degree of
Confirmation

PSQ Score

MATURITY OF SELF STRUCTURES

Integration

Weak	AVL:	Rel + (2).
	MMPI:	Hy (2); Nu (2); Pa (2); Pd (2); Re-r (2).
	SIQ:	Inac (2); Judge (2).
	SVIB:	PubA + (2).

Stability

Very strong	MMPI:	At (5); Ie (5); Sc (6); To (6).
	SIQ:	SE (7); SSE (7).
Strong	MMPI:	Dy (7); Es (4); F (4); Ma (4); Pt (4); Re-r (4); Si (4); Tot (4).
Confirmed	MMPI:	D (3); Im (3); K (3); Nu (3); Sr (3).
Weak	MMPI:	Do (2); Pd (2); Rgm (2).
	SIQ:	Auto (2); NI (2); Un (2).
	SVIB:	Y − Pd + (2).

Autonomy

Very strong		
Strong	MMPI:	Dy (4); Re-r (4); Tot (4).
	SIQ:	SE (4).
Confirmed	MMPI:	At (3); Do (2); Ie (4); Im (3); Pt (3); Sc (3).
	SIQ:	SSE (3).
Weak	MMPI:	Es (3; one other sample significant opposite direction);[f] Ma (2); Nu (2); Pd (2); Rgm (2); To (2).
	SVIB:	SalM + (2).

[a] See Appendix C for other validity correlates of PSQ scores.

[b] The number of samples for whom a significant relation at least at .05 *p* level was found.

[c] Sign of correlation given when no advance prediction made or correlate in opposite direction.

[d] Correlates not available for two American samples. Degree of confirmation may be underestimated as a consequence.

[e] Correlates available for only three American samples. Degree of confirmation may be underestimated for all SVIB scores.

[f] Score included though violates definition of weak confirmation. One Turkish sample, drawn from an American oriented college, gave inconsistent results on most measures related to autonomy, possibly because of a severe conflict in the college between Turkish and American role expectations of males about autonomy itself.

300

The Validity of the Interview Scores

The responses of each student given during his recorded interview were scored for the presence of any of the categories that defined maturing and immaturing. Chapter Four illustrates several scored interviews. Summary scores were secured for the number of maturing statements made about each self-structure and developmental dimension. A score indexing the degree of general maturing reported was defined by the

$$\frac{\text{Total number of maturing statements}}{\text{Total number of maturing and immaturing statements.}}$$

The different interview scores are used primarily in Chapter Seven to identify the most important effects attributed by the samples to each collegiate determinant. They were also used in Chapter Five to index how much the samples had matured on each dimension and self-structure that described the theory of maturing.

Just how reliable are such scores? Twenty randomly selected interviews were rescored two and a half years later by the same judge. The reliability coefficients for the total maturity and immaturity scores were .93 and .91; the median coefficient for the structural and dimensional scores indexing maturing was .82 and immaturing .80. A second but very minimally trained judge independently scored the same protocols. The agreement between the two judges was .89 and .85 for the total maturity and immaturity scores. The median reliability correlations for the individual maturity and immaturity scores were .69 and .70. Neither method of determining the reliability of the scores accurately reflects the consistency among the pairs of scores. The small size of the sample, combined with a very restricted range in the magnitude of some of the scores, meant that one or two large score discrepancies between the judges unduly reduced the correlation. For example, the judges agreed least about their scores for autonomy; yet, the largest discrepancy between their judgments for three of the interviews was only three score points. Although the judges agreed remarkably well in identifying the presence of a maturing or immaturing trend, they agreed less well in identifying the specific nature of that developmental trend. These preliminary reliability analyses suggest that the coding scheme can be made much more reliable by providing a judge with more detailed examples of the differences between some of the dimensions, particularly like stability and autonomy, which were frequently confused. The assumption that the dimensions are not independent and are only different ways of conceptualizing the organismic growth process inevitably means that precise definitional distinctions between the dimensions will elude us.

We did assume that the number of statements a person made in his interview about a particular type of maturing was, in fact, a valid measure of how much he developed in that particular way. So just how valid are the interview scores? Are they related to other measures of maturing? To anticipate our conclusion, given all of the troublesome factors that limit the validity of self-descriptions, most of the interview scores do covary with other measures of maturing.

What is the evidence? First, Chapter Five reports that there is a statistically significant relationship between the pattern of maturing changes measured by the PSQ and the pattern of similar changes reported in the interviews held four to six weeks later. Second, other tests and indices of maturity do, for the most part, consistently covary with the interview scores as predicted.

To summarize the extensive data from three samples, we follow the procedures adopted in Appendix B. Table C.1 describes the criteria that defined the degree of confirmation for three samples; Table C.2 gives the specific validity correlates for the most general score of maturing—the percentage of maturing statements made in the interview. Table C.3 summarizes the data for the remaining dimensional and structural scores obtained from the interview.

TABLE C.1

Definition of Degree of Confirmation

Degree	Criteria
Very strong	Two of three correlates are significant at least at $p < .05$; one significant at least .025; third correlate at least in mid 20's.
Strong	Two of three correlates are significant at least at $p < .05$; other near zero.
Confirmed	One of three correlates significant at least at $p < .05$; second at least in mid-20's; third near zero.
Weak	One of three correlates significant at $p < .05$; others confirmatory or at least none opposite direction in 20's.

What is a person like who gives many more statements about maturing than immaturing in his interview? Table C.2 shows he is self-confident, judges himself to be mature (SIQ SE) and stable (PSQ Stab), and accurately believes that other persons think similarly of him (SIQ SSE, Judge). He is an intellectually efficient person (MMPI Ie) whose good ego strength (MMPI Es) and assertive attitude toward problems (MMPI Do) probably contribute to his excellent academic work (Gd. Av.). He believes he is mature in his heterosexual relations (PSQ Fem) and has maturely developed values (PSQ Value).

On the other hand, a person who describes himself in interviews more frequently as immature than mature has more erratic but rigid controls (MMPI Pd, Rgm). He may be quite anxious, depressed, flighty, and concerned about his bodily health (MMPI At, D, Hy, Hs). He lacks a firm or stable identity (SIQ Un) and his beliefs about himself are not autonomous of outside influence. He may be quite autocentric (SIQ NA, Auto). While suggestive, these results are tentative for they don't consistently describe every sample. Yet, every significant correlate for which a prediction was made did confirm our expectations and the general interpretive pattern just described is consistent with other studies about the characteristics found to define a mature person.

Of the remaining interview scores, the most valid seem to be those indexing stability, integration, allocentricism, maturity of the self and relationships with women. Practically all of their correlates were in the predicted direction and each score covaried with a variety of personality measures, as Table C.3 indicates. The scores indexing the maturity of the students' values and relationships with other men were only moderately predictive of a variety of measures of adaptation, though again almost all of their correlates were in the expected direction.

The least powerful interview scores were those measuring symbolization, autonomy, and the maturity of intellectual development. This finding confirms the hunch made in Chapter Five about the inadequacy of the symbolization and autonomy scores. The pattern of the correlates of the symbolization score is inconsistent and does not confirm our expectations. Chapter Five also suggested that we probably misscored the interview statements about autonomy because we confused the narcissistic aloofness of highly individualistic students with more mature forms of autonomy. The validity correlates of the interview autonomy score are similarly confusing. On the one hand, persons who give many statements about having become more autonomous judge themselves on other tests to be mature and autonomous (PSQ Self, Aut) and are so judged by their peers (Judge Rtg; SIQ Judge) and by their Departmental Chairmen who rated them to be self-motivating and determined persons (DC Det). On the other hand, when they were freshmen as well as seniors, they were anxious and dependent persons (MMPI At, Dy) who did not have good reflective control (MMPI K). Although they did well academically (Gd. Av.), they undervalued theoretical and scholarly activity (AVL Theor);

TABLE C.2

Personality Correlates of Interview Score of % Maturity Statements

Degree of Confirmation	Samples		
	Freshman	Senior I[a]	Senior II
Strong			
MMPI Ie (T1)[b,c]	40**	42*	11
SIQ SE:	−14	47**	40*
SSE:	−19	56***	51***
Confirmed			
AVl Pol (T1)	15	−28	−40*
Soc (T1)	−02	50*	31
MMPI Do	06	46**	32
Ie	02	52**	26
Sc (T1)	−35*	−01	−25
PSQ Fem	03	37	36*
Stab	−16	50**	27
SIQ Judge	−05	45*	30
Un	−09	−40*	−26
Weak			
Gd Av. So.	16	16	41*
MMP At	−10	−63****	13
D	−37*	−06	−16
Dy	−07	−43*	11
Es	36*	17	−05
Hs	−34*	−11	−05
Hy	−45**	00	−22
Pd	−06	−13	−37*
Rgm	05	−55***	−15
PSQ Value	−18	43*	21
SIQ Auto	−47**	09	−19
NA[d]	−34*		−04

* p < .05
** p < .025
*** p < .01
**** p < .005

[a] N = 19 due to inadequately taped interviews.

[b] See Table 3, Appendix B for definitions of abbreviations.

[c] Parentheses (T1) indicate correlate is with test given at beginning of freshman year.

[d] SIQ Autonomy scores not available for Senior I sample.

and although they were socially introversive (MMPI Si), they over-valued social and altruistic forms of relationships (AVL Soc). If these apparent inconsistencies do not reflect errors in measurement and sampling problems, then they may reflect conflict and ambivalence about autonomy. The men's exaggerated individualistic autonomy, prized in the Haverford environment, may have kept them from securing gratification of their emotional and passive (MMPI Mf) needs for affection and care from others.

The pattern of traits that described those who reported that they had matured intellectually was also partially inconsistent. Such persons were very cultured as freshmen (CEEB Eng), had done well academically in college (Gd. Av.), were well adjusted (MMPI Tot, D), and judged themselves to be quite autonomous and maturely integrated as seniors (PSQ Aut, Integ.). Yet, on the Rorschach they produced many disturbing and threatening images which they were not able to integrate adaptively (Ror % DD, % Form).

We conclude that the method used to objectify the interview data was reasonably valid. Those who describe themselves to be mature in most of the ways defined by the theory of maturing were also more mature on other types of personality measures. The interview assessed less adequately, perhaps, the maturity of the men's intellectual skills, autonomy, and ability to symbolize their experiences.

TABLE C.3

Summary of Interview Score Correlates
for the American Samples

Degree of Confirmation		

MATURITY OF SELF STRUCTURES

Intellectual Skills

Confirmed	MMPI:	D(T1)[a]
	PSQ:	Integ.
	ROR:	%DD(+);[b] %Form(+).
Weak	CEEB:	Eng (+)
	Gd.Av:	Fr; So; Tot(+)
	MMPI:	D; Pa(T1); Tot.
	PSQ:	Aut.

Values

Confirmed	MMPI:	Do; R(T1, T2); Sr(T1).
	PSQ:	Male.
	SIQ:	Judge.
Weak	MMPI:	D(T1, T2); Eo (T1, T2); Es; Si; Sr; Tot.
	PSQ:	Fem; Symb.
	ROR:	%DD; %FAcc.
	SIQ:	Auto; Inac; NI; SSE.

Self-Concept

Strong	MMPI:	Do(T1).
	SIQ:	SE
Confirmed	AVL:	Pol(−)(T1).
	Gd.Av:	J; So(+).
	Judge:	Rtg.
	PSQ:	Fem; Intell; Stab; Tot.
	SIQ:	SSE
Weak	AVL:	Soc(+)(T1).
	CEEB:	Eng(+).

TABLE C.3 (*Cont'd*)

Summary of Interview Score Correlates
for the American Samples

Degree of
Confirmation

MATURITY OF SELF STRUCTURES

Self-Concept

MMPI: At(T1); Dy(T1); Eo(T1); K(T1, T2); R(+); Rgm.

PSQ: Integ; Self; Symb.

SIQ: NI.

Relations with Men

Confirmed AVL: Aes(+).

Gd.Av: Fr; So(+).

PSQ: Aut.

SIQ: NA.

Weak AVL: Aes(+)(T1).

CEEB: Eng(+).

Gd.Av: J; Tot(+).

Judge: Rtg.

MMPI: Pa(+)(T1); Pd(T1, T2); Re-r.

PSQ: Fem; Integ; Intell; Stab; Tot; Value.

SIQ: Judge; SSE.

Relations with Women

Very strong MMPI: Sr.

Strong MMPI: R.

SIQ: SE.

Confirmed Gd.Av: S(+).

MMPI: At; Es; Ie(T1); Ma(+); Rgm(T1, T2); Si(T1).

PSQ: Integ; Stab.

SIQ: Judge; SSE.

Weak AVL: Soc(+).

MMPI: D; Eo; F; Hs(T1, T2); Hy; Ie; Pa; Pt(T1); R(T1); Sc(T1, T2); Sr(T1); Tot(T1, T2).

PSQ: Allo; Fem; Male; Self; Symb; Tot.

SIQ: Un.

TABLE C.3 (*Cont'd*)

Summary of Interview Score Correlates
for the American Samples

Degree of
Confirmation

MATURITY OF SELF STRUCTURES

Symbolization

Strong	PSQ:	Allo($-$).
Confirmed	MMPI:	Re-r($-$)(T1).
Weak	AVL:	Rel($-$)(T1).
	MMPI:	At(T1); Dy(T1); Ie; K(T1); Sr.
	ROR:	%L1($+$).
	SIQ:	SE

Allocentricism

Strong	PSQ:	Integ; Stab; Value.
	ROR:	%DD($+$).
Confirmed	CEEB:	Eng($+$).
	MMPI:	D; Ie; Pt; R; Rgm; Sr; Tot.
	PSQ:	Aut; Fem; Male; Self; Symb; Tot.
	SIQ:	Auto; Judge; SSE; Un.
Weak	MMPI:	Hy; Sc.
	PSQ:	Allo; Intell.
	SIQ:	Inac; SE.

Integration

Very strong	Gd.Av:	So; J($+$).
Strong	Gd.Av:	Fr($+$).
	MMPI:	Do(T1).
	PSQ:	Stab.
Confirmed	CEEB:	Eng($+$).
	Gd.Av:	S; Tot($+$).
	MMPI:	Do; Ie(T1, T2); Pt(T1, T2); Rgm; Sc(T1); To(T1).
	PSQ:	Fem; Integ; Intell.
	SIQ:	SE; SSE.
Weak	AVL:	Aes($+$); Rel($+$).
	MMPI:	At(T1, T2); D(T1); Dy; Es; Hs; Pa; Re-r(T1); Sc; To; Tot(T1, T2).

309

TABLE C.3 (*Cont'd*)

Summary of Interview Score Correlates
for the American Samples

Degree of
Confirmation

MATURITY OF SELF STRUCTURES
Integration

ROR: %DD.
SIQ: Judge.

Stability

Very strong	PSQ:	Fem.
	SIQ:	Judge.
Strong	SIQ:	SE; SSE.
Confirmed	MMPI:	Do; Si(T1).
	PSQ:	Symb; Value; Tot.
	SIQ:	Auto; NA.
Weak	Gd.Av:	J; So; Tot(+).
	Judge:	Rtg.
	MMPI:	D(T1); Hy; Ie(T1); Pa; Pd; R(T1); Sc(T1, T2); To; Tot.
	PSQ:	Allo.
	ROR:	%DDxDE; %L2(+); MDE.
	SIQ:	NI.

Autonomy

Confirmed	AVL:	The(−)
	DC:	Det.
	Gd.Av:	S(+).
	Judge:	Rtg.
	MMPI:	Hy; Mf(+)(T1); R(T1).
Weak	AVL:	Ec(+)(T1); Soc(+).
	MMPI:	At(+)(T1, T2); Dy(+)(T1, T2); Im(+)(T1); K(−)(T1, T2); Mf(+); Si(+)(T1, T2); Sr(−) (T1).
	PSQ:	Aut; Self.
	SIQ:	Judge.

ᵃ Parentheses (T1) indicate correlate is with test given at beginning of freshman year. Correlates of Time 2 scores not followed by parentheses.

ᵇ (+) and (−) indicate direction of correlate; given when no advance prediction was made or when correlate was significant in direction opposite from that predicted.

References

ALLPORT, G. W., VERNON, P. E., and LINDZEY, G. *Study of Values.* (Manual 3rd ed.) Boston: Houghton Mifflin, 1960.

Amherst Alumni News. "A report to The Committee on Educational Policy from the Subcommittee to Study Student Life." Winter 1965.

ANGYAL, A. *Foundation for a Science of Personality.* New York: Commonwealth Fund, 1941.

ARSENIAN, S. "Change in evaluative attitudes during four years of college." *Journal of Applied Psychology,* 1943, *27,* 338–349.

ASTIN, A. W. "American Council on Education summary data on entering freshmen, 1966."

BARZUN, J. Speech at Hofstra University, Dec. 11, 1963.

BAYLEY, N. "On the growth of intelligence." *American Psychologist,* 1955, *10,* 805–818.

BELL, D. *The Reforming of General Education: The Columbia Experience in Its National Setting.* New York: Columbia University Press, 1966.

BLOOM, B. S. *Stability and Change in Human Characteristics.* New York: Wiley, 1964.

BODE, B. H. *Modern Educational Theories.* New York: Macmillan, 1927.

BRINTON, H. H. *Quaker Education in Theory and Practice.* Wallingford, Pa.: Pendle Hill Pamphlet, No. 9, Rev. 1958.

BROWN, D. R. "Nonintellective qualities and the perception of the ideal student by college faculty." *Journal of Educational Sociology,* 1960, *33,* 269–278.

BRUNER, J. S. *The Process of Education.* Cambridge: Harvard University Press, 1963.

CAPLOW, T., and MCGEE, R. J. *The Academic Marketplace.* New York: Basic Books, 1958.

CARTER, G. C. "Student traits and progression through college." *Journal of Educational Psychology,* 1949, *40,* 306–308.

CHICKERING, A. W. "Institutional objectives and student development." Unpublished manuscript, 1965.

CHICKERING, A. W. "The development of autonomy." Unpublished manuscript, no date.

CONANT, J. B. "Introduction" to *General Education in a Free Society: Report of the Harvard Committee.* Cambridge: Harvard University Press, 1945.

COX, R. Personal communication, 1968.

CURTI, M. *The Social Ideas of American Educators (1959).* Paterson, N. J.: Littlefield, Adams, 1963.

DAHLSTROM, W. G., and WELSH, G. S. *An MMPI Handbook; A Guide to Use in Clinical Practice and Research.* Minneapolis: University of Minnesota Press, 1960.

DEWEY, J. "What psychology can do for the teacher (1895)." In R. D. Archambault (Ed.), *John Dewey on Education.* New York: Modern Library, Random House, 1964.

DEWEY, J. "Interest in relation to training of the will" (1896). In R. D. Archambault (Ed.), *John Dewey on Education.* New York: Modern Library, Random House, 1964.

DEWEY, J. "Ethical principles underlying education" (1897). In R. D. Archambault (Ed.), *John Dewey on Education.* New York: Modern Library, Random House, 1964.

DEWEY, J. "The school and society" (1899). In R. D. Archambault (Ed.), *John Dewey on Education.* New York: Modern Library, Random House, 1964.

DEWEY, J. "Logical conditions of a scientific treatment of morality" (1903). In R. D. Archambault (Ed.), *John Dewey on Education.* New York: Modern Library, Random House, 1964.

DEWEY, J. "Progressive education and the science of education" (1928).

In R. D. Archambault (Ed.), *John Dewey on Education*. New York: Modern Library, Random House, 1964.

DEWEY, J. "The process and product of reflective activity" (1933a). In R. D. Archambault (Ed.), *John Dewey on Education*. New York: Modern Library, Random House, 1964.

DEWEY, J. "School conditions and the training of thought" (1933b). In R. D. Archambault (Ed.), *John Dewey on Education*. New York: Modern Library, Random House, 1964.

DEWEY, J. "Why reflective thinking must be an educational aim" (1933c). In R. D. Archambault (Ed.), *John Dewey on Education*. New York: Modern Library, Random House, 1964.

DEWEY, J. "The need for a philosophy of education" (1934). In R. D. Archambault (Ed.), *John Dewey on Education*. New York: Modern Library, Random House, 1964.

DEWEY, J. "Democracy and educational administration" (1937). In J. Dewey, *Philosophy of Education*. Paterson, N. J.: Littlefield, Adams, 1958.

DEWEY, J. "The continuum of ends-means" (1939). In R. D. Archambault (Ed.), *John Dewey on Education*. New York: Modern Library, Random House, 1964.

EDDY, JR., E. D. *The College Influence on Student Character*. Washington, D. C.: American Council on Education, 1959.

ERIKSON, E. H. "Identity and the life cycle." *Psychological Issues,* 1959, *1.*

FREEDMAN, M. B. "Studies of college alumni." In N. Sanford (Ed.), *The American College*. New York: Wiley, 1962.

FREEDMAN, M. B. *The College Experience*. San Francisco: Jossey-Bass, 1967.

FREUD, S. *The Interpretation of Dreams* (1900). New York: Basic Books, 1956.

GARDNER, J. W. "Fifty-first Annual Report, 1955–56, Carnegie Corporation of New York." New York: 1956.

GARDNER, J. W. *Excellence, Can We be Equal and Excellent, Too?* New York: Harper, 1961.

GOODSTEIN, L. D. "Regional differences in MMPI responses among male college students" (1954). In G. S. Welsh and W. G. Dahlstrom (Eds.), *Basic Readings on the MMPI in Psychology and Medicine*. Minneapolis: University of Minnesota Press, 1956.

HEATH, D. H. *Explorations of Maturity*. New York: Appleton-Century-Crofts, 1965.

HEATH, D. H. "But are they mature enough for college?" In *The Challenge of Curricular Change*. New York: College Entrance Examination Board, 1966, 32–41.

HEATH, D. H. "But are they more educable?" Talk for Twelfth Annual Counselor's Conference, University of Texas, Austin, 1968a.

HEATH, D. H. "The cool ones." *Journal of Religion and Health,* 1968b, *7,* 111–121.

HEIST, P. *The Creative College Student: An Unmet Challenge.* San Francisco: Jossey-Bass, 1968.

HOOK, S. *Education for Modern Man.* Toronto: Longmans, 1946.

HUNTLEY, C. W. "Changes in values during the four years of college." *College Student Survey*, 1967, *1*, 43–48.

HUTCHINS, R. M. *The Higher Learning in America.* New Haven: Yale University Press, 1936.

HUTCHINS, R. M. *Education for Freedom.* Baton Rouge: Louisiana State University Press, 1943.

JACOB, P. E. *Changing Values in College: An Exploratory Study of the Impact of College Teaching.* New York: Harper, 1957.

KATZ, J., AND ASSOCIATES. *No Time for Youth: Growth and Constraint in College Students.* San Francisco: Jossey-Bass, 1968.

KENISTON, K. *The Uncommitted: Alienated Youth in American Society.* New York: Harcourt, Brace, 1965.

KENNEDY, G. Personal correspondence, 1967.

KING, S. "Some early findings of the Harvard Student Study." Unpublished manuscript, 1967.

KINSEY, A. C., POMEROY, W. B., and MARTIN, C. E. *Sexual Behavior in the Human Male.* Philadelphia: Saunders, 1948.

KRIS, E. *Psychoanalytic Explorations in Art.* New York: International Universities Press, 1952.

LEHMANN, I. J., and DRESSEL, P. L. "Critical thinking, attitudes, and values in higher education." U. S. Department of Health, Education, and Welfare Cooperative Research Project No. 590. East Lansing: Michigan State University, 1962.

LOWRY, D. "Frustration reactions in 22 six year old boys." Senior Honors Thesis, Haverford College, 1967.

MACLEISH, A. "Professional schools of liberal education." *The Yale Review*, 1920, *10*, 362–372.

MCGRATH, E. J. *The Graduate School and the Decline of Liberal Education.* New York: Bureau of Publications, Teachers College, Columbia University, 1959.

MEIKLEJOHN, A. *The Liberal College.* Boston: Marshall Jones, 1920.

MURPHY, L. B., and RAUSHENBUSH, E. *Achievement in the College Years: A Record of Intellectual and Personal Growth.* New York: Harper, 1960.

NEUGARTEN, B. L. "Adult personality: toward a psychology of the life-cycle." Paper, American Psychological Association, New York, 1966.

NEWCOMB, T. M. *Personality and Social Change: Attitude Formation in a Student Community.* New York: Dryden Press, 1943.

NEWCOMB, T. M. "Student peer-group influence and intellectual outcomes of college experience." In R. L. Sutherland, W. H. Holtzman, E. A. Koile, and B. K. Smith (Eds.), *Personality Factors on the College Campus.* Austin, Texas: Hogg Foundation, 1962.

NEWCOMB, T. M., and FELDMAN, K. A. *The impacts of colleges on students*. San Francisco: Jossey-Bass (in press).

NEWCOMB, T. M., KOENIG, K. E., FLACKS, R., and WARWICK, D. P. *Persistence and Change: Bennington College and Its Students After Twenty-Five Years*. New York: Wiley, 1967.

NEWMAN, J. H. *The Idea of a University, Defined and Illustrated* (1852). New York: Longmans, Green, 1891.

NEWMANN, F. M., and OLIVER, D. W. "Education and community." *Harvard Educational Review*, 1967, *37*, 1, 61–106.

NICHOLS, R. C. "Personality change and the college." *American Educational Research Journal*, 1967, *4*, 173–190.

PERLOE, S. I. "To develop and partially validate a questionnaire to measure values relevant to good citizenship and to prepare a large scale project to study value change in a variety of colleges." Unpublished manuscript, 1967.

PERVIN, L. A. Personal correspondence, 1966.

PIAGET, J. *Judgment and Reasoning in the Child*. New York: Harcourt, Brace, 1928.

PINE, F., and HOLT, R. R. "Creativity and primary process: A study of adaptive regression." *Journal of Abnormal Social Psychology*, 1960, *61*, 370–379.

RAUSHENBUSH, E. *The Student and His Studies*. Middletown, Conn.: Wesleyan University Press, 1964.

RAUSHENBUSH, E. Talk to Quaker educators, 1965.

RUSSELL, B. *Education and the Good Life*. New York: Liveright, 1931.

SANFORD, F. H. "A faculty's goals for its students." In *The Challenge of Curricular Change*. New York: College Entrance Examination Board, 1966, 118–126.

SANFORD, N. (Ed.), "Personality development during the college years." *Journal of Social Issues*, 1956, *12*, 4.

SANFORD, N. (Ed.) *The American College*. New York: Wiley, 1962.

SANFORD, N. *Self and Society: Social Change and Individual Development*. New York: Atherton Press, 1966.

SANFORD, N. *Where Colleges Fail: A Study of the Student as a Person*. San Francisco: Jossey-Bass, 1967.

SHARPLESS, I. *The Story of a Small College*. Philadelphia: J. C. Winston, 1918.

STERN, G. C. *Scoring Instructions and College Norms. Activities Index. College Characteristics Index*. Syracuse, N. Y.: Psychological Research Center, 1963.

STEWART, L. H. "Change in personality test scores during college." *Journal of Counseling Psychology*, 1964, *11*, 211–220.

SULLIVAN, H. S. *The Interpersonal Theory of Psychiatry*. New York: Norton, 1953.

SUTHERLAND, R. L., HOLTZMAN, W. H., KOILE, E. A., and SMITH, B. K. (Eds.). *Personality Factors on the College Campus.* Austin, Texas: Hogg Foundation, 1962.

SYRKIN, M. *Your School, Your Children: A Teacher Looks at What's Wrong With Our Schools.* New York: L. B. Fischer, 1944.

TAYLOR, J. A. "A personality scale of manifest anxiety." *Journal of Abnormal Social Psychology,* 1953, *48,* 285–290.

THOMAS, R. B. *The Search for a Common Learning: General Education 1800–1960.* New York: McGraw-Hill, 1962.

THORNDIKE, E. L. *Education, a First Book.* New York: Macmillan, 1912.

THORNDIKE, E. L. "Mental discipline in high school studies." *Journal of Educational Psychology,* 1924, *15,* 83–98.

TIPPETT, J. S., and SILBER, E. "Autonomy of self-esteem." *Archives of General Psychiatry,* 1966, *14,* 372–385.

TRENT, J. W., and MEDSKER, L. L. *Beyond High School.* San Francisco: Jossey-Bass, 1968.

TRILLING, L. *Beyond Culture: Essays on Literature and Learning.* New York: Viking Press, 1965.

TRUMAN, D. B. "Forward." In D. Bell, *The Reforming of General Education.* New York: Columbia University Press, 1966.

VAN DOREN, M. *Liberal Education.* New York: Holt, 1943.

WARREN, J. R., and HEIST, P. A. "Personality attributes of gifted college students." *Science,* 1960, *132,* 330–337.

WEBSTER, H. "Some quantitative results." In N. Sanford (Ed.), "Personality development during the college years." *Journal of Social Issues,* 1956, *12,* 29–43.

WEBSTER, H., FREEDMAN, M. B., and HEIST, P. "Personality changes in college students." In N. Sanford (Ed.), *The American College.* New York: Wiley, 1962.

WEBSTER, H., SANFORD, N., and FREEDMAN, M. B. "A new instrument for studying authoritarianism in personality." *Journal of Psychology,* 1955, *40,* 73–84.

WHITE, G. "President's Annual Report." *Haverford College Bulletin,* LIV, 2, 1954–55.

WHITE, R. W. *Lives in Progress: A Study of the Natural Growth of Personality.* New York: Dryden Press, 1952.

WHITE, R. W. "Motivation reconsidered: The concept of competence." *Psychological Review,* 1959, *66,* 297–333.

WHITE, R. W. "Ego and reality in psychoanalytic theory." *Psychological Issues,* 1963, *3,* No. 3.

WHITEHEAD, A. N. "The aims of education" (1916). In *The Aims of Education and Other Essays.* New York: Macmillan, 1929.

WHITEHEAD, A. N. "Universities and their function" (1927). In *The Aims of Education and Other Essays.* New York: Macmillan, 1929.

Index